DISPOSSESSION AND DISSENT

DISPOSSESSION AND DISSENT

Immigrants and the Struggle for Housing in Madrid

Sophie L. Gonick

Stanford University Press

Stanford, California

Stanford University Press
Stanford, California

Library of Congress Cataloging-in-Publication Data
Names: Gonick, Sophie L. (Sophie Laura), author.
Title: Dispossession and dissent : immigrants and the struggle for housing in Madrid /
   Sophie L. Gonick.
Description: Stanford, California : Stanford University Press, 2021. | Includes bibliographical
   references and index.
Identifiers: LCCN 2020044889 (print) | LCCN 2020044890 (ebook) | ISBN 9781503614895 (cloth) |
   ISBN 9781503627710 (paperback) | ISBN 9781503627727 (ebook)
Subjects: LCSH: Immigrants—Housing—Spain—Madrid. | South Americans—Housing—
   Spain—Madrid. | Home ownership—Spain—Madrid. | Immigrants—Political activity—
   Spain—Madrid. | South Americans—Political activity—Spain—Madrid. | Social
   movements—Spain—Madrid.
Classification: LCC HD7288.72.S72 G55 2021 (print) | LCC HD7288.72.S72 (ebook) |
   DDC 333.33/80896804641—dc23
LC record available at https://lccn.loc.gov/2020044889
LC ebook record available at https://lccn.loc.gov/2020044890

Cover photograph: Olmo Calvo
Cover design: Rob Ehle
Typeset by Newgen North America in 10/14 Minion Pro

Contents

Acknowledgments

This book was produced across three continents, many years, and a variety of institutions. First and foremost, it is a story of the city of Madrid, where I took my first steps into adulthood, became a researcher, and developed deep ties to the city and many of its residents. I want to acknowledge the many anonymous women and men in Madrid who allowed me into their lives and gave me insight into their housing and activist experiences. This book would have been impossible without their voices. I am indebted to Marcela Maxfield, my insightful editor at Stanford University Press, for allowing me to share their story with the world. Sunna Juhn, also at Stanford, has provided welcome assistance. Both, too, were patient when COVID-19 made securing images nearly impossible.

I developed the bulk of this project at the Department of City and Regional Planning, University of California, Berkeley, at NYU's Center for European and Mediterranean Studies (CEMS), and in the Department of Social and Cultural Analysis (SCA), also at NYU. At Berkeley, Teresa Caldeira, Mia Fuller, and Ananya Roy were brilliant mentors who taught me not only how to be a scholar, but also how to navigate the ongoing gendered inequities of academe. I am forever thankful for their patient guidance, thoughtful critique, and consistently high (and often challenging) expectations. Also at Berkeley, I encountered wonderful friends and insightful interlocutors, including Julie Gamble, Sergio Montero, Oscar Sosa, and Matt Wade, who remain dear friends. The wider Berkeley DCRP crew continues to impress and inspire me: Gautam Bhan, Ricardo Cardoso, Sara Hinkley, Hun Kim, Chris Mizes, Sylvia Nam,

Lana Salman, and Alex Schafran have all provided stimulating discussions and fun memories. My earliest forays into planning and housing policy in Madrid, meanwhile, occurred as an undergraduate at Harvard, where I developed an undergraduate thesis on planning and placemaking in Madrid during the early years of the Franco era under the guidance of Adam Beaver. Some of that work has made its way, many years later, into this book.

NYU has been a wonderful home since leaving Berkeley. I am thankful to Larry Wolff for bringing me to CEMS. I had the extreme good fortune during my first year in New York to get to know Tom Sugrue and Kate Zaloom, who have gone on to become great mentors and friends. Both have helped me think through numerous questions of debt, crisis, and urbanism, and have offered substantive critique on versions of this book. SCA has been a great home, where my colleagues model politically engaged scholarship that extends the boundaries of academic work; Carolyn Dinshaw, Phil Harper, Kimberly Johnson, Jennifer Morgan, Michael Ralph, and Andrew Ross deserve particular mention. Elsewhere at NYU, Gianpaolo Baiocchi, Meredith Broussard, Joy Connolly, Steve Duncombe, Eric Klinenberg, Natasha Schull, Andrew Needham, Danny Walkowitz, and Barbara Weinstein have been great champions and fonts of good advice; while Becky Amato, Marlene Brito, Jess Coffey, Marty Correia, and Jay Mueller have provided logistical support.

Claire Colomb, Alberto Corsín-Jiménez, Natasha Eskander, Michael Goldman, Clara Irazábal, Maria Kaika, Cindi Katz, Geoff Mann, Margit Mayer, Nik Theodore, and Elvin Wyly provided valuable advice on various versions and portions of the text. Elsewhere, Kali Akuno, Emma Shaw Crane, Gordon Douglas, Hilary Angelo, Kenton Card, Daniel Cueto, Javier Gil, Eric Goldfischer, Max Holleran, Liz Koslov, Melissa García Lamarca, Miguel Martínez, and Andrés Walliser have been great interlocutors and friends who have helped me think through some of the major themes and questions that drive this book.

Todd Shepard and Raphael Reyes, Tom Sugrue and Luisa Valle, Jean Railla and Steve Duncombe, Vicky Bijur and Ed Levine, Loryn Hatch and Alp Aker, Mary Ann Newman, Oscar Sosa, Hiba Bou Akar, Nick McManus, David Rios, Brian Schiesser, Joe Gallagher, Kathi and Rich Jacob, Sue Tropio, and the three Amy's—Arbus, Kantrowitz, and Levine—in addition to Milo, Maggie, Henry, Stella, George, Simon, Joe, Luna, and Nicoletta, have provided friendship and solace amidst the anomie of New York. In particular, Todd and Raph have been invaluable friends during times of quarantine, for which I am eternally grateful.

In Madrid, Beth McGowan, Dennis Neiman, Mia and Tessa, Lee Douglas, Carolina Pulido and Ivan Rizos, Virginia Eschelman, Amy McAllister, Daysi Silva, Paisaje Transversal, Oscar Martínez, La Taberna Tintorería, María José Vicente, and Monica Bobadilla remain dear friends who have provided sustenance, places to stay, late night fun, and friendship through many bouts of fieldwork.

Several funding sources were crucial to the research and writing of this book. At Berkeley, the Center for Middle Eastern Studies, the Institutes for European Studies and International Studies, and the Department of City and Regional Planning all provided continuous professional and financial support. The Social Science Research Council and the Mellon Foundation have provided funding for fieldwork and additional research. At NYU, the Dean of the Humanities, the Provost's Office, the Institute for Public Knowledge, and NYU's Madrid campus have provided crucial support. Finally, the Institut Ramon Llull's Faber Residence, in the magical town of Olot, provided a much-needed writing retreat. I am forever grateful to Faber and the other members of the thematic residency on "Diversity Policies," for an unforgettable time in La Garrotxa. An additional big thanks to photographer Olmo Calvo for the cover image.

The events of the last year have illuminated the absolute necessity of healthcare and the work of medical professionals. To that end, I am lucky to be able to rely on Joseph Alban, Shirin Ali, Juan Gamboa, Joe Helms, Julie Nissim, Javi Rosas, Lenny Rosenblum, and Thomas Stephanos for health and happiness. The pandemic also complicated the production of this book: I had intended for there to be many more images throughout the text, but most are only available in the Spanish National Library, impossible to access in time for production.

Finally, and most important, my family sustains and supports me unconditionally. My parents, Larry Gonick and Lisa Goldschmid have been unfailing in their love and generosity. I am thankful that in 2007 my father prompted me to apply for city planning programs as I flounced about Madrid looking for my next adventure, and then encouraged me to choose Berkeley. Anna Gonick and Devin Reitsma are also great sources of support. I am grateful to the community my grandparents created on Harstine Island over half a century ago, which has been a source of solace and refuge. Finally, little Jasper has been my constant companion, and helps me see the city in new ways—a great four-legged urban ethnographer. During the production of the book, meanwhile, we lost my beloved aunt Johanna. The book is dedicated to her memory.

Terms

15M	Spain's anti-austerity movement born on May 15, 2011, when thousands of people occupied Madrid's Puerta del Sol.
Afectada	I use the term *afectada*, in its original Spanish, to designate people who are directly under the threat of foreclosure and eviction. I use the feminine version to reflect the gendered dynamics of the PAH.
Aval	A guarantor or guarantee for a financial transaction such as a mortgage loan.
CONADEE	The Coordinadora Nacional de Ecuatorianos en España–National Coordinator of Ecuadorians in Spain.
FRAVM	The Federación Regional de Asociaciones de Vecinos de Madrid–The Regional Federation of Madrid Neighborhood Association emerged from the neighborhood struggles of the late 1960s-1980s, and straddles activist and electoral politics.
IU	Izquierda Unida (United Right) is a leftist party that unites a number of smaller left groups, including the Communist Party.
Madrid Community	In the democratic era, Spain created a governance system of autonomous communities, political and administrative territories with most major competencies. The Madrid Community is the regional government that manages the metropolitan area of the city and holds much more political power than Madrid city hall.

PAH   The Plataforma de Afectados por la Hipoteca (Platform for People Affected by Mortgages) is an autonomous, nonpartisan activist collective with over 200 groups throughout Spain dedicated to the right to housing.

PP   Partido Popular (Popular Party) is Spain's mainstream right-wing party.

PSOE   Partido Socialista Obrero Español (Socialist Worker Party) is Spain's mainstream left-wing party.

SAREB   Sociedad de Gestión de Activos procedentes de la Reestructuración Bancaria (Company for the Management of Assets proceeding from Restructuring of the Banking System) is the "bad bank" that manages assets from four nationalized Spanish banks.

Timeline

2005	PSOE-led government issues amnesty for all undocumented immigrants.
2007	Global financial crisis begins.
Dec. 2008	First anti-evictions protest in Madrid
2009	The PAH is founded in Barcelona.
Early 2011	The PAH Madrid is founded.
May 15, 2011	The 15M movement begins.
June, 2011	The PAH Madrid blocks an eviction for the first time.

1   Immigration, Homeownership, and Activism

Toward the end of 2006 Maribel decided to buy a house in Madrid. An immigrant from a poor suburb of Quito, Ecuador, she had lived in the Spanish capital for eight years, where she worked first as a live-in nanny, and then as a housekeeper to a series of wealthy families.[1] She had managed to save a bit of money, which she hoped to invest in the urban boom that was taking place all around her. Many in her immediate network had purchased housing in the city. A real estate agency in her neighborhood that catered specifically to an immigrant clientele helped her find a forty-square-meter flat in an older building. While the place needed work and was far from the subway, Maribel was excited to become a homeowner.

She would not be a homeowner for long. As the global economy collapsed in 2008, her mortgage rate shot up. She lost her job at the beginning of 2009. When she fell behind on monthly payments, her lender foreclosed on the property. In early 2010 she was evicted from her home but under Spanish law she remained responsible for the paying the outstanding debt, which totaled some 180,000 Euros.[2]

Dispossession and Dissent reveals the multiple ways that homeownership fuels dispossession and drives urban inequality. Much more than simply a model of housing, homeownership promises incorporation, urban inclusion, and the accrual of equity. However, its costliness, its reliance on outsized investments, its ties to debt, and its consumption of land can deepen exclusion and produce new forms of vulnerability. On the other hand, this book also illuminates how homeownership as a target for activism can bring together diverse groups to imagine radical collective futures. In the case of Madrid, Andean immigrants such as Maribel were the first to protest against the extant terms of the prevalent model of private property.[3] In the process, they sparked one of the world's most exciting and paradigmatic urban housing movements, which now serves as a model for similar struggles across the globe.

Indeed, when I met Maribel in 2013, she had become a seasoned activist with the Plataforma de Afectados por la Hipoteca (PAH—Platform for Mortgage Affected People), which had emerged to fight to the panorama of crisis that engulfed the nation. Her trajectory from immigrant to homeowner to activist reflects the broader transformation of a city and a nation that experienced numerous, rapid changes over the course of a decade. Spain became an immigrant nation within the short span of a single decade. From 2001 to 2008 its foreign-born population grew fivefold. A country long accustomed to emigration soon saw itself transformed into a site of lively and complex diversity. In Madrid Ecuadorians fueled this transformation.

Madrid has long been a site of arrival. Since the turn of the last century, rural peasants had flocked to the capital in search of employment, a trend that intensified during the brutal economic depression of the Franco era. But mass foreign immigration is relatively new. In 1998 only 10,000 Ecuadorians lived in Spain. By 2005 that number had reached half a million.[4] Almost all of this population lived in the Madrid region, where working-class neighborhoods soon became bustling ethnic enclaves. Ecuadorians established cultural associations and businesses, and on weekends flocked to the city's parks for barbeques and soccer tournaments. Assiduous at saving, they also sent millions of euros home, contributing to Ecuador's economic development.

These demographic and urban transformations occurred alongside other changes that would lead to profound economic crisis by the end of the first decade of the twenty-first century. As Spain entered the European Union and then Euro Zone, it pursued a number of measures to make itself competitive within the global marketplace, including banking and finance deregulation and the introduction of novel forms of credit. The securitized mortgage soon became a key tool to bolster both personal and municipal bank balances. The explosion of credit opportunities, meanwhile, coupled with the liberalization of land use laws, allowed for the complete transformation of the urban landscape. Madrid built to the extent of its capacity, constructing hundreds of thousands of new housing units and glittering new centers for leisure and commerce, investing in cutting-edge business infrastructure to attract multinational corporations, and extensively expanding its metro and regional rail systems.

By early 2008 the city found itself on the brink of disaster. Both the municipal and regional governments soon went broke and subsequently slashed services. Myriad businesses that sustained the boom—construction companies and development firms, real estate agencies and financial franchises—closed up shop. The first to lose jobs were immigrant workers. Soon subprime mortgage payments ballooned, and thousands of people faced foreclosure and eviction. In late 2008 and early 2009, however, a few pioneering members of the Ecuadorian community began to challenge increasing housing precarity, both drawing on their own experiences of dispossession and deploying strategies from their community's past activism. In so doing, they created the foundation for Spain's most successful social movement. Their participation in the PAH and the broader housing movement, as I argue in this book, was not accidental. They were not mere victims of predatory lending, but rather transformative figures in forging a politics of outrage.

I examine their history of struggle to draw out the intersections of housing, immigration, and urbanism, a crucial task given that cities are currently being remade through regimes of both property and migration.[5] Within contemporary urban landscapes, housing is at the epicenter of fierce debates over our collective futures.[6] Urban residents spend disproportionately on their place of residence, a reality that has inspired innovative and exciting forms of social protest. In Madrid, credit opportunities, housing speculation, and migration all surged together over the course of a single decade, followed rapidly by a devastating crisis and subsequent popular outrage. The confluence of people, capital, and crisis makes the Spanish capital an important site to observe how immigrants navigate both boom and bust, and how extant systems contribute to their experiences of settlement and survival in the city.

Homeownership lies at the heart of this story. Most critical scholarship on homeownership examines the United States. Yet systems of ownership of housing and land manifest themselves in myriad ways across the globe, each with its own variegated history. We cannot read them merely as transplants of the American model.[7] Examining the histories and lived experiences of homeownership in Madrid, I came to understand that this housing system offered a particular means of incorporation for the Andean community during the city's boom. But as I dug deeper, homeownership revealed itself to have been an engine for a number of different transformations. It was an integration policy for immigrants, but also a means of economic inclusion for members of the working class long denied upward mobility. Homeownership was a state strategy to spur Madrid's growth across the twentieth century, but also a technique for discipline, domination, and dispossession. In 2008, however, homeownership became an engine of exclusion that devastated households and splintered communities. By 2012 housing insecurity had become the focal point of Spain's most vibrant social movement. Through my research, I discovered that Ecuadorian immigrants had catalyzed that movement, transforming their experiences of vulnerability into outrage and then vibrant, plural contestation.

Scholarship on migration and cities often looks to placemaking and public space, labor, or immigrant social movements.[8] Yet as revealed in this book, housing is central to the immigrant urban experience, for processes of settlement and emplacement and for claims-making and protest.[9] My attention to immigrants as they navigate and contest urban housing markets led me to the book's central arguments. First, homeownership fuels urban inequality and multiple forms of dispossession against promises of inclusion, advancement, and economic growth. Such negative effects, however, can also rupture historical attachments to the ownership model, transforming it into a target of social and political protest. As the Madrid case reveals, immigrants discern and formulate dissent to propertied dispossession, catalyzing protest by drawing on past experiences with exploitation and activism. Resulting struggles such as the PAH model new forms of inclusive collaboration and imagine radical alternatives.

Immigrant Homeowners

This book challenges mainstream assumptions about migration and homeownership, which are based on the premise that homeownership facilitates social, political, and economic inclusion. Scholars rarely justify the use of homeownership as a variable for immigrant integration. They see homeownership as the endpoint of an immigrant's settlement, a fruitful conclusion to a difficult and lengthy process of dislocation, migration, and incorporation. Thus, while migration scholarship has been attendant to where and how immigrants live in cities, homeownership is the *sine qua non* of full settlement within a variety of geographical settings.[10] Homeownership suggests permanence, stability, and successful entry into the mainstream against forms of economic marginalization, racialization, and discrimination.[11] For many migration scholars, homeownership offers proof of integration—economic, social, and cultural. In this analytic, becoming a homeowner means one has gained full access and can thus reap its rewards, including the accrual of equity and the guise of permanence.

In this book I take immigrant homeownership as a starting point, something to be analyzed in its own right rather than understood as a metric of a group's success. I interrogate the idea of homeownership as a tool for social amelioration and upward mobility, emphasizing instead its fraught and fragile nature. The great financial crisis has inspired work that looks to homeownership's racialized regimes of predation, including the prevalence of foreclosures within immigrant communities.[12] Yet despite attention to the inequities of subprime lending, prevailing scholarship largely treats homeownership's capacity for violence as an anomaly, ignoring the much longer histories of exclusion that animate homeownership as it has been extended to marginal populations.[13] Critical work on homeownership, moreover, has drawn out the ways it propagates inequality, mostly through attention to who and how it excludes.[14] Homeownership constitutes a central strategy to alleviate inequality and include disparate social groups into the mainstream; however, it often fails to fulfill that mandate.[15] As I found in my research in Madrid, groups that buy into its promises experience variegated outcomes. In particular, homeownership's ties to debt and finance mean it can no longer guarantee upward mobility and economic security, generating inequalities for those who take part. Those ties, in fact, can serve to transform it into an engine for dispossession, furthering rather than ameliorating abjection.

Accounting for timelines of economic prosperity and crisis, my approach offers a model for immigration scholarship that must contend with novel and more generalized forms of housing and urban precarity that now ravage the globe. Gentrification and urban revitalization have changed cities, while low interest rates and an abundance of cash have configured urban real estate markets into key sites of investment.[16] As a result, housing in the city is ever more prohibitively expensive. Attention to lived experiences of homeownership allows me to draw out its inequalities. I demonstrate in this book how a bullish urban real estate market meant that immigrant homebuyers moved to degraded areas at the city's literal and metaphoric peripheries. Rather than allow them greater access to the city and its amenities, therefore, homeownership exacerbated socio-spatial exclusion and inequality even before the onset of crisis. Historicizing Madrid's real estate market, moreover, allows me to draw out how homeownership furthered other forms of urban dispossession by producing an urban economy centered wholly on construction and real estate. This account thus reveals the centrality of housing—as an industry, a necessity, and a consumer good—in the lived experience of urban immigration and the ways it can produce paradoxical outcomes.

The Promise of Homeownership

Indeed, homeownership is paradoxical. The home is a key site for the making of domesticities, the extraction of capital from everyday people, and processes of urbanization. The prevailing explanations of spatial relations of debt, finance, and housing emphasize the construction of markets and indebted subjects. A wealth of scholarship on geographies of housing and mortgage lending has drawn out the ways in which place has become dictated by complex systems of securitization and financialization, linking Main Street to Wall Street, a Spanish deed of sale to complex transactions in foreign currency markets.[17] Property investment is not about securing a roof over one's head, but rather securing a role, albeit small, in the circulation of debt, credit, and money.[18] To perpetuate itself, this capitalist system manufactures consent, creating modes of common sense that make participation in neoliberal systems seem like rational choices that might offer great reward.[19] But to treat mortgaged homeownership as a biopolitical tool of financial extraction cannot alone elucidate people's decisions to become homeowners.[20]

Why did immigrants buy into a system that shunted them into the peripheries and burdened them with outsized debts? Portraying Madrid's latest crop of homebuyers as simply caught in capitalism's "web of life" cannot fully capture their decisions to participate in the real estate market and would "limit understanding of the manifold ways [homeownership] matters in social life."[21] Rhetoric about the "dream" of homeownership hints at the kinds of promises that activate and sustain property markets. But for immigrants that dream was constrained by structures of discrimination and domination, interwoven with the micro-racisms of mundane urban life. Thus in this book I pay attention to the production of consent through neoliberal financial technologies and to the fine-grained everyday realities, imaginaries, and aspirations of people themselves in order to understand how the "contagion" of the mortgage (as one interlocutor described it) spread through both immigrant and native working-class communities. I argue consent for homeownership was produced through a tangled net of statecraft and policy, aspiration and social reproductive needs, popular culture, and the daily fabric of uneasy co-existence.[22]

Understanding the promise of homeownership helps to explain why its loss is so devastating. Several analyses of subprime borrowers have examined how these subjects interact with, submit to, or resist systems of housing, money, and finance.[23] This book, however, looks to the loss of the home and the death of homeownership as embedded within a broader terrain of urban life. Inspired by diverse scholarship from feminist political economy to development studies, I examine homeownership's dispossession as a process that invokes financial vulnerability as it is entangled with kinship and community ties, neighborhood identity, gender roles and gendered violence, and racialization and differentiation.[24] But I also articulate how, prior to the onset of urban crisis, homeownership instantiated a number of other dispossessions. Thus while foreclosure and eviction splinters communities and produces variegated abjection, those who suffer the consequences must face other inequalities produced through reliance on homeownership as an engine for growth. As I detail, these experiences often atomize people, discouraging mobilization as debtors consider their ruination to be individuated products of their own moral deficiency. The question then remains how to confront a system whose victims understand their abjection in terms of singular failure?

Homeownership's Activisms

The politics of homeownership often rest on regressive and exclusionary ideas of community in which property rights supersede other forms of democratic engagement. The private interests of homeowners often trammel the public good.[25] In California in the 1970s, for example, homeowners pushed for lowered property taxes through Proposition 13, which defunded public education, transforming the state's school system from one of the best in the United States to one of the worst. Meanwhile, homeowner's associations have become vehicles of exclusion, exacerbating spatial inequalities in the interest of maintaining property values. We observed the trend of exclusionary homeownership reach its violent apogee in the killing of Trayvon Martin by George Zimmerman, a neighborhood watch coordinator in his Floridian gated community. Such violence was largely absolved as legitimate self-defense in the interest of maintaining order in a private community of homeowners.

This book tells a different story to reveal how homeownership became a potent site for robust and inclusive activism that sought to undo its punitive logics. Spain has long been home to squatting struggles that articulate sophisticated alternatives to dominant modes of dwelling in the city.[26] What was unusual about the emergence of the anti-evictions struggle in Madrid was that those who had adhered to the homeownership model now openly confronted its exclusions and violence.[27] Rather than advance their cause from a conservative position as self-interested property owners, those *affected* by mortgages, to use the Spanish framing, instead appealed to more inclusive forms of justice and cooperation. Drawing on community ties, experiences with marginalization and racialization, and past activist histories, Andean immigrants were the first to transform experiences of exclusion and financial ruin into civil disobedience. As a result, they sparked one of the globe's most potent housing movements.

Scholars of urban social movements and immigration have produced a wealth of literature detailing immigrant involvement in forms of protest, though mostly within the realm of citizenship and rights.[28] The sophisticated political imaginaries and activism of subaltern populations more generally inspire a rich literature, with recent work attuned to immigrant involvement in radical struggles.[29] But while immigrants emerge as savvy political actors, we see little of their actual *influence* within radical movements and spaces. In this book, however, I document the role of immigrants in broader struggles over collective consumption. I draw out their role as central protagonists in the fight over evictions and foreclosures. Indeed, Madrid's Andean immigrants revealed the fragile character of homeownership and its potential to do grievous harm. Immigrants brought new perspectives to Madrid's system of homeownership, debt, and mortgage finance. Their distinct histories with other systems of land and governance in their places of origin and their past experiences as political actors provided them with alternative interpretations of society and space. As such, they forced the urban populace to see anew that which is taken for granted. Madrid's displaced homeowners offer a powerful framework to show how sites of abjection can also inspire solidarity and new repertoires of action that challenge and unmake the status quo.

The Silence of Numbers

The question of immigrants and housing in Madrid emerged while I lived in Madrid from 2005 to 2008, immediately after graduating from college. It was difficult to find an apartment—the rental market was an unregulated afterthought to the primacy of homeownership. Apartments varied tremendously in price, particularly depending on one's demographic profile and willingness to forego a legal contract, which would allow the landlord to earn undeclared income.

In the same moment, migration was surging, and Madrid became noticeably more diverse. Caught within the patchwork web of Spanish urban housing, I thus wondered, how were the city's newest members finding housing? When the multiethnic PAH burst onto the scene during the exuberance of 2011's 15M movement, I realized many immigrants had in fact purchased homes.

While PAH assemblies made evident immigrant acquisition of homeownership, official data were inadequate in accounting for their role in the housing market. The Andean community began to migrate to Spain in the late 1990s. Most became homeowners during a very short window of time, between 2003 and 2008. With the onset of crisis in 2008, many lost homes, and some returned to their countries of origin. But the Spanish government only collected census data on homeownership in 2001 and 2011. It gathered data on immigrant communities, including their housing patterns, in 2006. Meanwhile, data on foreclosures and evictions are notoriously difficult to obtain. The national government only recently began keeping authoritative data on home repossession. Previously data were collected on an ad hoc basis and could only be found by combing through individual judicial records. These official silences thus demand other methods of inquiry in assessing patterns of ownership and its devastating loss, particularly in a community that has gone largely uncounted in government records.

The story of immigrant homeownership and subsequent foreclosure, then, required methods of inquiry that extended beyond official numbers alone. During 2013 and 2014 I spent my days with the anti-eviction movement in the Spanish capital, working with people experiencing foreclosure and dispossession. Some had already been evicted from their homes; others were anticipating an upcoming foreclosure notice; still others were trying to negotiate with banks to alter the terms, quantities, or conditions of mortgages that they could no longer manage to pay. I went to protests and bank branches. I attended meetings with lawyers and financial officers. I sat in numerous assemblies and counseling sessions where a wide variety of individuals discussed the mortgages that had become their manacles. In the latter half of the book, I deploy standalone quotations from these fora that are in conversation with and illustrative of my analysis. Quotes are drawn from interviews, popular media, and my own fieldnotes.

I conducted extensive archival work to complement my ethnographic immersion. Part of the book's emphasis on historical analysis emerges from the research site itself. Madrid's urban activists are acutely aware of urban histories as complicit in producing the current political, economic, and social terrain.[30]

For example, one of PAH's slogans is "From the real estate bubble to the right to housing." That phrase illustrates a common theme that runs throughout current protests: protestors explicitly link their claims to particular historical trajectories of spatial change and make connections with similar processes elsewhere. Furthermore, in conceptualizing the problem, my research took as its starting point the issue of immigrant foreclosures and evictions. That issue necessarily conjures up spatial histories: the act of foreclosure is predicated on a particular sequence of events, with eviction as the punctuation mark at the end of a much longer process of dispossession.

To understand boomtime narratives of acquisition, I created an archive of real estate and banking advertisements directed at the immigrant public gleaned from the newspaper *Latino*, a free weekly paper distributed at metro stops and businesses in immigrant neighborhoods. What emerged from both these materials and the narrations of immigrants themselves was the singular importance of homeownership. Homeownership was also given weight and heft in its loss, in the experiences of civil death many interlocutors conjured poignantly. Thus I also wanted to understand homeownership as a historically produced category in order to untangle its contemporary devastation. I inflect my analysis with material drawn from popular culture, which illuminates how notions of the home, the city, and then the later crisis circulated through everyday channels. As such, homeownership brought together the state and civil society, individual homeowners and various tiers of governance. To untangle the property model meant that I arrived at the inception of this contemporary system under the Franco dictatorship. Through careful ethnographic and archival work, therefore, this book demonstrates how autarkic pasts and indigenous presents are integral components of contemporary urban politics in Spain.

This book is built around two central paradoxes: First, for both immigrants and native members of the working class homeownership promised to ameliorate inequalities and promote modes of inclusion, but instead deepened exclusion and vulnerability. Second, the collapse of homeownership and the precarity it engendered provided the terrain for new forms of activism, alliance building, and sociality. The death of a model that was meant to integrate provided new avenues for inclusive claims-making. These entwined paradoxes demand we place homeownership at the center of an account of immigrants as they navigated Madrid's boom and bust.

2   Mortgaged Inclusion

In 2006, after almost fifteen years in Spain, Betsy was ready to buy a house. She had moved to Madrid from her native Lima in 1991, during the major neoliberal reforms of the Fujimori government. Her arrival to the city in the early 1990s presaged the coming wave of immigrants from South America to Spain. Most settled in the Madrid region. Upon Betsy's arrival the Latino immigrant community in the capital was small; by the mid-2000s it had swelled to more than half a million people. Their fortunes soon rose, as work was easy to find amidst the city's booming economy. Betsy toiled long hours in a catering company that serviced one of the city's fanciest hotels. There she served bankers and titans of industry, many from the construction world, as they dined at extravagant conference dinners and elaborate cocktail parties. Her immediate environment, while fairly modest, nonetheless brought her into close contact with a society replete with riches that appeared easily in reach. Betsy meticulously saved her earnings. Soon she witnessed her friends buying homes. Modest salaries allowed them to purchase housing in peripheral neighborhoods, where real estate prices were skyrocketing. Betsy wanted to eventually return to Peru, but purchasing a house might aid that return. By staking her small claim on Madrid's boom, she dreamed of the future return on her investment. Imagined profits would make for a wealthy and comfortable retirement when she finally went home. If the Lima of her past was one of strife, brutal austerity regimes, and declining household finances, the native city of her future might be one of middle-class comfort and well-earned earthly possessions. Returning to the former metropole might then, too, develop the post-colony, raising humble families, many of Indigenous origin, from the depths of poverty into a much-longed-for middle class. Homeownership would provide the vehicle for that transformation.

To qualify for a mortgage, Betsy decided to buy a house with her brother Cesar in the suburban town of Coslada, southwest of the city. She had never been to Coslada, despite its relative proximity to Madrid. It was an inner-ring suburb, right at the edge of the capital. If she couldn't afford a place in Madrid proper, this option was certainly her next best. Coslada, like myriad other small towns across the plateau, was booming, too. Cranes dotted its horizon, announcing growth and progress. There Betsy and Cesar found a new development of small apartment blocks. While it was far from the center of town, with few amenities, the development hinted at a lively urban future. A new stop on the commuter rail line was to open at the end of the street, promising to whisk future inhabitants briskly to the center of the city. A small bar and a café had opened to cater to the first pioneering residents. Betsy and Cesar decided to stake their claim on this new urban frontier. They purchased the house with a combination of cash, personal loans, and a mortgage. The total amount of their debt hovered around 250,000 euros.

Betsy and Cesar—two immigrants making their way through the decadent landscape of Madrid—are modest protagonists within the city's transformations. Yet they are also emblematic of a millennial moment of transformation and consumption during which tens of thousands of Andean immigrants also purchased homes. These urban denizens flocked to bank branches and real estate franchises, eager to take part in the property boom. This chapter examines the qualitative experiences and everyday desires that made possible and even necessary immigrant entry into homeownership. It is concerned with the terrain against which homeownership became legible in order to make sense of immigrants' decision to become homeowners.

Homeownership's legibility was produced through a plethora of considerations. Social chatter, visual culture, policymaking, rapid demographic transformation, individual aspirations, and daily hostilities all contributed to the decision to become a homeowner. By deploying immigrant accounts alongside state debates on integration, real estate and banking advertisements, and popular news sources, I argue homeownership became a mechanism of integration and inclusion in a moment of uncertainty, growth, and possibility.

Strangers in the City

In the late 1990s, Spain suddenly became a country of immigration.[1] Through-out the twentieth century, in light of poverty, famine, war, and dictatorship, the country saw scores of people leave to make their lives elsewhere. Civil war ex-iles settled all across the Americas, while poor youth under Franco sought out better opportunities closer to home, as unskilled labor in France and the United Kingdom. This history suddenly reversed itself toward the end of the twenti-eth century. Through processes of decolonization, development, outsourcing, and deregulation, migratory flows shifted dramatically with major changes to the global economy. Spain, once repressed and depressed, was now an attrac-tive site for entrance into Europe. In addition to its booming economy, its lax border controls made it a target for immigrants looking for egress to Fortress Europe.

Betsy's move to Madrid was thus part of a larger wave of migration that began in the 1990s and would reach a crescendo in 2012, when almost six mil-lion foreign-born residents lived in Spain, a 300 percent growth since 2001.[2] At that point, foreigners represented over 12 percent of Spain's population. In Madrid Andean immigrants accounted for much of the city's immigrant boom during its early years. In the late 1990s, numerous countries throughout that continent struggled through a series of violent and sometimes deadly crises. In Ecuador and Peru financial collapse condemned already modest households to deep poverty. Interlocutors in Madrid all point to this earlier economic crisis as impetus for their departure. With aging parents and young children to sup-port, many people left behind families and spouses to seek economic refuge elsewhere. Ecuadorians, many of them women, often chose one of two places: Queens, New York, or Madrid, Spain. This migratory pattern created a major demographic shift for both Ecuador and Spain: the Ecuadorian community in Spain grew from 20,000 in 1998, to 200,000 in 2002, to 500,000 in 2005. Al-most all of this growth occurred in the capital, where this diasporic commu-nity's population was greater than in most Ecuadorian cities.

In popular culture immigrant narratives often begin with the decision to emigrate. These tales highlight the promise of the destination, replete with eco-nomic opportunity and the pleasures of modernity in the global north. Here we can think of Robert de Niro as he traverses New York's Little Italy in *The Godfather II*.[3] There is hardship but also opportunity, ripe for those who have the audacity to seize it. Even in our current moment, one of unprecedented movement, we think of boat trips and train rides toward the sanctuary and refuge of the west. The horrors of war-torn Syria, the bloodied shell left behind by Empire's exploits in Iraq and Afghanistan, the gang violence in El Salvador and Honduras, are never foremost in our mind. It is always the journey toward riches and progress that defines our understanding of migration, often with emphasis on the pioneering individual.[4] Yet migration always constitutes a loss, as people leave behind identities, communities, and home life. In the case of Andean migration, dispossession at home prompted the journey. Betsy was essentially kicked out, banished by a failing economy. Similarly, Aida, a middle-aged Ecuadorian woman of Indigenous origin, related that "everything was cut off for me and I couldn't take it anymore," with the crisis that engulfed her native Ecuador. She saw migration to Spain as her only recourse in a moment of deepening vulnerability and rampant debts. Similarly, Morton, a soft-spoken former lawyer from Quito, could find no work and absolutely no resources in order to sustain his family. He decided to head to Spain where he would "work in whatever, wherever there were possibilities to generate [enough] resources to be able to maintain the family back home." His law degree was unusable in Madrid, where he would have to pass an additional thirteen courses in order to have the state recognize his diploma.

Such heart-wrenching domestic dramas played out against a broader landscape of ruin. While Spain was flourishing thanks to a global marketplace of capital, finance, and land, Ecuador and much of South America were collapsing under the great strain and punitive logics of structural adjustment. Ecuador, Peru, and a host of other countries throughout the continent saw markets crash and the economy retract.[5] Morton, in recalling his migration to Spain, explicitly connected his departure to the crumbling political economy of Ecuador. There, in a country "that didn't have any international economic significance," the lords of economic science could come in to "experiment" with shock and austerity. Morton, Aida, and Betsy not only couldn't find work but they also found themselves consumed by debt. The Ecuadorian Sucre was completely devalued, leaving behind scores of invoices that went unpaid. The reality of material lack engulfed much of the continent. In 2003 I was in Buenos Aires for an extended stay. The elegant metropolis had fallen on hard times as its currency, previously tied to the dollar, collapsed. Buildings sat in ruin, while the streets of the historic center were littered with beggars. Their skeletal frames spoke of the crisis's violences as hunger crept through a once prosperous society.

Acquaintances referred to urban legends of the wealthy fleeing town in vans laden with US dollars. In Ecuador, a country suffering a similar fate, Morton recalled "a bank strike," where the technocrats running the country determined "there's no credit for anyone, nor are we going to repay any debts." He couldn't even retrieve money from the bank. At the same time, imposed austerity dictated "labor reforms that increasingly cut workers' rights, more rights for businesses, unions were decapitating their members, who accused them of being corrupt, and corruption was everyone." "In the middle of all this," he recalled, "we had to migrate." These forms of economic collapse prompted both poor and middle class alike to search for brighter futures elsewhere.

For many, economic exile was particularly painful because it required leaving loved ones back home. Bringing the entire family was prohibitively expensive. The cost of the plane tickets alone meant that families might only be able to send one member at a time. For many interlocutors, this reality dramatically altered extant familial relations. Women drove Ecuadorian migration to Spain, an unusual pattern within broader demographic trends that usually observe male heads of households making the initial journey abroad. While Betsy was a single woman with no offspring, other interlocutors described the pain of saying goodbye to their children. Mabel, also Peruvian, for example, was determined to triumph in Spain, but her determination was tinged with sadness as she bid goodbye to her daughter. Aida, meanwhile, left part of her family, in addition to her close community of Indigenous activists. She hardly told anyone of her decision to emigrate to Spain in order to avoid the reproach of her community. Her decision meant wrenching herself away from a movement that was finally attaining some of its key demands. But her personal circumstances and feelings of obligation toward her family required she abandon the movement even in its decisive moments. Thus migration meant wresting oneself from a particular environment at the behest of economic interests. That process was disruptive to families, but also to broader social ties and community relations.

Bringing the entire family was also not an option because of the dire housing situations that awaited recent arrivals. Not only would émigrés, often already deep in debt, need to purchase plane tickets, but they would also have to worry about finding a place to live for multiple people. Aida, who came with her husband, wanted to bring her little sister, whom she had helped raise. She lamented, however, "where will I receive her? How are we going to live three to one bedroom? How would we live like that?" Morton described the conditions upon his arrival as *paupérrimas*—pauperous or completely abject. He described moving into what is colloquially referred to as a *piso patera,* a name that derives from the slang word for the wooden boats full of immigrants commonly associated with Mediterranean crossings.[6] In many such apartments, individuals rent shifts in a bed, a system known as *cama caliente,* or warm bed. Morton stayed in a house run by an Ecuadorian family, a situation that he relates "made me terribly outraged . . . four people in a family reduced to one bedroom when [the baby] was still nursing. . . . Thirty people lived in the rest of the house, where they charge each one of us water, electricity, this, that and the other thing." Interlocutors describe finding their first place to sleep through friends and family. They entered into such precarious situations with the knowledge and hope that soon they might find something more permanent. Eduardo, a soft-spoken Ecuadorian man in his fifties, explained to me the common pattern of settlement: first sharing maybe even a bed for a few days or weeks, then finding a shared room, finally perhaps a room of their own, when they can begin to contemplate bringing over other family members. Aida's experience bears out this pattern; during her first years she lived "in Tetuán, then in Tribunal, then around Carabanchel, then around Pueblo Nuevo," before she purchased her house in San Blas. These itineraries of settlement speak to a constant hustle in which these individuals could only really concentrate on the immediate needs of social reproduction. Mabel, a middle-aged woman from Lima, related: "Out of twenty-four hours in a day, we worked twenty. Work and work. Work, eat, sleep. We didn't allow ourselves any leisure." Constant toil was at the service of getting ahead and accruing some small amount of capital.

Such precarious situations furthered exclusion and difference. As described in the next chapter, the rental market had been neglected throughout several generations of housing policy that has encouraged homeownership. As a result, urban rents fluctuated wildly with little regulation. When faced with prospective immigrant renters, landlords essentially held all power. Throughout interviews, immigrant interlocutors related similar early histories in their adopted city. Upon arrival, they desperately needed housing, yet could not find places that were not degraded or poorly located; usurious landlords saw them as either crooks and criminals or ignorant peasants from whom they could extract extra money. Immigrants often relied on their rapidly expanding social networks: the cousin of a friend from Guayaquil, or an ex-neighbor from Mancora. Many landlords, meanwhile, asked to see work contracts and pay stubs. Yet many jobs provided neither, which made securing a rental contract difficult. Without such documentation, landlords demanded exorbitant down payments and inflated rents, or refused to rent to immigrants entirely. Even so, legal status or formal employment was no guarantee against the predations of xenophobic landlords.[7] Housing was thus another site of ambiguity and anxiety. In the absence of a well-regulated rental market, immigrants relied on their own informal networks in order to house themselves.

Legal ambiguities and informal arrangements were constitutive parts of a more generalized system. Loopholes and informal practices dot the Spanish legal and legislative landscape, particularly in the realm of housing and employment. When I lived in the city in 2005, I went to look at a three-bedroom apartment. It was in the historic center of the city, immediately behind the regional government headquarters in the Puerta del Sol. The owner was a bureaucrat in the Treasury Department. After I expressed interest in renting the apartment, the owner quoted me two prices: with a formal contract, it would cost 1200 euros. Should I be inclined to rent without a contract, he would let it for 800. I didn't rent the place but remained bemused by the thought of the taxman cheating on reporting his own income. Such everyday illegalities permeate many aspects of the economic sphere. Subcontracting or simple illegal bookkeeping allows many companies to keep workers off their official payroll. When contracting services through my work, I was often quoted two prices: one the official price with invoice, and the other, much lower, to be paid under the table. This seemingly harmless flaunting of the rule can in fact create ambiguities for people who rely on official paperwork to achieve or maintain their immigrant status. Legality might appear a simple technicality, but it in fact implicates a complicated terrain of policy and practice veiled in uncertainty. Many immigrants came over on tourist visas and overstayed. Thus entry was legal even while residence was not.[8] To maintain legal status, some immigrants also must maintain work. Yet the Spanish economy is shot through with irregularities and marked by informal practices. Many immigrants work in industries rife with potential for abuses, including domestic labor, agriculture, and construction.

The way in which labor law and employment practices intersect with immigration and integration requirements is not necessarily an accident. Kitty Calavita has documented how the Spanish state institutionalizes irregularity through the creation of legal loopholes and contradictions. In her analysis, immigration policymaking largely serves to perpetuate liminal spaces immigrants are forced to inhabit, both physically and metaphorically. The legal often serves to maintain immigrants in this murky state as "others," acting as a mechanism by which these xenophobic attitudes can persist and flourish. She writes: "Immigration laws, anchored by temporary and contingent permit systems, build in illegality," creating a kind of "institutionalized irregularity" that allows both the economy to rely on immigrant labor and society to regard immigrants as a class apart. Rather than act as a means of obtaining citizenship and representation, the regulatory system often manages to obfuscate, creating an almost Kafka-esque state of confusion riddled with irregularities. Such a system serves "to provide not just a supplemental workforce, but a particular *kind* of workforce, i.e., one that will do the jobs, and under conditions, that local workers no longer accept despite double-digit unemployment."[9]

Difference was unwanted as a substance of daily life, yet necessary for both production and reproduction. Yvette, a middle-aged Ecuadorian, worked as home help upon her arrival without papers and narrates a similar story, in which she slept four hours a night and was at the mercy of an imperious boss. In her scant free time on weekends, all she desired was to sleep, so exhausted she could barely make conversation with her husband. Her boss wanted to hire a woman without papers, who could be made to work long hours with low pay. The conditions of her employment cut her off from her community and family. Meanwhile, Mabel described her first days in Madrid: "I arrived at 9 AM, and by 12 I was working. The next day I went to pay all my Social Security taxes. I paid Social Security. It was their obligation, but you eat all your own expenses. You pay Social Security." Mabel knew employers were supposed to pay Social Security, but she did it anyway, always cognizant of completing those responsibilities that might accord her full membership. Motivated to escape the corruption and brutality of Peru under Fujimori, Mabel set to work in whatever kind of employment she could find in order to one day bring over a daughter still behind in Lima. Ambiguities and illegalities of everyday also provided openings in which immigrants could perform their ready willingness for full membership. Mabel strived to do everything by the book, meticulously following through with her duties as a newly arrived immigrant. She went on, "I came without making one mistake as a citizen." Her invocation of citizenship hints at the ways in which that category might confer rights but certainly demands responsibility and obligations. It is not just a piece of paper or legal status, but rather an entire performance of civics. Demonstrating the ability to follow through on obligations and perform civic responsibility is what then might allow formal access. Exclusion to formal and informal membership, however, is what accorded the nation its informal economic foundation, keeping costs low while the economy boomed. The new trove of immigrant labor allowed for another host of economic activities: women could go to work rather than care for children or the elderly, construction companies could keep their costs down, and agricultural products continued to be cheap. Immigrants paid far more into Social Security than whatever they received in public benefits. Soon, too, they would come to sustain the housing boom as it reached its apogee.

The Discourse of Integration

Homeownership would become a means by which immigrants further demonstrated their capacity for full membership. State discourse encouraged homeownership as a particular kind of fix for the problem of migration and the emergent question of integration. The institutional irregularities that proliferated, allowing easy exploitation of immigrant labor, emerged against a backdrop in which the state was ambivalent if not outright hostile toward immigrants. Tracing the Madrid government's attitudes will unearth how the immigrant as a *social subject* was perceived as problematic and even a threat.

Integration lies at the heart of many sociological debates on immigration, which look to social and political structures to explain diverse outcomes.[10] Such perspectives also attend to those systems and policies that are not particularly targeted at immigrant populations—for example, integration policies per se—but instead shape everyday life.[11] Different political structures, historical citizenship regimes, anti-racist and multicultural policymaking, racialization, labor market segmentation, and colonial histories are all important variables that might determine outcomes.[12] Within such an epistemological understanding, however, integration "is a normative goal rather than a description of reality."[13] Indeed, rather than constitute a process of assimilation or acculturation, we can also think of integration "as a control strategy that aims to incorporate targeted populations into governance structures."[14]

Approaching integration not as a social process of settlement but rather as a normative goal meant to control populations provides fruitful terrain for investigation. As such, it turns integration into a political project that works through a variety of arenas, including discourse. Discourse is a key site to understanding relations of power and creates different subject positions. In *Encountering Development*, Arturo Escobar examines what he calls the "discourse of development" in order to map how power operates within a collection of different arenas that produce both development and consent for particular rationalities of international intervention under the rubric of expert aid.[15] Similarly, discourse drawn from the nascent days of integration policymaking in Madrid is a rich site to interrogate competing ideologies and emergent politics of managing difference. During the mid-2000s, the discourse of integration emphasized individual responsibility and an aversion to dependency and "handouts," and was one variable that encouraged homeownership when read in conjunction with other facets of daily life. Attention to discourse, too, draws out how statecraft demands integration, while also inscribing difference and managing foreigners as separate from and not quite equal.[16]

Sociological approaches to integration and incorporation, moreover, often privilege the national arena, "tak[ing] the existence of a bounded national 'society' for granted."[17] The Spanish case, however, demands a different lens, one that emphasizes the scale of the city and region. In Spain the national government establishes the norms and regulations by which foreigners can enter, stay, and work within the country. These laws have gone through several rounds of major overhaul since their inception in 1985. With changing political sensibilities and powers, each evolution either relaxed or strengthened barriers to entry. Further, each new regulatory phase addressed different issues, such as family reunification, or amnesties for undocumented immigrants. These concerns, as to who could gain admission and how that person would then establish herself legally, from entry all the way to the acquisition of citizenship, fall under the jurisdiction of the national government. But integration is another matter: rather than establish cohesive, national integration programs that would then be devolved to the scale of autonomous communities, provinces, and metropolitan areas, the state determined subnational governance arrangements would be responsible for integration.[18]

One quirk of the Spanish context, however, is that integration policy fails to identify exactly how and into what an immigrant would integrate. The question of integration remains ambiguous because of Spain's refusal to address the broad definitions of Spanish identity: "there has been a lack of tradition to openly debate the meanings and substance of the national identity within which [immigrants] should or could be integrated."[19] In large part, this unwillingness springs from the troubled history of twentieth-century Spanish nationalism and its association with Fascism and the ever-present Basque and Catalan questions. Franco demanded unity, prohibiting the regional identities that make up contemporary Spain. In light of the diversity of traditions, languages, and identifications, Spain does not advance one vision for the model citizen, and instead adjudicates integration policymaking and competencies to regional governments.[20]

In the late 1990s and early 2000s, the country struggled to craft adequate policy amidst these shifting considerations. As migration increased rapidly, the various tiers of the state scrambled to produce a coherent response. Early Socialist efforts conceived of integration as a social project that encapsulated a variety of issues and angles and, because of the nature of Spanish immigration, addressed and accorded certain rights and recognition to populations with and without documentation. Integration policy, in its infancy, addressed the contextual situation, with attention to such issues as family reunification, social capital, education, and health care, beyond the simple question of legal status or employment. Yet this moment was short-lived; as soon as the Partido Popular achieved absolute majority in parliament in 2000 under José María Aznar, they threw out that idea of integration. Instead, the new policymaking "represented an important regression as regards the status of both regular and irregular [immigrants]."[21] Policy focused on restricting access to rights and recognition, conferring that privilege only on those with legal status. Further, it obligated new conditions for the regularization of legal status, including permanent residence deemed "adequate" by the state, which was also necessary for family reunification petitions.

Immigration and integration were not central to policymaking efforts in Madrid until 2004. The Al Qaeda train bombings on March 4, 2004, dramatically transformed the political landscape, and José Luis Rodríguez Zapatero, a Socialist, won in a surprise victory against Aznar.[22] Elected on March 14, Zapatero vowed to reform Spain's immigration and integration policies in order to better address the actually existing landscape, in which hundreds of thousands of people were stuck in legal limbo. The national shift in priorities immediately influenced regional policymaking. On March 18, four days after the general election, the Madrid Assembly convened the Study Commission on Immigration in the Madrid Community. The inauguration of the commission marks the beginning of Madrid's formal integration policymaking.

The Study Commission invited representatives from various civil society groups, including immigrant associations, in order to assess the social panorama of migration within the region. On May 20, 2004, a representative from Rumiñhaui, an Ecuadorian association, visited the commission. Throughout her comments, the representative pointed to the difficulties surrounding housing, particularly regarding legal ambiguities and loopholes, housing pre-carity and economic toil. The confluence of irregular status and poorly en-forced labor laws conspired to produce precarious situations in which Ecuador-ian immigrants found themselves largely defenseless. This situation also had gendered implications within the community.[23] Women working in domestic service were poorly paid, forced to work at all hours of the day and night, of-ten lived with the families for whom they worked, and had little protection against abusive employers. Many were subject to sexual harassment, which was treated as simply another hassle of getting and keeping work. The Rumiñhaui spokeswoman revealed how conditions of vulnerability, rampant throughout all aspects of economic life, of course influenced housing. Domestic servitude offered little in the way of housing security; one anecdote brought to the com-mission related the story of a maid turned out in the middle of the night. She had no money and nowhere to go, abandoned fearful and alone on a posh street in the darkness. Irregular employment practices exacerbated this situation—she was, of course, not accorded any kind of severance. Other narratives from different immigrant associations portrayed similar situations of vulnerability, workplace abuses, and necessary resiliency in the face of unregulated hostility. With little in the way of protections against these kinds of situations, the vari-ous immigrant populations in the Madrid region had to rely on members of their community or the benevolence of strangers in order to get ahead.

Madrid's politicians often responded with skepticism and even hostility to these testimonies of toil and isolation. The cognitive disjuncture between the immigrant experience and the response of the state is evident in discussions over the *empadronamiento*—registration within local government records. Re-gardless of legal status, residents of Spain can register in a municipality's *pa-drón,* a local ledger that tracks the population. Once registered, a person has access to basic services such as healthcare and education. But the study com-mission found many immigrants failed to exercise this basic right. As asso-ciations told the committee, their reasons were myriad: to register, one needs proof of physical residency, yet many immigrants could not produce a rental contract or utility bills because of ad hoc housing situations (and many land-lords' desire to rent under the table). One also needs some kind of valid govern-ment ID, but many immigrants either lacked such documents depending on their form of entry or were wary of producing documentation that might reveal their irregular status. Finally, when the government wanted to crack down on immigration, news reports proclaimed the state's intention to cross-reference the *padrones* to locate irregular residents. Engaging with the state was an experience fraught with tension, anxiety, and fear; why risk such engagement if it might end in deportation or arrest?

March of 2005, a year into the commission, one lawmaker asked incredulously of an immigrants' rights activist, "Why are they not registering in the *padrón?* What causes the fact that they're not registered?"[24] Three months later the same politician, from the Socialist Party, once again interrogated an expert from the pro-immigrant organization Red Acogida. He stated:

> You have told us some things that have worried and surprised me. One of them is that [immigrants] are not susceptible to registering in the *padrón.* According to current legislation, everyone has the ability to inscribe, including in a bank, any person can register, he just needs to have a place in which to do so; I insist, I know people who signed up in a bank in a particular place, so I don't understand why those people aren't susceptible to the process and I would like it if based on your experience, you could explain it to us.

Such an easy process, he implied, what is wrong with the immigrant that he does not follow it through? Ignoring the testimony of a diversity of experts who had explained exactly why the *empadronamiento* was such a charged issue, the representative revealed an unwillingness to understand the broader situation that might make the immigrant subject feel excluded. It was not about whether an immigrant can enter a bank or not, but rather the feared implications of an act that was for this politician wholly benign. By disavowing that reality, such an account served to further notions of incompatibility: the immigrant could not carry out the most basic of Spanish tasks. Further, in such a rendering the responsibility resided completely with the immigrant rather than with the greater system at large.

This emphasis on responsibility reverberated through these testimonies, and situations of exclusion were then rendered into examples of immigrants' failure to become proper social subjects. In a presentation by a representative from Cruz Roja, the Spanish Red Cross, Joaquín Pérez Gil-Delgado drew a bleak portrait of life at the urban margins as "immigrants arrive from other countries and they integrate and take up part of the most negative aspects of our society," which is violence against women.[25] Further, within immigrant communities, drug use was rampant and alcohol consumption was "out of control." Finally, immigrants often lived in "conditions that were less than hygienic," in situations of "*cama caliente,*" despite possessing work permits and steady employment.[26]

To the Red Cross representative, such a situation derived from immigrants' desire to save as much money as possible to send to their countries of origin, with little regard for the dominant habits of the society at large. Yet while immigrant experts had repeatedly told the commission such situations arose out of exclusion, poverty, and hostility, here what emerges is a sense of cultural incompatibility. Madrid's immigrants simply failed at becoming productive members of Spanish society, taking to drugs and alcohol while dwelling at the absolute edges of civilized life.

Pérez Gil-Delgado's intervention raised an important question that animated another theme haunting these discussions: the specter of remittances. At various points representatives and lawmakers remarked upon the capacity of immigrants to save money to send back to their country of origin. Yet while policymakers appeared to laud these communities for their ability to save, they were simultaneously troubled by its implications, namely that large sums of money accumulated in Spain was being sent elsewhere. Further, Spain had no further influence in how that money might be used in its final destination. Here emerged another tension. While people like Morton and Aida came to Spain precisely because of opportunities to make money and thus help family back home, lawmakers viewed the flow of remittances as antithetical to processes of integration. For Pérez Gil-Delgado, for example, sending money abroad instead of investing in their own social situation in Spain meant immigrants chose to live in conditions of penury with little regard for society at large. Immigrants here were good *financial actors,* but negligent to their social responsibilities.

Two competing visions of immigrants and their urban lives translated into the ideological frameworks that underpinned policymaking. As such, the broader project of integration—as an idea, as an object of policy, as a process, and as a discourse—was fraught with its own ambiguities, shot through with myriad tensions. Many of the experts who appeared before the Study Commission spoke somewhat philosophically about the idea of integration. Mustafa El Merabet from the Asociación de Trabajadores Inmigrantes Marroquíes de España (Moroccon Immigrant Workers Association) offered his vision regarding immigrant integration to the committee. He spoke of integration as implicating a host of social actors, each with a different notion "because even though we speak the same, we each situate things as we sense them."[27] Here again uncertainty and ambiguity emerged as key themes. Later in his presentation, he came to a dilemma that runs throughout each expert testimony: is integration a process for which the immigrant is solely responsible? Or is it more dialectical, implicating both native and newcomer? He wondered to the commission, "up to what point is the law going to obligate the citizen to tolerate me?"[28] Such a question raised the possibility that tolerance can be inscribed in law. But it also hinted to the reality of mid-2000s Spain: tolerance was still something that had to be mandated at times, potentially through the vehicle of legislation.

Integration, of course, is not solely a question of mutual tolerance. Instead it implicates an array of variables. Ibarra Blanco, from the Movimiento contra la intolerancia (Movement Against Intolerance), spoke of the difference between economic and social integration. For the most part, immigrants were finding jobs and helping to grow an exuberant economy. Indeed, as many experts detailed, immigrant contributions to Social Security far outweighed their financial costs to the system. But integration, he pointed out, is not simply an economic barometer of activity, particularly when so much of immigrant work was poorly remunerated. For him, integration accounted too for issues such as "poverty, loneliness, and sadness" and required that Spaniards themselves worked to "neutralize their prejudices."[29] As such, the task of integration was one that befell all citizens and civil society actors, constituting a field of action rather than normative prescription.

While immigrants themselves continuously spoke of exclusion, loneliness, and marginalization in a new and foreign place, authorities read delinquency, ghettoization, and the specter of violence. The policy solution emphasized individual responsibility, placing the onus on the immigrant. When the Study Commission concluded in 2007, the Assembly put together another commission for integration and cooperation, in which the regional government's policies regarding immigrant incorporation into urban life took shape. The head of the commission ended his first appearance before the committee by stating: "I believe in freedom; I believe in the capacity of every man or woman to get ahead with his/her own effort. . . . I do not believe in paternalism."[30] In another appearance, he stated: "We bet on individual development. We do not believe in multiculturalism. . . . We believe in the individual, who we respect and who we consider primarily responsible in integration."[31] Integration as individual project of amelioration is in direct contrast to the idea of integration as social project implicating an array of actors. Instead, it is a personal, liberalized concept of incorporation. Responsibility rests wholly with the immigrant, who must be given the barest minimum so that she might then grow into her role as a new Spaniard. To extend more privileges or benefits would, in the eyes of the state, be a form of paternalism. As such, the Madrid government sought to create "equality of opportunities, mutual responsibility, social cohesion, and normalization."[32] After that, the immigrant could through participation, "encourage his own integration."[33]

Meanwhile, translating personal responsibility and individual advancement into policy proved a difficult task. The commission failed to enunciate the benchmarks or processes by which an immigrant would become integrated. While it mentioned the acquisition of proper papers, the use of healthcare services, and educational attainment as arenas in which immigrants might more actively participate, no clear image of an integrated society emerges beyond vague nods to issues of social cohesion. Without addressing underlying questions of tolerance and prejudice, the commission presented no cohesive vision of what immigrants are supposed to integrate into or how such an ill-defined process should take place. Thus the Community 2006–2008 Integration Plan, the first of its kind, included a lengthy diagnosis of the migratory experience in the Madrid region. Following many pages of analysis, the plan proposed a series of interventions, which further reveal the state's anxieties over migration— namely that immigrant financial gains would not then be channeled back into productive circuits of capital. The devaluation of the immigrant as *social subject* served to valorize her role as economic actor, but one whose fortunes needed discipline and direction. In particular, one program addressed the problem of remittances through the creation of co-development programs. The plan elaborated that remittances, when "used well," could "help development in countries of origin." As such, the Community would create development policies that would "incentivize productive investment of remittances" in such countries."[34] What this idea meant in practice, according to the plan, was "the development of financial products in local banks, which could capture part of the *private remittances,* with the goal of directing them towards profitable and sustainable economic activities (checking accounts with advantageous conditions, mortgages, microcredits)."[35] Such a proposal revealed the anxiety of lawmakers. Despite abjuring paternalism in their public interventions, lawmakers nonetheless wrote it into law, the implication of course being that countries of origin— Ecuador, Senegal, Morocco—needed to be told how to use these surging flows of capital properly. What emerged, too, is the idea that the financial and real estate sectors are key sites of investment rather than, for example, infrastructure or agricultural production.[36] In a moment in which financial services were increasingly interconnected, moreover, such a proposal served to direct immigrant gains into global markets.

The plan also encouraged channeling money back into the Spanish economy by increasing immigrant homeownership, which emerged as the de facto form of integrating immigrants through housing. In the section discussing housing patterns among immigrants, the document points to the correlation between length of stay and housing tenure, revealing that groups with longer histories in Madrid tended to acquire private property rather than rely on the rental market. Within the broader context of Spain's cultural attitudes and policies toward housing, such data within this context were evidence that Madrid's immigrants were in fact integrating. The plan called for "promoting access to mortgages for the immigrant populations."[37] To promote immigrant homeownership, the state worked with an organization called ProVivienda, a private entity that received public funds to elaborate housing strategies, including helping immigrants take out mortgages. The goal of the organization's work with the immigrant community was "a long term project" to "influence within real estate negotiations." This association offered to mediate with banks on behalf of immigrants, easing their access to credit. According to a July 29, 2005, article in *Latino*, the organization intervened to ensure the bank waived the requirement of an indefinite work contract, then necessary to receive a mortgage. In its stead ProVivienda provided a certificate confirming the client had at least two years of steady work. Additionally, it advocated mortgages with monthly payments equivalent to 40 percent of people's monthly incomes, against the standard 35 percent, because "the ability of the immigrant to save when sending remittances to his country of origin is admirable." Within a crowded field of programs and social centers—each with often-illusive goals—the ProVivienda program offered tangible help with measurable outcomes.

Official integration discourse produced its own ambiguities and tensions. While it failed to provide a holistic portrait of integration—as a process, a goal, a normative framework for the elaboration of policy—it reveals the Madrid government viewed the immigrant other with skepticism regarding the immigrant's capacity to be a productive member of society. At the same time, it placed great importance on economic abilities and contributions. Yet if an immigrant was left to her own devices, those abilities might be wasted as her financial gains might not be put to good use.[38] These anxieties then left room for the important role of the banking and real estate industries to provide ameliorative mechanisms to address a host of issues for both immigrants and the state. Homeownership, for Madrid's Latin American community, became a key tool to resolve myriad tensions, aspirations, anxieties, and contradictions of the moment.

Good Financial Subjects

The state's integration discourse reveals a profound ambivalence toward the immigrant as a *social subject*. However, her role as a *financial subject,* participating in international remittances flows, was greatly valorized. How, then, to direct those flows back into the Spanish economy? Indeed, while the state struggled to define their goals and plans for integrating its immigrant populations, the private sector had already alighted on the foreign born as the newest frontier for the spread of credit and capital. During the same period of the early to mid-2000s, banking and real estate firms began to elaborate sophisticated marketing campaigns explicitly directed at an immigrant public. In keeping with the state's anxieties and appreciations, we see great value placed on the immigrant as a savvy financial consumer. If her role in society at large was up for extensive debate, her role within the economy was singularly positive, particularly in her capacity to participate in relations of credit, risk, and urban speculation. Homeownership thus became the tool that could capture immigrant money and channel it back into the booming economy.

The attitudes of politicians and policymakers, which demonstrate ambivalence and at times outright hostility toward immigration, and their concrete proposals for integration worked in concert with the banking and real estate sectors. Not only were the boundaries between the state, finance, and the construction and real estate industries incredibly porous, but they also produced contradictory messages that conspired to push homeownership on an immigrant public. While the state in its many permutations could be sneering and even punitive toward the immigrant other, banking and real estate services welcomed this new customer base with open arms.

Real estate and banking were eager to explore new frontiers for capitalization. Met with hostility and confusion within many arenas of public life, immigrants found themselves courted by these industries, their dreams for incorporation accessible through participation within the explosive marketplace. Yet it was not just a strategy for procuring a roof over one's head; homeownership also allowed for a whole host of other opportunities tied to the immigrant experience to take place. While it permitted easier family reunification, additionally it was a vehicle by which marginal groups—never accorded full membership even with the acquisition of legal status—could stake their small claim on Spain's ebullient boom, as a means of securing imagined futures both within their adopted country and back home.

Thus far I have mostly treated the integration discourse as wholly within the purview of the state. As Madrid became more heterogeneous during the late 1990s and early 2000s, however, integration became a question animating social, economic, political, and cultural relations. While perhaps not named as such, integration—that is, how immigrants would settle, survive, and become part of Spanish society—was a question that traveled freely between the halls of government, popular material culture, political economy, and the aspirations of immigrants themselves. Social, ideological, and material realities produced their own registers and understandings of incorporation, inclusion, and the increased heterogeneity of urban life. The recuperation of this historical memory complements official government narratives to deepen understandings of the political economic moment.

Before the state had fully developed its integration programs and policies, the banking industry saw immigrants as prime customers for their financial services. Early financial penetration was sold as a social mission that would help the immigrant in her economic journey. La Caixa, one of Spain's biggest banks, began to penetrate the immigrant community in 2002 through the creation of transfer services for remittances.[39] Establishing agreements with banks throughout Latin America, Eastern Europe, the Philippines, Pakistan, and Senegal, La Caixa captured clients within immigrant communities, establishing themselves as a potent link to back home. During the same period, it created ties with various civil society organizations directed at immigrants, allying financial and social concerns. In its 2007 annual report, the bank declared that "facilitating immigrant integration is [our] singular priority."[40] By offering services directly targeted to the immigrant experience, it began to infiltrate those segments of the population that were largely ignored by the rest of civil society. In the process, it spread a message of trust, confidently connecting immigrants with their families back home through ubiquitous financial ties. Thus the bank was not only a useful service, but also a benevolent patron aiding immigrant settlement.

The newspaper *Latino*, which had several local editions within Spain, including Madrid, was a free weekly paper that began in 2005. It was mostly distributed at metro stops in heavily immigrant neighborhoods, and by 2006 their circulation was around 100,000 copies in Madrid, Barcelona, and Valencia. Because of its extensive reach and tailored local content, the newspaper provides a lens into the visual and material culture of the South American community in Madrid. Regular articles spoke to issues in both Madrid and countries of origin, connecting its reading public to an international social geography. By 2006 and 2007 the paper was awash in banking and real estate advertisements, in addition to coverage of the role of Latinos within those sectors. The paper also featured a regular column on the housing market in the interest of helping readers become homeowners.

Initial advertisements in *Latino* mainly addressed the issue of access to credit. Peppering the interior of the newspaper, these ads often specified credit products tailored to immigrants. Finanfácil, for example, advertised early and often, their large images plastered with *"hipoteca especial extranjeros"* (special immigrant mortgage). This franchise assured readers of the "over 50 offices at [their] service," as images of immigrants of different backgrounds stared back. Using the informal second person (*tú*), such an advertisement presented a different reality to immigrants used to the hostilities of their adopted country. Informal language transmuted amiability and casual hospitality, while phrases stressed the painlessness of the process. Finanfácil and CrediÁgil contained within their names references to facility and ease (*fácil* and *ágil*). Both were early and frequent advertisers in *Latino,* appearing almost weekly with at least one very large ad. These allusions to agility and ease are in contrast to the narratives of toil and trouble of immigrant interlocutors.

For example, Yvette's first years in Madrid were marked by incredibly long hours for which she was paid poorly. Even after she acquired legal residency, her work situation remained precarious. At one point, she had seven jobs at once; while contracted employment paid her a part-time wage of 300 euros/month, hourly work in six other places provided supplement. Such a work life was defined by constant movement; the hustle of daily life meant nothing was easy. In contrast to such hustle, these advertisements promised painlessness and facility. Further, in a world dominated by bureaucratic hurdles and *papeleo*—the daily bureaucracy of endless paperwork—such a promise was an enticing offer, a glimpse of relaxed normalcy in a sea of struggle. By mentioning their widespread presence in urban life, too, Finanfácil establishes itself as mainstream; rather than some backwater operation clandestinely catering to the immigrant public, the chain asserted its strong public presence.

These campaigns spoke directly to an immigrant public. Hipoteca Grátis (Free Mortgage), for example, plastered its campaigns with images of immigrant faces; the backpage of the November 4, 2005, issue of the newspaper was covered with a large image of "César," "a 32-year-old Colombian," clearly of Afro-Caribbean descent. By taking advantage of the novel products of this financial entity, César was able to leave behind his rented room to acquire his own place, more spacious and accommodating, a small slice of Spain to call his own. If this young man from Colombia could make such a financial move, so too could many of the readers of *Latino*, who at present were "throwing away their money on rent." Indeed, another Hipoteca Grátis ad, which proudly displayed the Jaramillo family, claimed purchasing a home was in fact cheaper than renting. In text purporting to be from the young family of three, the ad proclaimed, "We now know that it is cheaper to buy an apartment than to rent." As such, they seemed to share their newly acquired wisdom with readers, letting them in on a secret previously closed to foreigners.

In many advertisements providing financial services, various firms claimed to offer special deals for foreigners so that they could achieve domestic bliss and get out from under the great weight of renting. With the subtitle, "if you're Latino, this is your real estate agency," one Century 21 ad (December 23, 2005, p. 20) asked rhetorically, "Why pay rent when you can now buy your own home?" The profound barriers to the rental market were not only major inconveniences on the path toward settlement and stability, but also severe impediments to reunification plans that demanded housing adequate for numerous family members. Yet in the pages of *Latino*, a solution to such a problem emerged. Why attempt to navigate the precarious and pernicious *madrileño* rental market, in which landlords are unscrupulous and prejudicial, when one could just buy a house? No longer would the immigrant have to suffer through the predations and whims of the landlord. Here was a solution both beneficial and specifically addressed to immigrant needs.

While state practice and discourse read delinquency and deviancy into immigrant urban life, these campaigns presented a different reality, a potent promise that appealed to people's desire to settle with dignity. In addition to portraying homeownership as a tangible and immediate facet of urban reproduction for immigrants, credit and real estate entities disseminated a vision of comfortable lifestyles laden with opportunities for upward mobility, middle-class comforts, and great choice. The back page of the January 20, 2007, issue, for example, was dedicated to an ad for Fincas Mendel, a real estate company

NO TIRE MAS SU DINERO
EN ARRIENDOS,
LA CASA DE SUS SUEÑOS
POR EL MEJOR PRECIO

FIGURE 2.1. Detail of advertisement for Fincas Mendel. Source: *Latino,* January 20, 2007, back cover. Used with permission.

that "had the key to your future." Clearly Latino, a young, modern couple on the bottom right-hand corner of the page stared at a blue rendition of a quaint pitched-roof house with a family of four, mother and father flanked by daughter and son. Under the oft-repeated adage regarding throwing away one's money on rent, Fincas Mendel promised "the house of your dreams for the best price." For a population that largely toiled long hours on the margin of urban life, few opportunities catered to or even allowed their dreams and desires. Further, the images of young families reflected their aspirations for stolid domesticity and private family life. In a world in which people took whatever they could get, here they were being offered possibility, expansive opportunity, and an imagined future that actually resonated with their dreams of settlement.

Concurrent to these consumer visions, the newspaper's own coverage of real estate, mortgage markets, and immigrant participation in the banking sector covertly promoted participation in this marketplace. Throughout the pages of the newspaper, regular stories and features gave advice on how immigrants could best attain a mortgage. During one period of time, Hipoteca Grátis even offered a short column on various aspects of purchasing a home; the lines between editorial and advertising were blurry, thus ensuring the influence of such financial entities. Alongside such materials on the practicalities of the market, meanwhile, regular stories trumpeted the importance of immigrant consumption within Spain's decadent economy. For example, a March 24, 2006, feature announced to readers, "Immigrants will sustain the housing market. This year they will buy 170,000 units." While their bodies sustained that market by providing the crude labor, their hard-earned euros would sustain it through new consumption opportunities, too. Through economic integration, Madrid's Latino population would demonstrate to society at large their importance as consumers actively contributing to the expansion of the economy.

What emerges throughout these pages is a portrait of the immigrant as a consumer who exemplifies dignity and worth, integral to the booming Spanish economy. For example, an October 11, 2007, story carried the headline, "The immigrant, the great client for the banking industry." Such language placed great prestige and weight on immigrants as financial subjects, carrying out their duties and responsibilities within the realm of the market. If society at large often viewed such individuals as delinquents leeching off the goodwill of the state and social services, here they emerged as diligent workers with great capacity to manage and extend their small domestic economies. That rendering, in turn, reverberated with the performative qualities of good citizenship. Immigrant interlocutors impressed upon me their impeccable financial histories. They were exceptionally worried they might "*quedar mal*" (rub the wrong way) by falling behind on payments. Cognizant of dominant opinions that often read foreigners as spendthrifts and wastrels, many felt that assiduously carrying out their financial obligations was a means of demonstrating common decency and moral fortitude, a way to dismantle and disprove the sea of voices critical of increased heterogeneity. To be a good client implied both a desire for and an ability to attain full membership.

This imbrication of consumption, financial capital, and citizenship emerged in one ad from the now-defunct Caja Madrid, featured on July 1, 2005, early on in the newspaper's history. The ad, which occupied the bottom half of the third page, depicted stairs leading out of an airplane onto the tarmac below. A welcome mat read "*Bienvenido*" at the bottom. The text accompanying the ad stated the bank had "placed at your disposal all financial services you need to feel at home." Through the formal *usted* address, the ad treated its audience with great respect, offering to them a portal into the Spanish financial world. The invocation of home lulled the reader into a feeling of security, while also establishing that she will need banking services to fully settle. Visually, the ad

FIGURE 2.2. Advertisement for Caja Madrid. Source: *Latino,* July 1, 2005, 3. Used with permission.

allied the experience of migration—tied to the image of the plane—to sentiments of hearth and home, and personal finances, uniting three disparate entities into a composite whole.

In addition to promising inclusion and even full membership, banking and real estate made homeownership easily within reach for immigrant clientele. Betsy spoke of the "contagion of having a mortgage," as "everyone around you was buying." Aida describes attempting to rent an apartment, yet the real estate agent with whom she was in contact offered purchasing a place as vastly preferable. She had gone to the Centro Hipotecario del Inmigrante (CHI-Mortgage Center for the Immigrant) after hearing an ad on an Ecuadorian radio station. She relates, "They were really supportive, [with] marketing about how they wanted to help us." She interpreted their reaching out to the immigrant community as an act of goodwill, a means of helping out people in need. She believed in the moment she had found a firm that understood her particular concerns and predicaments in a way others did not so as to "include immigrants in society." In many cases, they promised monthly payments much lower than current rents. Having scrupulously cared for their household finances in order to send ample resources back home, people like Mabel and Betsy, Yvette and Aida saw this as their next rational economic decision. Even if they hadn't thought much of buying a house, they thought they must do it today for fear the price would double tomorrow. The common sense of acquisition—that contagion—was disseminated throughout their immediate environments, from the chatter of real estate agents, the gossip of friends, and the visual assault from the media.

That wisdom was of course bolstered by the endless rise in prices, authoritatively narrated throughout the immigrant community. If one did not buy immediately, the price would have risen considerably the next day. Within Madrid's Latin American community, many people worked in the construction industry and were thus quite familiar with the industry's explosive growth. Everyone had a friend or relative who was employed somewhere in the sector, who would pass along the latest news of the outsized growth of the housing industry. The city around them was rapidly transforming, and their friends and neighbors were buying into the frenzied property market. The environment was saturated with consumption, and everywhere one looked there was an opportunity to participate. Eduardo, who worked construction for several years, would chat about the market with his fellow day laborers as they set foundations and put up new walls. After work under the hot sun, as the day came to a close, they would find themselves bombarded by real estate agents offering deals on housing. At the café across the street, a phalanx of financial professionals awaited their arrival for an after-work drink. Sweaty and tired, Madrid's immigrant laborers could ponder and take part in the easy fantasy of homeownership. During the weekends, at barbecues around the soccer field in the Casa de Campo, more agents would come to pitch their wares to young families and singletons. In their dark suits, these figures were indiscriminate in their pursuit of clients. The dream of homeownership was egalitarian, open for all those who dared to dream of its promises.

Many in the dark suit, moreover, were also immigrants themselves. Increasingly, the lines between consumption and labor market participation were blurred, furthering the spread of credit and its common sense. As firms sought out immigrant clients, they often employed foreigners to serve as ambassadors within their communities. Indeed, the advertisements that dotted the pages of *Latino* not only promoted homeownership to readers; they also invited immigrants to find employment in the sector as vital links that could extend the homeownership model to others in their community. One June 7, 2006, ad sought "*captadores*" and "*vendedores*" for a new agency in expansion.

By participating in this economy, not as unskilled labor but rather as the suave, suited representative, people could realize their goals of upward mobility and the accumulation of wealth. The spread of homeownership to immigrants relied on these interlocutors, who connected finance capital with the world of the foreign born. When I lived in Madrid during this time, I knew a number of employees of Tecnocasa, Spain's largest real estate franchise. Most of these acquaintances came from elsewhere and sold housing to other immigrants. Thus when one went to buy a house, the agent might also be a relative newcomer. The loan used to purchase the house might be arranged through financial entities such as Centro Hipotecario del Inmigrante, clearly created for the immigrant community.

The close-knit ties of the Andean community aided this frenzy of acquisition. The early days of settlement, in which newcomers had to rely on friends and acquaintances, helped to deepen ties. As Morton described, those ties were necessary not only for housing, but also for employment, for tips about bringing over family and then educating children. Within a society that could be hostile, moreover, social ties were also important for self-preservation, as they allowed people to navigate a new environment and make a home for themselves in the city. Banks and the real estate industry took advantage of these informal ties as a means of spreading financial risk. Often, banks or financial franchises would employ people not as real estate agents but rather as informal *captadores*—capturers sent out to snare clients. Charismatic members of immigrant communities, they worked on a commission basis, using their knowledge of a particular community to spread the dogma of homeownership and overleveraged debt. Mabel, for example, was induced to purchase through her relationship with one such man, who she describes as "of great confidence," well known throughout the Peruvian community. She said, "he knew everyone, he knew the banks." He was an "*enchufe*" (literally an electric plug) connecting his community to the complicated web of financial and real estate services. For Mabel, however, this man appeared as an advocate, allowing her to realize her dream of homeownership. In the moment, immigrant interlocutors interpreted the attention lavished on their communities as coming out of solidarity, a kind of benevolence or goodwill that would allow them to take part in this explosive economy and cut through its morass of paperwork and regulations. As members of the community purchased housing, therefore, they shared their tips and tricks with friends, helping to spread the mortgage "contagion." Here, finally, was a solution to a host of problems. Becoming a homeowner would allow people to bring over family, in addition to securing a permanent roof over one's head. It was also a symbol of success that would telegraph to society at large one's worth to society. Homeownership offered a solution to housing problems, a means of demonstrating ability, a comfortable future, and at times a job, as immigrants moved up the economic ladder from day laborer to *captador* to real estate agent to owner of a financial franchise.

Finally, it was a strategic economic tool that would secure futures of comfort. What drew many to this form of housing tenure was the fact that it might line the coffers for a comfortable old age in the country of origin. While homeownership is perhaps a marker of permanent settlement, here it allowed for forms of greater permanence, but also dreams of comfortable destinies back home. Such a decision was meant to allow for greater opportunity later on. In a study by the Colectivo IOE, an Ecuadorian woman related:

> A lot of immigrants like me decide to buy a house, because it's money after all. It's basically like you're saving that money, because if I want to leave, I'll take the apartment and sell it and I know that the money I have, the little bit that I've invested I have there (in the house). I sell it and if I earn something well great, but at the very least I take out what I've invested. So the majority of people think that for what they pay in rent, well it's better to pay for something that'll be mine.[41]

This logic makes further sense when considered against the recent financial history of Latin America. As Morton related, the economic crisis inaugurated policies that prevented people from collecting on debts or withdrawing their money. A house, however, is a tangible asset, one that might depreciate in value (which was thought highly unlikely in the present climate of Spain at the time), but that cannot be disappeared like money in the bank.[42] As such it can be a tool for investment that allowed for people to think about comfortable, secure futures. The endless rise in prices implied that when one hoped to move back to Quito or Lima, selling the house would repay the mortgage amount with an ample nest egg to take home, where euros would go much farther than local currency. Thus immigrant homeownership was in part paradoxical. While it implied greater settlement and stability, it was also designed as a tool for future departure and return. In this guise, too, it also subverted the narrative of the Madrid government. While gains were to be momentarily directed into the Spanish economy, the end goal was for further remittance money to flow back to the country of origin.

Interlocutors describe making this decision in part because of the great trust they assumed they could place in the Spanish system. One element many hoped to escape was the petty corruption that animated so much of urban life in cities back home, a theme many interlocutors raised unprompted. Betsy describes her mother purchasing a house, a process that demanded she hire a lawyer, an economist, and a host of other experts to ascertain that everything about the sale was above board. In friendly conversation with Celi and Margarita one day, I laughed with them about their erroneous beliefs. At home in Ecuador, they had to pay off someone for even the simplest task. Driving down a rural highway, they might find themselves confronted with a patrolman's bribe. Europe, however, promised a different reality, in which everyone operated with honesty and straightforwardness. Thus, as Celi and Margarita impressed upon me that day, in Madrid, "you trust the man in the tie." The man in the tie, whether he is the banker or the broker or the notary public, must be by the book. If immigrants were delinquents and deviants, as they were often portrayed in the media, then their Spanish counterparts must surely be reliable and decent, acting in the best interests of their clients. After all, one could drive the length of Spain without bribing someone. Thus when they walked into the bank offices, they assumed that the people who sat across from them at the desk, those holders of professional knowledge, gave of that expertise as obligation to transparency. The confidence one could place in the system, even if it had proved to be so treacherous at times, was the great benefit of being in Spain, a nation ruled by international doctrines on human rights, fair trade agreements, and consumer protection regulations.

The possibilities that bedecked the pages of *Latino*, the proliferation of financial entities and real estate offices in immigrant enclaves, the scores of suited professionals offering access to the world of mortgages and homeownership, and extant impressions of the Spanish economy all nourished the imaginations of modest immigrant families. Tales of economic predation and seduction, of con men dressed as bankers and credit access that's too good to be true, can render people such as Betsy and Mabel into dupes and victims. Yet their entry into homeownership was made possible through their own aspirations. Their financial desires came to be entangled within this great political economic web, which in turn offered them the possibility of consumption. As recent settlers in the brave new world of millennial Madrid, people like Mabel and Yvette had come to the city primarily to make their fortunes. Homeownership was a logical next step within their settlement in the city. To see their reflections in popular media as the good client, to be courted by financial professionals, to grasp the possibility of investment opportunities, and to take part in the urban spectacle of construction and consumption all affirmed and upheld their own sense of purpose and aspiration.

The Question of Integration

For the state, homeownership offered quantitative proof of immigrant integration, a benchmark to encourage through both policy and laissez faire edicts on industry. The state's seemingly benevolent, economically liberal attitude allowed the banking and real estate industries to infiltrate the lives of Madrid's immigrant communities, fostering a common sense that covertly, though forcefully, encouraged consumption of housing. In a moment in which immigration and integration policy often served to confuse and confound, maintaining the immigrant other in a liminal state, homeownership provided a tangible means that would ameliorate the conditions of quotidian urban life.

This account forces us to confront the notion of integration as a normative goal. In both policy and the academy, the question of integration relies on specific variables such as voting patterns, language acquisition, and educational attainment. Yet partitioning the immigrant experience into such categories seldom captures or accurately reflects the complexity of daily life, in which competing systems propagate different norms and rules. Thus we can observe a lacuna between statecraft and the urban experience, a problematic but productive terrain. Indeed, such disjunctures are key sites to examine the relation between official policy, economic imperatives, and the immigrant quotidian.

If we look qualitatively to the homeownership apparatus, as it interacted with and influenced the immigrant experience, we can also see the ways in which integration is far from a normative process that sees the direct, scaled progress of an immigrant's assimilation into society. Rather, the imbrication of political attitudes, policy, industry, personal considerations, and family histories produces a plethora of outcomes. Crafting effective, reasonable, and politically sound immigration and integration policy is a difficult task, often influenced by ideological positions that occlude and ignore existing practices. Within such a landscape, homeownership is an easy fix, particularly when the onus for inclusion is largely placed on immigrants themselves. But the Madrid system, which saw widespread ownership as a form of integration and economic advancement, was deeply flawed, predicated on outsized debts and financial fraud.

I have not provided official numbers for Ecuadorian, or Andean, or immigrant patterns of homeownership; these are notoriously difficult, if not impossible, to ascertain. The 2007 *Encuesta Nacional de Inmigrantes* (National Survey of Immigrants), found that of the 346,272 households that originated in the Americas, 67,728 lived in owner-occupied housing. Of the 441,0181 households that were mixed Spanish American, 160,349 lived in owner-occupied housing. What are we to make of these numbers? Are they sufficient data to corroborate my evidence? The data do not show us how many Ecuadorian households owned property, or how many Latin American households in Madrid owned property. What they demonstrate instead is that a majority of households clearly didn't own property. That being said, a number of immigrants were only just purchasing housing in 2007, as the pages of *Latino* make evident. If crisis hadn't struck immediately thereafter, these numbers might have steadily risen, such that a majority might have soon found themselves as homeowners. But for something to be disseminated as common sense does not require the full participation of all members of a group. Instead it can be a sentiment, an imperative, or, in the words of Betsy, a "contagion," caught in the web of everyday urban experiences, something that easily fills the liminal spaces between statecraft, policy, and the quotidian chatter of friends and neighbors.

3 Homeownership's Urbanism

At the southeastern edge of Madrid, a long boulevard leads to the ghostly streetscapes of the PAU Vallecas urbanization.[1] The boulevard is mostly empty, devoid of trees that might shade the few pedestrians from the hot Spanish sun of the summer months. It leads the *flaneur* to large housing blocks that sit half occupied. Many balconies are obscured by "for sale" banners, while chain-link fence protects several building sites that lie fallow, their developers having gone broke in the crisis. From the higher floors of a new housing block, homeowners can catch a glimpse of the city's changing skyline. Here one can espy the towering glass and steel of the new financial services center that defines Madrid's northern edge, proclaiming its multinational modernity in a moment of European integration. But those developments are at a distinct remove from the dusty half-finished streets of the PAU Vallecas. In the mid-2000s, the region inaugurated the extension of the train line to this far-flung locale, allowing *vallekanos* to travel to the center of the city with relative ease.[2] Yet urban life within this ghostly village remains contingent and precarious.

Similar landscapes dot the Madrid region. The PAU Vallecas was one of a series of such developments, which sought to urbanize greenfield sites at the peripheries of the city during the early and mid-2000s. As European money gushed into Spain, planners extended transportation networks and improved existing infrastructure. They created new urban destinations with budgets bloated with extravagance. After a severe housing shortage, the city would also plan to add 300,000 new units, despite estimates that the deficit was only about half that amount. But these new peripheral neighborhoods would not only solve a deepening housing crisis; designed wholly under the tenure of homeownership, they would also provide property taxes in perpetuity. Future municipal revenue was thus assured by the spread and success of the housing market

It is tempting to locate the city's recent crisis of homeownership as the after-effect of the boom. But to do so would miss the distinct role of homeownership within a longer urban history. The predominance of owner-occupied housing, and its importance within the Spanish economy, had historical roots that explain Madrid's contemporary landscape. The extant literature on "The Spanish Model," as Isidro López and Emmanuel Rodríguez term it in their seminal piece on the Spanish crisis, hints at the centrality of the construction industry in the Spanish economy, to the detriment of comprehensive economic growth.[3] Yet such explanations do not fully uncover the significance of homeownership in Spain, nor its salience in Madrid's model of urbanism. Unlike other accounts that trace the emergence of the construction sector and thus homeownership back to the late 1950s, when Franco opened up the country to outside investment and influence, this chapter locates the seeds of this model during the very early years of brutal autarky.[4]

Privatized urban development was born out of economic necessity. Part of an economic strategy, speculative projects have long dominated planning agendas, which use the gains of homeownership to produce elite spaces for international consumption. Rather than change the city's planning logics, the recent moment of easy credit and explosive growth simply allowed for the speed and scope to change. This history illuminates the myriad inequalities and dispossessions that homeownership produces as a central mechanism for expansion.

Dictatorship, Devastation, and Dwelling in the City

After three years of brutal civil war (1936–39), General Francisco Franco claimed political victory, having vanquished his Republican foes. Madrid was one of the last strongholds to fall to his Nationalist Army, which had strengthened its clout through more peripheral and conservative regions. Against the democratic ideals, antireligious intellectualism, and egalitarianism of the Second Spanish Republic (1931–36), Franco espoused a Catholic ideology tied to autarkic self-reliance. He sought to cut Spain off economically from the rest of the world while exalting the Church. The progressive strides of the Republican era were to be undone in favor of a repressive regime of intolerance and fear.

Autarky, which Franco prescribed during the first two decades of his dictatorship, was the overarching policy of isolationism and stoic dependency on national products and economies alone.[5] The country was cut off both ideologically and financially from the rest of the world. As the Second World War engulfed the globe, Franco's policies literally severed the country from the international marketplace. The country allowed no international trade and mandated exclusive self-sufficiency. Yet the civil war had decimated the nation, condemning it to economic depression and material lack. While the young dictator dreamed of imposing his will upon the country, uplifting Catholic tradition and agrarian domesticities, he had to contend with a deepening crisis of hunger, poverty, and resource deficiency.

Despite his celebration of tradition and the agrarian roots of Spanish society, Franco also determined his capital city must be the crucible for his political power and prestige. After the war, Madrid was dirtied and dingy, made into rubble through many rounds of blockades and bombings. To reach the city from the hinterlands one had to pass through wide tracks of shanties that ringed the formal capital. According to the regime, its Republican predecessors had left the city disgusting, with "the most repulsive dirtiness that invaded everything."[6] Franco bemoaned the experience of entering the city, "contemplating the miserable slums, these shanties that surround the city."[7] The city was encased in a ring of misery and sewage, while certain areas "suffered from dirty and excessively overcrowded housing."[8] In order to move into the new era of Catholic authoritarianism, "the new political system decided that Madrid had to purge herself of her sins," which "had converted her into an 'emporium of terrifying filthiness.'"[9]

Madrid was a small city, rife with poverty, no match for Barcelona or Bilbao, where industry had long ruled. Additionally, the regime worried that the city paled in comparison to other European capitals; while Berlin and Rome proclaimed the splendor of their leaders, Paris and London displayed centuries of political power and industrial might, in addition to more recent exploits of imperialism. Central to the government's agenda was consolidating all efforts in the capital, repressing regional differences, and creating the majesty and splendor of a true European capital city.[10] Madrid, then, must reflect these various ambitions of political centralization and international prestige. Postwar reconstruction had to both rehabilitate the city and enhance its glitz and glamor.

In order to promote and transform Madrid into a grand and cosmopolitan city, Franco immediately ordered a new urban plan upon taking office. In

1939 J. Paz Maroto created a preliminary plan for the city; however, it lacked an overall vision that might reflect the regime's ambition.[11] Thus Franco turned to Pedro Bidagor in an effort to mount an exhaustive plan. Three new boulevards proclaimed the vision of the new regime. The *Vía Europa* would rechristen the northern portion of the Castellana boulevard to better enunciate an emerging multinational relationship between this country and its capital, and the continent at large. The *Vía de la Victoria* would run south from the city to Castilla La Mancha and Andalucía, connecting the capital to the newly conquered hinterland. The *Vía Imperial* would lead from the city northwest to the historic site of El Escorial, where Philip II had ruled his court (and where Franco would construct a giant mausoleum in the side of a mountain using prison labor). The imperial spirit of the city would also be celebrated through renovations of the historic center that had been badly bruised and the creation of a *madrileño* "façade," which allied historic architecture to Franco's new imperialism.

The regime also annexed outlying districts in order to bring them under control and eradicate the specter of impoverished informality. The city's overall size thus swelled as it added once-rural villages to its administrative territory. Carabanchel, Villaverde, and Vallecas, for example, went from being small independent towns to the urban fringe. The Bidagor plan, which prescribed this annexation, extensively detailed the transformation of these areas into orderly and disciplined neighborhoods. Social services would complement this physical planning. Alejandro Acha, an architect influential within the regime, elaborated the ideal type for the urban neighborhood, which would mimic the community and Catholic harmony of the small town within the anonymous and immense metropolis.[12] Here a medical center, recreational facilities, and a local school would serve the residential area. The church would sit in the center, radiating Christian goodwill to the local inhabitants. These planning efforts sought, too, to banish any lingering red sentiment, which the regime worried still flourished in the more impoverished corners of its untamed capital city.[13]

Yet this vision of urban harmony and imperialism could not easily come to fruition. The city was beleaguered and poor, its economic fortunes reflecting the tragic consequences of autarky. Scores of workers could not find employment. And Madrid faced a dire housing crisis, its stock decimated by years of warfare. Rather than dissipate, the shantytowns only grew and proliferated as more people came to call them home.[14] As the country experienced economic depression and physical devastation, the regime concentrated natural and material resources in the capital, prompting tens of thousands of migrants to make their way to the capital city. During the period 1940–45, the population of the city grew by just under 100,000.[15] They too took up residence in the city's informal edges, exacerbating urban poverty and disadvantage. Soon the city overflowed with people in desperate need of both housing and work. While Bidagor's plan had dedicated extensive space to the question of housing, the state lacked funds to realize his program. By the fifth anniversary of Franco's rule, under 2,000 new units had been constructed.[16] As Franco incited planners to realize his dreams for a capital city, they were confronted with deeply entrenched urban poverty and acute material lack.

As the regime directed its scant funding toward more emblematic urban works, Franco's economic policies prevented large-scale construction of social housing.[17] In the throes of autarkic self-reliance, the regime had no funds to spend on housing. Early efforts by the Falange, Franco's fascist group, sought to provide housing for the poor as a means of both fulfilling their Catholic duty and incorporating people into the city. Real estate speculation, in its view, constituted a nefarious practice that undermined religiosity in favor of lucre. But other factions within the new government were staunchly against such intervention. César Cort, a member of the town council and architect, advocated investing in and encouraging the construction industry, allying capitalist interests with the question of housing. In the infancy of the dictatorship, a tension emerged between housing as a social right and need and housing as an industry.[18]

In light of these economic considerations, the regime soon embraced homeownership as a tool that might resolve a host of problems. Designed to reduce unemployment among the working class, the Decreto Ley of November 25, 1944, encouraged new housing construction as a means to create jobs. Rather than pursue measures to encourage further industrialization, which Madrid lacked, Franco instead saw in the construction of housing a potent new frontier for economic development. Yet to make such a system work, these houses would of course need occupants with economic means. As such, this law also sought to encourage the acquisition of housing under the rubric of private property. To do so it put in place a new system that would promote private property among the middle class, offering incentives to purchase brand-new construction.[19] Thus, since its inception homeownership has been closely allied not only to housing needs but also to labor and employment, hinting at the central role of the construction industry in the Spanish economy.

Drawing on Bourdieu, Jane R. Zavisca writes: "Housing [homeownership] is the market, bar none, that the state must create."[20] Of course, dispossession is implicit in the creation of new land markets.[21] The case of Madrid illustrates the state's singlehanded role in the creation of a housing market and the dispossession it entailed. Until the early 1940s, the city had largely been a city of renters.[22] Those children of rural landowners who were not first born would make their way to the capital and purchase large, stately housing blocks within the city. This situation also ensured that the political interests of rural, landed gentry—*caciques* who ran daily life in agrarian Spain—were represented in the capital. These second and third sons, in addition to maintaining close ties with Madrid's political classes, would make their money from the rents charged to inhabitants. Madrid's famous nightlife emerged in part from this system, which ensured a large, moneyed population of individuals with no full-time employment tied to a workday. Everyday citizens lived in housing units they did not own, and the idea of the individual ownership of a private unit was anathema. Instead one either owned the entire building or one rented. This system, however, was soon completely undone as the regime made private ownership of individual units a central goal to Spanish economic development. What was uprooted and then largely banished was the traditional method of dwelling in the city.

Franco's homeownership legislation created "two systems of state protection of house building: That of 'protected dwellings' . . . and that of 'subsidized dwellings,'" the latter being "typical middle class dwellings."[23] These units could be sold to individual families, thus disrupting the traditional form of *madrileño* housing tenure. The government offered the same financial incentives for both kinds of construction: loans were issued to construction firms at up to 60 percent of the value, with an annual interest rate of 3 percent. Further, the state would contribute 26 million pesetas annually to housing construction.[24] With no incentive to pursue low-income housing construction, firms could carry out projects as they saw fit. They would receive the same state benefits regardless. Meanwhile, housing clearly would no longer fall under the purview of the state, which rejected the earlier *falangista* premise that it was the regime's duty toward its subjects. Rather, it sought to privatize the provision of this good. Thus from its inception, consolidated housing policy loosened state control and encouraged private investment. While that decision was born out of necessity, it removed housing from the battery of goods and services provided under welfare systems. So, too, did it create deep connections between housing as shelter and investment, the construction industry, and economic development.

Incentives to construct middle-class housing resulted in a boom in higher-end construction at the expense of protected housing projects for more modest urban residents. While the companies could receive the same benefits to construct lower-class housing, the middle-class alternative was more profitable: companies could sell units rather than just putting them up for rent.[25] We can see a profound shift after the Decreto Ley took full effect. Soon after the 1944 law, for example, the pages of architecture and design magazines are suddenly awash in new projects, all designed for a discerning clientele. For example, a 1946 edition of *Revista Nacional de Arquitectura* featured a story on a new building on Ayala Street, in the Salamanca neighborhood. Notions of cleanliness and community peppered descriptions of the project: "the service staircase, open to the patio, gives more light and cleanliness . . . and the open access ventilates the rooms." The building was grand, on a posh street in Madrid's nicest neighborhood. The façade featured small wrought-iron balconies, numerous windows, and a pleasing mix of brick and stone, "the construction, in all its details, of the best quality."[26] The floorplan was spacious, accommodating servants if necessary. Two mirror-image flats occupied each floor, with terraces both in the front and to the rear.

Within such architectural projects, meanwhile, there is the realization of certain middle-class, western fantasies of domesticity and cosmopolitanism. These invocations of light and hygiene conjure up sophisticated, modern lifestyles and livelihoods that go against the misery and decay of the street, recalling ancient tropes that turn to logics of dirt and filth to produce both value and inequality.[27] Working through such imaginaries, property as both economic miracle and consumer affair offered a means to produce the bourgeois city, counteracting the long years of war and misery. In a city surrounded by grime and urban shanties, such developments hinted toward a glamorous urban future.

The regime designed this push toward homeownership, meanwhile, as part of a broader plan for economic recovery following the war. The construction industry was key because it satisfied several requirements. First, it was well suited for the demands of autarky as it demanded no outside resources or investments. Spanish architects could design buildings to be built on Spanish soil by Spanish construction workers using Spanish timber, brick, cement, and steel.[28] Second, it could reconstruct the country after the devastation of war. Bombed-out remains and rubble could be replaced by new construction. Third, it might provide wages for the scores of unemployed men who lived at the edges of the city, seeking work to no avail. Finally, it would help to solve the housing question, perhaps providing those same men with better residence so that the city might eradicate its outer rings of poverty and blight. The buying and selling of individual units, however, would be the key ingredient that would encourage the flow and accumulation of capital.

Emphasis on homeownership allowed the construction industry, and thus the regime, to eke out new frontiers for capitalist expansion in ways that were unavailable through traditional industry. Housing policy during the 1950s perpetuated this push toward property ownership. Changing land-use laws facilitated new construction, while tax breaks encouraged people to purchase new homes, that is, homes that had just been constructed. At the same time, urban rental laws froze rents at very low levels, discouraging landlords from renting or maintaining units and depriving them of rental incomes. The endeavor to create new housing under the rubric of homeownership and against rental tenure schemes allowed for the ruination and degradation of much of the historic housing stock.

Adjudicating development to private businesses allowed capital to circulate through the economy, but it also profoundly changed the nature of Francoist urbanization. Rather than direct the gains from this nascent industry into comprehensive growth, the regime and its developers—the emergent group of "empresarios de Franco"—channeled funds into spectacular projects that might proclaim the grandeur of the city.[29] An early project, inaugurated in 1948, was the Edificio España, which was to act as one bookend for Franco's imperial urban façade. The building was designed and built by the Hermanos Otamendi, important Basque planners and architects who had produced some of Madrid's finest architecture of the early 1900s. This project, however, was much larger in scale and scope. Occupying an entire city block at the edge of the historic center, the building was to be the tallest in both Spain and all of Europe. When it was finished in 1953, it became an enormous luxury hotel that might cater to the emergent tourist industry.[30] In a full-page photograph from a 1953 architectural publication, a bird's-eye view of the city shows the Edificio de España in the foreground, its marble and brick light against the city that stretches out beyond it.[31] It soon became an important emblem. In a Madrid guidebook from the late 1950s, Bonifacio Soria Marco, a celebrated author in Franco's Spain, pointed to the development as one of the city's most notable buildings.[32] It was no mistake that the building shared a name with the nation: this gigantic construction was a portrait of the New Spain, even if it bore little relation to the imperial past.

In a history written soon after Franco's death, one author describes the Edificio España as "a symbolic building, a building that summarizes the meaning of the autarkic moment."[33] Indeed, the kind of development embodied by the Edificio España would soon become the norm. In handing over urban development to private interests, the state was able to place a bet on an imagined future. The project was highly speculative, sacrificing modest gains to wager on the success of Madrid's nascent tourist industry. The building, made possible through homeownership—albeit indirectly—pursued audacity and spectacle. The city, in this moment, was still mired in the depths of urban poverty, which would linger long after Franco had opened the country up to foreign investment. But despite misery at the peripheries, the center might be a lively European capital, replete with the kind of infrastructure necessary for visitors on the grand tour. In its name, the Edificio España reveals itself to be the symbol of the new nation, a hulking behemoth that proclaims grandeur, wealth, and expansion. The gains from private ownership—mostly middle and upper class—were then channeled into reimagining central parts of the city deemed emblematic for an outside audience. Thus various firms, often intimates of the dictatorship, inaugurated new hotels and leisure palaces along the Gran Via and Castellana.[34] Their clean lines and imperial facades proclaimed a kind of Francoist modernity. Yet at a stone's throw entrenched urban poverty continued to engulf the majority of the city's population.

The kind of urbanization that the Edificio España exemplifies allows us to reflect on debates in urban studies that examine strategies of urbanism as a means of competing within the global marketplace. This recent strand of scholarship has explored the concept of "worlding," a process by which cities use placemaking strategies and outsized speculative urbanism in order to claim the world's attention.[35] It is, as Ananya Roy and Aiwha Ong write, "the art of being global." Such accounts present processes of privatized speculative excess as recent, aided and abetted by multinational flows of money and influence. Analysis rarely locates speculation and worlding within longer trajectories of urban history. Yet since the inception of the Franco regime in 1939, Madrid's urbanization privileged spectacle and emblematic placemaking projects over comprehensive growth. Homeownership and the central role of the construction and real estate industries served as the fuel for this model of urbanism, a model that endured into democracy and Europeanization.

Indeed, Franco had alighted on a lucrative formula. The homeownership model allowed construction firms to get rich: they sold off new, light-filled units in elegant neighborhoods to those families with capital to spare. Those neighborhoods soon replaced any dingy remnants of postwar poverty with the bourgeois atmosphere of a cosmopolitan city. In turn, firms could redirect their gains into other kinds urban development, further remaking the city for an international audience. By the late 1950s and early '60s, the regime could finally pursue massive investment in social housing. It planned for enormous new residential communities at the periphery of the city and channeled subsidies to companies to carry out the construction of new neighborhoods. A propaganda video from 1959 proudly depicts the great progress of housing construction under the regime.[36] Middle-class women visit the housing office to secure their spots within one of the thousands of new units then under construction. Aerial shots pan over building sites, and the viewer is awed by the sheer size and scope of these projects. The narrator reads a laundry list of neighborhoods that will soon be home to new, modern housing blocks. The shanties that had marred the city would be replaced by these rational beacons of good urban living.

What the film does not show, however, is the street life and quotidian experiences of these new neighborhoods. With new housing did not come well-serviced neighborhoods. Orcasitas, Villaverde, Usera, and other new peripheral neighborhoods, would have new housing but little else. In Villaverde a "*poblado de absorción*," that is, a new neighborhood meant to "absorb" former shack dwellers, new housing suffered from "infrastructural deficiencies and a nonexistent urban fabric, without access or transport, what gave rise to 'colonias de barro' [mud estates], without any services, and without connections to the urban core."[37] Madrid's planning under Franco thus did little to ameliorate the entrenched inequalities of the city. The city remained starkly divided between rich and poor, with little in the way of comprehensive growth.

The story of the country's economic development in most accounts often begins with the process of opening up that began in the late 1950s. During that period, the dictatorship abandoned its cruel policy of autarky. Autarky, rather than cause the economy to flourish with new Spanish-made substitutions, instead maintained the country in a state of depression. Yet in the late 1950s, as Europe embraced the aid of the United States and its Marshall Plan, Spain turned toward technocratic rationalism against isolation. Its new embrace of the international order was famously satirized in the film *Bienvenido, Mr. Marshall,* in which a small village in the central plateau remakes itself in the guise of the "typical Spanish" town in order to welcome Marshall on his voyage through the continent.[38] Of course, his visit is but a brief car ride through the center of town, now replete with whitewashed walls, flowerboxes, flamenco dancers, and *toreros.* No longer sealed off from the rest of the continent, Spain also felt the warm embrace of the United States, its ally in staunch anticommunism.

Similarly, literature on the construction industry and urbanization, including housing policy and homeownership, also looks toward the modernization efforts of the latter half of the dictatorship.[39] During this time, the country "caught up," while also experiencing a boom in tourism. Looking toward those moments of progress and economic growth, however, ignores the ways in which autarkic policy contributed to later processes. Madrid's particular model of urbanism, seemingly wholly aligned with a particular era of millennial excess, instead emerged in a different moment of crisis. Certain economic logics were well suited to the economic demands of autarky, technocracy, and subsequent democracy, even if their devastating effects would only be laid bare almost a century later.

Democracy and the Enduring Promise of Europe

When Franco died, Madrid was a sprawling city still struggling with poverty. The formalized working-class areas that emerged at the peripheries in the late 1960s and '70s greatly improved the housing stock through sweat equity. Yet these areas, as Manuel Castells documents in his early work, were poorly serviced, without proper infrastructure.[40] Thus while people had housing, it was far from centers of employment, without schools or medical facilities, proper transportation systems, or even adequate water supplies. This reality inspired the emergence of a robust neighborhood movement that demanded more egalitarian city-making.[41] Despite advances in both citizen participation and overall Spanish prosperity—the late dictatorship had seen the emergence of consumer culture and a strong middle class—the country soon suffered economic depression. Spain, and by extension its capital city, was not immune to the crises of accumulation that took place during the 1970s. Throughout the early years of democracy, then, a tension emerged between the exuberant, liberal, and open culture of postdictatorship and the strident demands of a recessed economy.

Following the social movement struggles of the late 1960s and 1970s, Madrid became a haven for left-wing politicians during early democracy. Many made their way from neighborhood mobilizations into the formal walls of electoral politics. Throughout all layers of the government, the PSOE experienced triumphant success in 1982. A staunchly left-wing, intellectual coalition of municipal planners soon found themselves tasked with planning the democratic city. As protagonists within battles over municipal services during the previous decade, these young planners sought to reshape Madrid after Franco's rule, using space to insist upon democratic and egalitarian lines of social justice and the Lefebvre-ian right to the city.[42] The resulting 1985 General Plan hewed closely to these ideals, espousing the *derecho a la ciudad* as a foundational analytic for the new democratic capital city. As such, the plan attempted to prevent future urban speculation and to provide infrastructure to the southern areas of the city that had experienced explosive growth with little service provision during the late dictatorship.

Yet Spain's rapid transition to democracy did not erase the vestiges of its Francoist past. Nor, too, did it erase dominant practice, as a generation of scholarship concerned with historical memory and Spain's mandated amnesia has diligently documented.[43] Further, dominant planning paradigms that had dictated development in the capital city continued to exert influence, as Madrid still pursued spectacular placemaking projects to the detriment of comprehensive development. The city's planners would not see their visions come to fruition: policymakers and planning professionals immediately expressed their disdain for a plan labeled too Marxist in content and one unable to satisfy the demands of an international city. As with the early Franco years, a depressed economy precluded the realization of a project many architects and planners deemed far too utopian in scope and edict.[44] While local planners preached the language of social justice, city hall could not carry out their plan and called for a different kind of urban development and concomitant planning regime that once again privileged elite interests and privatization. Lacking public funds to carry out projects, the municipality ceded land—both public and private—to private companies for development. The urbanism that emerged from this web of public interest and private initiative often followed the dictates of the latter. The private sector funded many large-scale projects in which "the emphasis on slick outward appearances did not always coincide with the planner's diagnosis of the city's problems or the solutions they presented."[45]

Planners were also thwarted by extant systems of urban development. The early years of the Franco dictatorship established a complicated, Napoleonic planning system that emerged directly from the reality of the capital city. National law enshrined a highly circumscribed, hierarchical, and authoritarian planning system in 1956. That law, which reflected the Madrid case, ensured a dense, intricate, and top-down structure in which national policy laid out frameworks for development to which city planning must comply; this structure worked through the local, provincial, and national scales.[46] The central state then had the authority to veto a plan and guarantee that urban development took place exactly as laid out in a plan. It required all plans work through a hierarchy of uses and scales, addressing the general city, the partial zone, and the project, that is, the actual construction, a system that continues to this day.[47]

This planning bureaucracy has been further complicated by the evolution of governance over the course of the democratic era. The political structure of Spain has given increasing competencies to autonomous communities, which in turn inflate state spending through the creation of additional layers of bureaucracy.[48] Autonomous communities developed to undo the centralization demanded under Franco, in which regional particularities were squashed in the name of a Spain that was *una, grande, y libre*. To empower regions and redress previous political repression, the state developed subnational arrangements, devolving governance responsibilities and promoting autonomy. The result has been the emergence of a muscular bureaucratic system at the regional and provincial scales. The impact on municipalities has been significant, as public funds were channeled into regional governments, making city halls reliant on their subnational counterparts. Such a structure deprived municipalities of tax revenue, redirecting funds to regional initiatives and programs.[49] The result of contemporary planning and governance has been twofold. First, municipalities are incredibly reliant on tax revenues from land development and real estate. As such, both rising housing prices and homeownership are very attractive as they offer greater tax gains. Second, town halls can't easily pursue holistic growth and planning efforts because they are incredibly expensive.

During the 1980s and 1990s this situation produced a very particular regime of planning focused on the project, which is often conceived as a question of urban design and architecture. One comparative analysis points to Spanish urbanism as marked "by abandoning *plans* in favour of *projects*" in which architects, rather than technocratic planners, play a decisive role.[50] In this system, larger institutional governance mechanisms create a political climate and policy framework for such projects to take place, and while master plans are not anathema they exist by and large to facilitate the elaboration of projects and to meticulously detail the uses for each parcel of land. Such projects, emerging not from planning offices but rather from architecture studios, necessarily focus on morphology, form, and the architectonic qualities of the urban experience. Another analysis argues in favor of this morphological approach because of it allows for agility and malleability of project-based development against the functionalism of other planning paradigms that hew closely to the plan.[51] Indeed, in Spain the figure of the planner doesn't really exist; *planificación urbana* is a technical exercise concerned with land-use arrangements and laws.

The emphasis on the project meant Madrid's city hall focused on those efforts that might attract international capital and so continued to pursue speculative place-making projects. If "worlding" in Dubai or Delhi is born out of a desire for international prestige, here it emerged out of economic necessity, as one of the only ways in which the city might develop in a moment of strangled budgets. López and Rodríguez argue that this arrangement meant the emergence of the local scale as a growth machine: "Local units have typically acted as growth machines in competition with each other. Indeed, local governments have become boosters of their localities."[52] Instead of holistic development that would take into account the needs of the entire metropolis, Madrid instead pursued highly uneven planning goals centered on specific projects. Those projects that could attract outside, private investment took precedence. As a result, planning efforts privileged elite spaces and uses and placed great weight on design; aesthetic concerns trumped less-sexy infrastructure and housing needs. Consequently, while certain parts of the city experienced revitalization, neighborhoods at the periphery became increasingly degraded. As a result, urban inequality deepened. Modern masterpieces and bold architectonic statements co-existed in close proximity to areas of degradation and growing despair. Planning during the democratic era therefore largely hewed to the same logic of the Franco era, where bold projects were erected at the expense of integrated development.

Large-scale urban development also became a key site for international investment and "worlding" aspirations. The new multinational Madrid of the democratic era came to invest its fortunes in development along the north-south axis of the Castellana.[53] Central to this development was the construction of the Plaza Castilla, a new gateway to the city from the north. A revamped design for the plaza was meant to be a centerpiece for the city's democratic-era urbanism. There, the *Torres KIO* leaned toward one another from either end of the plaza. The buildings were financed by the Kuwaiti Investment Office (hence the KIO), located in London. Philip Johnson's Burgee, Johnson and Associates was responsible for the design, and the land was made available by two men known as the "dos Albertos," Albertos Alcocer and Cortina, married to two heiresses of El Corte Inglés, Spain's main department store founded under Franco with intimate ties to the regime. Upon their construction, the towers were rechristened the *Puerta de Europa* (Gateway of Europe), "signaling that at the end of the Paseo de la Castellana, these inclined towers would finish off the city's North-South axis, creating an allegorical gate along the road that led towards the Europe of prosperity."[54]

While large-scale land deals and high-end development allowed for international accumulation of wealth and the growth of the Spanish economy, smaller-scale property investment was an accessible way for foreigners to stake a claim on an emergent European capital city.[55] Residential property became a vehicle for investment during the 1980s and '90s. During the 1980s Spain entered the European Community, which gave new prominence to the city: Madrid was the capital of a Western European country strategically located on the Mediterranean and with important EC neighbors. As a large city with international aspirations, Madrid also began to attract multinational firms, often by offering them enticing deals on land development, so that they too were able participate in this exciting moment of Europeanization. Well-heeled international executives could easily buy into a very undervalued property market. For the equivalent of a tiny garret in a lesser neighborhood in Paris, a French businessman could instead purchase a stately home in Madrid's baroque Plaza Mayor, steps away from the thrilling nightlife and *castizo* charm of the old city.[56] Thus international capital, already infiltrating the reaches of large-scale urbanization, took hold in the Spanish housing market, steadily pushing both prices upwards and people outwards.

In his cinematic meditation on Europeanization, *Carne Trémula*, Almodovar reveals the deep inequities produced by this urbanism.[57] A wealthy European elite lives in contemporary splendor, having had easy access to the city's relatively cheap property market. Elena, a rich though troubled Italian, dwells in a glamorous apartment with high ceilings and elegantly appointed rooms, recalling both Spain's baroque past and its European present. Yet Victor, the Spanish protagonist, lives in the upgraded remnants of a shantytown. This small community, housed in one-story buildings that evince a tough history of sweat equity, sits literally in the shadow of one of Johnson's towers. Emerging from his dark, modest dwelling one morning, Victor stares up at the glass-and-steel edifice so tall its top is shrouded in the early haze of dawn. This visual juxtaposition between the squat shanties and the tower reminds us of the vestiges of Franco-era urban poverty, while also unmasking democracy's inadequacy at restitution. Democracy has meant simply higher, fancier skyscrapers rather than the substantive improvement of life at the urban margins. Democratic Madrid was thus defined by both yawning inequality and privatization through direct foreign investment in property.

During this same moment, much of the center of Madrid was also in ruins. Because of Franco's frozen rents, which only allowed minimal increases, property owners had neither incentives nor *pesetas* to maintain the old building stock of historic center. Narrow brick housing blocks and old *corrallas*, while perhaps still charming from the street, were increasingly in shambles. One famous story that circulated through the EMVS (Empresa Municipal de la Vivienda y Suelo—Municipal Housing and Land Office) involved a man taking a bath, when the floor under the tub gave way, surprising and horrifying neighbors below. Further, many of these old buildings were poorly equipped for contemporary demands: units still lacked individual toilets, sharing one per floor.[58] These old buildings were the remnants of the pre-Franco housing model, where families would rent from wealthy landlords. Now, however, those landlords were neither wealthy nor living, having passed on these old building across generations. Thus property was held in the hands of multiple offspring who had little desire or capital to invest in rehabilitation. Selling off such buildings was also difficult, as it would require multiple family members, sometimes distant and dispersed, coming to a common agreement.[59]

The national government, meanwhile, attempted to reform the rental market: in 1985 the PSOE unfroze the minimal rental increases in an effort to stimulate supply. The law was implemented to encourage private investment, increasing rental housing against the near monopoly of the private property tenure system. So, too, was this liberalization effort designed to lower new rents by increasing supply. Yet prices rose sharply as landlords and property speculators found a new niche in which to exploit the housing market.

When juxtaposed against the history of autarkic planning, Madrid's urbanization during early democracy bears striking similarities. Even while the country threw off the veneer of Catholic authoritarianism, many of the logics and rhythms of policy and planning remained. Rather than pursue comprehensive growth and reforms, planners once again looked to spectacle that declared Madrid to be a major international destination—this time for globalized business. As a consequence, the same problems continued to emerge, most notably within the realm of housing.

The Millennial Moment

Madrid suffered another housing crisis. Housing had become incredibly expensive, and families were quickly leaving the city because of its prohibitive cost. Further, there were simply not enough adequate units to house the city's population. Significant amounts of housing stock were substandard and expensive to renovate. Many also preferred new units, a holdover from the Franco era when legislation provided subsidies to homebuyers for purchasing newly built stock. Yet the city had built to the limit of its capacity. There was no more available land upon which to erect housing. Following the 1985 General Plan, the city had developed all available plots, yet acquiring more land for development was a difficult, protracted legal and legislative battle. While real estate was integral to Spanish prosperity in the late 1980s and early 1990s, Spain still adhered to a land market model that many felt thwarted growth, allying development too closely with strict Napoleonic planning edicts and denying property owners full authority over development; property rights did not necessarily include the right to development.[60]

The historic system of ownership stressed the social function of urban land. Extremely detailed land-use plans dictated what was allowed, and landowners had to follow legislative planning obligations, their rights as property owners superseded by the state's right to dictate urban development. Indeed, despite imagining a country of homeowners, Franco pursued a hierarchical structure of planning that wrested authority from landowners and localities; control over territorial development ultimately resided with the central state. The right to own was separate from the right to build, and "development [was] only accepted if carried out in accordance with the plan."[61] Additionally, land classification was controlled by state planning agencies, which were tasked with a laborious process to determine whether a plot might be reclassified for development. Many Spanish lawmakers identified their territory as illegible, too susceptible to expropriation and forms of eminent domain that were incompatible with urban development goals. Here the arbitrary vision of a planner, enshrined in a master document, could supersede the property rights of an individual. The famed neoliberal development economist Hernando de Soto, envisioning a world of property owners, argues these kinds of regulatory frameworks stymy economic growth and the accrual of wealth.[62] His prescription, of course, is the elimination of "red tape" in the service of creating robust property markets.

Policymakers across the political spectrum began to evince a belief in the need to change existing land use laws. In 1993 José Borrell, Minister of Public Works under the socialist government, lamented the stagnation of development within the pages of *El País*. He pointed to "the lamentable and slow process of [land conversion], due to a complex set of disfunctions."[63] Borrell, however, was opposed to untethering development rights from planning codes entirely, insisting on the need for cautious revision instead of the complete deregulation of land and land markets. In a moment in which cities were expanding, planning lacked the agility with which to respond effectively to mounting urban issues. So, too, did economic crisis feed into responses to this situation: stimulation through urban development—so integral to previous economic recoveries—was no longer possible given the scant availability of land. Consensus began to emerge around the idea of land and its ownership as productive economic assets that would further Spain's project of modernization.

Land—as commodity to be owned, as crude good necessary to compete through the production of urban space—also emerged as a key vehicle for Europeanization. When Spain transitioned to a democracy, it also gained membership within the European Community, prompting the country to seek mechanisms for integration into the continent's markets. The current system—slow, antiquated, with little rights accorded to landowners—was unattractive to foreign investment, incompatible with European markets that privileged private initiatives.[64] As foreign capital flooded Spain's cities, through the arrival of multinational corporations, wealth pooled in elite hands, but that wealth no longer had to be directed into the productive circuit of capital.[65] Madrid, and indeed much of urban Spain at the time, suffered from what David Harvey designates as a crisis of accumulation, whereby surplus cannot be directed efficiently back into circuits of capital.[66] In such a moment it needs new avenues for the generation of additional wealth. What the mid-1990s crisis—both urban and capitalistic—meant for the city's economic geography was renewed interest in investment in real estate. As the central motor of the urban economy, real estate had long ago pushed out the light manufacturing that previously occupied urban peripheries. Yet Madrid was unable to pursue new projects. Additionally, its tax base was shrinking as people moved out, driven by high prices and a shortage of adequate housing.

The rabidly conservative, pro-market group the Defense of Competition Tribunal—convened under a socialist administration, yet a steadfast advocate for liberal economic ideologies of competition and liberalization—argued the country had to greatly increase the availability of urban land throughout the peninsula.[67] That argument was couched in the language of self-determination, free will, and the expansion of opportunity. Such a framing speaks to an attitude akin to manifest destiny, in which greatness might be concretized and made visible through the colonization of space. The tenor of this argument would soon find an audience within the executive leadership, as the PSOE lost the prime ministry after many years of rule. The country elected the conservative José María Aznar of the Partido Popular to lead the way out of the recession and toward prosperity. The son and grandson of *falangistas,* the new president emerged from the crucible of Spanish conservatism.[68] Aznar's victory in 1995 signaled the rejection of the Socialist era, and perhaps the consolidation of a new kind of conservatism for Spain, centered on liberal economic policy and European integration. Prior to their victory, the PP had already designed new legislation to liberalize land use. This measure was justified as a means to drive down the cost of housing, but it was also necessary, in the words of a party member, for "the market economy and free enterprise."[69] Lubricating the channels for urban development would stimulate the free and open economy the conservatives imagined for their country. The proposed law would permit municipalities and regional governments to rezone and annex rural territory with ease, allowing for urbanization to occur on vast new tracks of virgin land.

Within economic visions of land, meanwhile, a specific liberal ideology animated their approach to property ownership, which sharply differed from current land use regulation. *El País* reported the *populares* believed "the right to urbanize and build is inherent to the right to property."[70] This concept of property, closely aligned with many of liberalism's ideologies, is a contrast to the Francoist system. While the regime espoused a deep belief in the transformative power and great necessity of homeownership, property in land was something to be tightly controlled by the state, which would have very deliberate decision-making power over every aspect of development. Now, however, the conservative party embraced an economically liberal framework in which the property owner has inalienable rights, a naturalized system that ties together an individual with his plot of land. While the PP still clung to many vestiges of its Francoist past, its belief in economic modernization through the vehicle of liberalization clearly differed greatly from the tight central control of the regime. In keeping with broader political and economic trends, the PP married its regressive social values with the rapacious neoliberalism of many of its global counterparts.

In addition to efforts bringing more land onto the market, the drive to expand property rights reflected circulating ideologies of development and prosperity through individual initiative and autonomy. Land and property rights were in fact linked, as the law would "foreground the landowner within the production of 'new' urban land."[71] Even while this new legislation was meant to break the monopoly of tightly prescribed planning codes, it created "the monopoly of owners in the appropriation of the development project created by the community, and also the high priority attached to this project within land development activity."[72] Public entities, previously major actors within urban economic development, would take secondary roles as guarantors of the free market and the immediate relationship between property and its owner. Now property owners had expansive control over the development of their land. Private gain found itself greatly privileged over the public good, while the social function of ownership diminished.

Such a drive to reclassify and make legible land and its development reflects larger questions of power, government, and state control. James Scott, in *Seeing Like a State,* writes of the emergence of systematic land tenure regimes, property rights, and authoritative cadastral maps as mechanisms by which the state enacts control over its territory.[73] With the emergence of unified nation-states, previous systems, legible only to inhabitants themselves, demanded standardization in part to make territory legible from the outside. Indeed, de Soto's vision for a world of homeowners is not about securing housing for everybody, but about securing market access.[74] Cadastral maps make territory easily read, and thus easily governed and dominated, a technology that aids formations of power. Spain's complex systems of ownership and development were opaque to the outside, which was quickly growing more important in this moment of multinational integration. As such, they demanded legibility, an ordering and making sense, that might make Spanish territory and its concomitant planning apparatuses easily grasped and dominated from above. Here state power makes territory "work" for certain political ends by turning complex environments into divisible, obvious parts.

The drive towards legibility energized the Spanish shift in land use governance, determining the property owner to be the master and commander of his own territory, both building up that land and reaping the economic rewards derived from such development. Such a shift is crucial, meanwhile, because it cemented individual initiative as central to economic progress, reflecting the broader emergence of a global sensibility centered on atomized enterprise.

Previously, public administrations had played lead roles in land development; despite ensuring urbanization projects were linked to private industry, the state closely guided processes of urban change. Now, however, the state took on the role of liberalizing facilitator, opening new channels for industry and territorial competition, an episode of Spanish political economic history that illustrates how previous promises of socialism were rejected in favor of neoliberal rationalities of competition, expansion, and development.

This ideology of expansion—both territorial and capitalistic—through the guise of property animated other portions of the new law. While policy reform greatly encouraged private initiative and investment, so too did it untether growth from the prescribed boundaries laid out in previous planning efforts. In approaching the troubling issue of land classification, conservative policymakers decided to toss out existing codes and regulatory frameworks that dictated development. Instead, they put into place a new system in which the logic of classification is reversed, from positive designation of certain territories for urbanization to the negative logic of only classifying those areas unfit for urbanization. The law represents a radical theoretical and legislative shift: rather than prove that a piece of land is necessary for inclusion into an urban plan, policymakers had to demonstrate that a parcel is of some unique value that demands it be left off the cadastral map of development. If land was of agricultural use, tied to some aspect of cultural heritage, or particularly environmentally sensitive, it could acquire the designation of "not to be urbanized." But the de facto status of all land within the Kingdom of Spain now became *urbanizable*, that is, available for urban development. Essentially the entirety of the peninsula was now urban. While several autonomous communities and politicians on the left attempted to block the legislation, Aznar and his government were ultimately successful in passing the new land law.

Policy debates, the popular press, and academic discourse portrayed expanding access to territory for development as the only solution to housing the thousands of households experiencing difficulty in attaining adequate housing. The relationship between property in urban land and homeownership is not necessarily obvious or straightforward. In the Spanish case, however, the national government pursued the expansion of available urban land in order to also expand the ownership model, as political discussions on land were ultimately tied to the housing question. The implication, bandied around television shows and the pages of daily newspapers, was that new land meant new housing. Across these new tracks of virgin territory, developers could construct new estates that might house Spain's emergent middle class. If thousands or even millions of new housing units were added to the market, astronomical prices would finally begin to fall, allowing families, young people, the working class, and even the emergent immigrant community access to a home. Also implied was that in keeping with more than half a century of housing policy, these new units would be for owner occupation.

In looking to the expansion of territory as a solution for a whole host of issues, Madrid's urban planners designed a new plan that would substantively remake their city.[75] This plan took into account large areas of territory previously designated as rural, greatly extending the city's existing borders to well beyond their current scope. Rather than tackle the problem of the historic center's badly needed restoration, the 1997 *Plan General de Ordenación Urbana* sought the new—new space, new land, new neighborhoods, and new housing. It would incorporate almost 3,000 hectares of virgin land at the periphery of the city to be transformed into residential neighborhoods such as the PAU Vallecas. Planners justified this annexation because it would provide the crude product to solve Madrid's housing problem. Despite estimates of a shortage of 120k–170k units, the General Plan allocated space for 300,000 new housing units, all new construction primarily located in greenfield sites on the periphery.[76] The growing waves of immigration also provided a justification to plan and create oversupply. Planning Madrid to its limits would mean the end of the housing shortage and guarantee lower housing costs.

Municipal planners further justified these new areas because of their potential to generate employment. However, in keeping with Spain's boom-time logic, most of that employment would come from the very construction of these areas themselves; their long-term uses would after all be as residential warehouses to house lower- and middle-income families driven out by the rising prices of the 1980s. Such a plan for economic growth reflects the paradoxes of an economy built on property and construction. Anthropologist Timothy Mitchell writes on rising property values and investment into property markets: "Such investment simply draws existing capital away from more productive ventures, exacerbating broader problems caused by the lack of investment in activities that create employment."[77] These were not, indeed, to be sites of new industry—instead the construction itself could potentially employ myriad workers. Rather than plan for economically integrated neighborhoods, planners designated only 2.37 and 1.36 percent of the land for tertiary and industrial uses. In addition to residential housing blocks, the vast majority of remaining space was for parks and recreation.[78] Here property was to be both the means and the end, generating employment while also allowing everyday citizens to take part in this new multinational marketplace.

Many years later, I would head to the city's posh Aravaca suburb to interview the economist Julio Rodríguez López in his home. Rodríguez has held many important positions within the banking industry and the Socialist Party, including as head of the Banco Hipotecario de España, a defunct entity that used to regulate the mortgage market, and then as president of the Caja Granada, the Andalucian province's regional savings bank. That day he explained to me the allure of housing for municipalities all across the country. Reflecting on the governance arrangements that have privileged regional and provincial state entities, he related how housing under the rubric of homeownership became the de facto urban economic development policy for town halls both big and small across Spain. The construction, sale, and eventual occupation of housing units by their owners meant huge amounts of tax money would flow directly to municipal coffers. Homeowners, invested in the built environment and the maintenance of property values, meant revenue in perpetuity. Thus for a city like Madrid, where global aspirations continued to dictate planning agendas, homeownership provided a stable stream of euros. As other sources of public money flowed towards the regional government, the capital city could be assured long-term finances.

Madrid was of course not alone in liberalizing land and following this path toward economic prosperity. The Madrid Community, following the 1998 Land Use Law, also completely deregulated and liberalized its land, allowing municipalities across the region to craft their own policies and practices. The region has not approved a general plan for its metropolitan territory since the mid-1980s. As a result, each municipality has pursued its own development, abetted in large part by the powerful construction industry. Local planning authorities throughout the region's numerous municipalities aggressively pursued measures that would allow them to capitalize and develop land. During this same period, myriad suburbs also read promise and potential prestige into these shifting frameworks, as they sought out new ways to position their municipalities within this economy of space. The region produced an astonishing cartography of urban growth: in several municipalities, particularly in the poorer regions of east and south, the amount of land available for development increased by over 100 percent.[79]

Such development was also abetted by the ready availability of credit, often flowing from other parts of Europe, for the construction of new regional infrastructure.[80] Securitized bonds allowed the state, in partnership with private industry, to completely overhaul its highways and public transportation, making rapid connections between the city center and the distant hinterland a reality. Made possible by the ready availability of European money, large-scale infrastructure projects, such as the creation of these multiple ring roads, have encouraged dispersal and the growth of new suburban centers.

As a result, the urbanism of the Madrid region changed considerably over the 1997–2007 decade. Both the capital and its suburban hinterland experienced unprecedented rates of urbanization. Much of this development was oriented toward housing; during my tenure in the city from 2005 to 2008, I would regularly read about the inauguration of housing estates with tens of thousands of units in both Madrid and rapidly expanding suburbs such as Mostoles and Alcala de Henares, bastions of the traditional working class where old factories and sites of light manufacturing were now being remade into residential complexes. Part of this logic was animated by the promise of property taxes in perpetuity. Whereas the economic gains from industry take time to trickle through municipal economies and into state treasure chests, here that relationship was immediate.

At the same time, these lesser satellite cities, following Madrid's lead, went about pursuing emblematic urban projects that would establish their authority within some social or cultural niche. As mentioned above, the huge investments in infrastructure aided this development. With the inauguration of rapid connection to the capital city, suburbs could then visualize an extravagant urban project that might provide a lucrative future; visitors would be able to travel easily from the capital to these new regional nodes of prominence. This urban imperative, moreover, crossed political and party lines, as socialist, conservative, and communist city halls became infected with the fever of urban speculation. One particularly misbegotten project in Alcorcón, a southwestern suburb, hoped to create a world-class arts center, replete with concert halls, dance studios, restaurants, cafes, gyms, circus ring, circus school, and a motley crew of other cultural infrastructure provisions. A product of the decadent late years of the boom, this project only got underway in 2010 and drained municipal coffers of 120 million euros. Directly south of Madrid, meanwhile, the suburb of Parla debuted a top-of-the-line electric streetcar in 2007; the route is eight kilometers in length and cost an estimated 130 million euros to service a city of 120,000 occupants. Such public works, which many in the Spanish press have labeled "pharaonic" for their outsized pretensions and inflated budgets, are commonplace throughout the country, and pale in comparison to such absurdities as Valencia's half-a-billion-euro Santiago Calatrava–designed City of Arts and Sciences, which is now also falling apart.

Belonging in the City

The Spanish capital, and by extension the country's boom, was made through homeownership. A policy created under Franco served to drive the city's urban economy across most of the twentieth century and provide a key investment device for explosive growth at the dawn of the new millennium. The combined power of land liberalization and new flows of credit dramatically transformed the urban landscape of Madrid, inaugurating a frenzy of development and acquisition. The city spent 5 billion euros to submerge a Franco-era ring road and create a verdant multiuse park in its place. The north of the city, always a point of intense urban speculation, was soon home to new enormous skyscrapers and gleaming office parks, where Europe's multinational firms might take up new headquarters. Chief amongst Madrid's development was the immense and rapacious construction of housing, which rose at astonishing rates throughout the region. Thousands of new units flooded the market. The periphery of the city, once dotted with shantytowns and urban misery, was now home to an army of cranes. As discussed in the next chapter, their constant activity, raising steel beams and glass, incited *madrileños* to imagine exciting urban futures. These futures were replete with comfortable housing units in gated estates with pools, large patios, and shaded balconies, where the newest generation might live urbane lifestyles. The expanded transportation network meant places like Villaverde, once isolated and muddy, were now just several stops away from the Puerta del Sol on the commuter rail. Leaving the city for the suburbs no longer seemed a form of exile, as wide highways and public transportation easily connected the urban core to the once distant periphery. Star architects flocked to the city to design new projects. And everywhere money gushed and pooled in the hands of developers and construction executives through the vehicle of homeownership.

Indeed, homeownership sustained the urban economy of expansion. Soon on nearly every block bloomed a bank branch or a real estate office. Their windows would promise comfortable material futures to the urban *flaneur*. Each bank would advertise special mortgage promotions, which included new dishes, or bedding, or even furniture, in addition to favorable rates. The windows of estate agencies would be plastered in advertisements for numerous housing units of every kind of type. If only ten years prior the city had been plagued by a housing shortage, now new estates rose with enervating speed. In *Tintin in America,* the Belgian boy detective finds himself somewhere within the central plains of the United States, when suddenly an oil reservoir blows, sending him flying in the air.[81] Ten minutes later, developers show up to buy the well. By the next morning, an entire city has sprung up seemingly from nothing. Where once there were fields of greenery and low mountains, now there is brick, concrete, cars, and cranes. Hergé's portrait of oil-based urbanization resonates with the pace and scale of development in millennial Madrid. While his is a comic-book vision, it nonetheless evokes the frenzy of the transformation of virgin soil into urban land. In the case of Madrid, homeownership served as the engine for that transformation, which, as will be seen in the next chapter, necessarily also transformed the modes of inhabiting and belonging to the city.

The specter of dispossession haunts this account, evident, too, in Tintin's America. In the fictional comic-book world, we see the transformation of Indian land into an urban property market, hinting at legacies of settler colonialism.[82] The dispossessions at work in Madrid are perhaps more subtle and hint not at the individual but instead toward the collective and its urban opportunities. First was the transformation of housing from rental to ownership, which served to extinguish more traditional modes of dwelling in the city, while also depriving landlords of rental income. In discouraging the rental market, the regime condemned a swath of the city to the slow violence of ruination, while also denying housing to those without enough capital to buy a home. The concentration of resources in the city, meanwhile, forced people to abandon land and traditional villages, bringing them streaming into the city.

At the same time, more damningly for labor and employment, homeownership banished manufacturing and other kinds of production, as construction became the main urban industry. The regime thus dispossessed the city of economic diversity, and it never fully experienced industrialization or its benefits. Housing under the logic of homeownership displaced other land uses, consuming territory and subjecting it to the dictates of the propertied order. Homeownership as economic development policy lay the groundwork for later inequities in the labor market. During the democratic era, moreover, Aznar's land use law also dispossessed numerous actors previously integral to the development process, consolidating a monopoly within the hands of the landowner. Finally, the speculative excess of the boom years leveraged future labor and its taxes to finance audacious projects using cheap European loans. Future populations were thus dispossessed of the ability to decide how and on what their taxes might be spent, or, as anthropologist Julia Elyachar writes, "the power to decide what matters."[83] Homeownership as a motor for transformation, then, relies on multiple dispossessions in order to continue unabated. In this respect, it not only transforms the built environment and instantiates property market, but also profoundly alters its modes of everyday life, its horizons of possibility. Homeownership's dominance in producing the urban landscape demands, then, an examination of the ontologies of dwelling in the city.

4 Citizen Homeowner

We're used to a life with a partner and a mortgage. The Spanish dream is to have a partner and house with a mortgage, and when you're done paying it off, a house at the beach.

Iñaki

Iñaki is a young man in his early thirties. While he never went to college, he was enterprising from a young age. He worked in bars and restaurants, moving from busboy to waiter to manager within the span of a few years. In the mid-2000s, he saw he could make far more money in financial services. With a business partner, he opened a franchise that offered loans and credit products to people who had trouble acquiring them at more traditional banks. He worked closely with people in the real estate sector. In 2007 he purchased a townhouse in a suburb of Madrid. While he acquired the property with the idea of flipping it, he nonetheless clung to the idea of homeownership as integral to his future plans for partnership and a family. Homeownership was a key component to his Spanish dream.

Where did that dream come from? As members of the lower middle class, Iñaki's family had long worked hard for modest rewards. The comfort they now enjoyed in a traditional neighborhood in Madrid's working-class periphery would have been unimaginable to a previous generation. Iñaki's grandparents had migrated to the city from a small *pueblo* during the bleak years of early dictatorship. As rural to urban migrants, they toiled long hours with little remuneration and lived in substandard housing like much of the urban population. When they were finally able to access adequate housing, they settled into a miniscule two-bedroom apartment in a concrete complex at the edge of the city. After many years, they upgraded to a slightly larger house in a slightly better neighborhood. The old black-and-white television was replaced by a large color set with an integrated VCR, and then a flatscreen with a separate DVD player where they could watch the latest Hollywood films. They still drove modest cars and rarely ate at restaurants, but their fortunes had improved considerably from a generation ago. Their son, however, dreamed of more extensive creature comforts. Iñaki's millennial bounty meant he could enjoy the full range of middle-class pleasures, wholly out of reach to his forbearers.

The distinct history of spatial and economic expansion through homeownership that animated Madrid's twentieth-century development influenced the kinds of lives and livelihoods that were possible for the city's many denizens. Homeownership was central to that expansion, and as such had to be incorporated not only into planning and policy, but also into an ideological project of building the city and its citizens. Replacing other forms of housing tenure, the ownership system became the means by which urbanization was possible. But it was also, crucially, a central component to full membership within the city. As it proved to be successful for economic development, homeownership soon became incorporated into Francoist ideology, against previous notions of Catholic charity and responsibility. But the piecemeal nature of urban development, the high cost of urban living, and the enduring precarity of labor markets meant comfortable city living and the material rewards we associate with homeownership were kept out of reach for a large portion of Madrid's populace. Iñaki's Spanish dream had long been an aspiration, but only recently could it be translated into material reality.

Visions of domestic bliss and economic attainment emerged out of a particular historical trajectory that emphasized homeownership as a means of self-actualization and personal initiative. However, ordinary urban dwellers were often locked out of that vision, kept at the periphery and unable to partake in consumer culture. While many generations of politicians and planners had sought to make Madrid into a global, cosmopolitan capital awash in possibility, upward mobility for citizens of the global city was a fantasy. Millennial deregulation, the proliferation of credit opportunities, and the shifting logics of labor markets would suddenly correct for a long history of material lack. Homeownership through the accrual of mortgage debt became the vehicle that allowed for other types of consumption to take place. Consumption opportunities, made possible through indebtedness, offered a powerful antidote to the long absence of Fordist structures of class and employment.[1]

Crafting the Homeowner Subject

In conversations, Madrid's planners and architects often remind me that the Franco era extolled the virtue of the *propietario* (property owner) who might offer a corrective to the dangerous memory of the *proletario* (proletarian). Yet in drawing out the histories of homeownership and its subjects in Madrid, I came to realize this ideological fairytale only emerged after the regime had discovered the magic fix of private property as a tool for economic growth. The entanglements between ideology and policy are myriad, particularly in the realm of housing. Critical scholars of gender and race bring our attention, for example, to the ways in which heteronormative notions of domesticity and the private sphere influenced suburban planning and development, or how racial tropes justified colonial exploits and housing types.[2] But many of those same scholars incite us to think about such relations as dialectical, produced through an assemblage of practices that implicate not only policy, but also popular culture, material histories, iconography, and discourse. We tend to think policy flows from ideology, yet the reverse can also be true. In the case of Franco's Madrid, the revered figure of the homeowner only emerged as a powerful trope once homeownership proved to be successful.

In the infancy of the dictatorship, a tension emerged between housing as a social right and need, and housing as an industry. The Falange, Franco's fascist group, viewed social housing as part of their responsibilities toward the Spanish people. The far-right group was explicitly opposed to speculation in the real estate market and sought social measures to provide for the large numbers of people living in substandard housing.[3] The Falange viewed the provision of housing as central to the mission of Catholic autarky. To perpetuate proper subjects, the regime must provide dwellings to its most vulnerable. This ethic of care would foster fealty toward and obedience to central rule, in addition to following a biblical doctrine of responsibility toward others. Initial urbanization projects in the city bore out this mandate; several small social housing projects cropped up throughout the city. Public funds promoted social visions of Catholic harmony, centered on the neighborhood unit. One project, in the Usera neighborhood, provided modest homes oriented around a church. Yet the regime soon abandoned such efforts.[4] These small-scale projects did little to absorb the vast tide of urban poverty. With little funding and a stagnant economy, the central state could not pursue a vision that demanded massive public investment in housing infrastructure.

César Cort, town council member and architect mentioned in the previous chapter, had a vision for homeownership that influenced the rejection of social housing in favor of owner-occupation. Indeed, he identified the provision of social housing as a means of rewarding a working class that was known for its communist sympathies. Providing housing to this segment of the population would not advance the Catholic cause because it would allow red elements to remain and fester. Instead he sought to defend the interests of the "capitalist property owner."[5] His particular approach to the housing question looks not only to housing but also to the power of property ownership as a transformative tool for the realization of certain political ends, in which economic rather than social necessity takes precedent. But his ideas also promulgated a particular vision of the good urban subject. The *petit bourgeois* property owner was the figure who needed uplift and support during these bleak years of economic austerity. The poor, understood to be allied with the Republican army, required instead further punishment. To give them housing would be to reward and potentially exacerbate their disloyalty rather than turning them into docile subjects. In scapegoating the working class, Cort rendered them outside and against the national rebuilding project, not fully in need of the state's support and aid. Such rendering was shored up by political understandings of the popular classes and the areas in which they lived, as remnants from the failure of red Spain, enemy combatants to be weeded out or beaten into submission to the Catholic way of life.[6]

This distinct vision of the petit bourgeois subject was still in its nascent form during the emergence of the homeownership model. During a conference on the "Future of Madrid" in 1945—shortly after the regime passed its first homeownership policies—Madrid's head architect German Valentin-Gamazon y Garcia Noblejas spoke at length about the housing crisis in the city. For him, the problem was not merely a question of substandard dwellings or overcrowding. Rather, the lack of adequate housing in the city had also provoked a moral crisis that had devalued the home as the domestic heart of the family. In order to insist on housing as not only a material good, but also a key site for the development of family values and Catholic ethics, ownership of one's own home was crucial. He stated, "No one makes a better home than the man who makes it for himself and his family," rather than renting from someone else.[7] "One's own house," he went on, "is the most perfect social and economic formula for the production and use of housing." Madrid's chief architect was most concerned with how best to provide housing and foment harmonious, Francoist social relations. Owner-occupation emerged as a tool for stability and the eradication of urban poverty.

While *homeownership* was gaining traction as a useful housing and urban economic development policy, reverence for the figure of the *homeowner* would take longer to emerge. Only once the homeownership model proved successful did this subject take on a more central role within the regime's ideology as a central pillar of *franquismo*, allied with both economic policy and popular depictions of the good urban subject. In order to consolidate housing, urban, and land policy, the regime created the Ministry of Housing in 1957. This development was part of a more generalized effort to institutionalize some of the key tenets and political goals of *franquismo*, particularly in a moment of increasing economic prosperity and consolidation. But it was also a period of ideological consolidation. The chief housing minister, José Luis de Arrese, spoke of homeownership as the vehicle by which both Spain and its inhabitants would better their economic futures through an emphasis on private enterprise. In an interview with the newspaper *ABC*, Arrese spoke of the duty of his ministry: "It is not to do, but rather to help and procure so that others do."[8] Here emerged an idea of the state as facilitator of the market rather than direct provider. Housing, rather than fall under the jurisdiction of the central state, was instead left to private interests. Arrese also clearly aligned the broader economic landscape with the question of personal amelioration. In another speech, he spoke of "private initiative," which would be encouraged through "developing the construction industry."[9]

Arrese's vision of economic growth became entangled with the elaboration of a specific vision of the good subject, couched in terms of social welfare, individual progress, and the importance of family life for Falangist ideology. Here discourse married various concepts of property, personal advancement, housing, and the family to produce a coherent vision of the model urbanite. Homeownership was "the laboratory for the best of man's virtues, for his quality as a man and for his eternal destiny, he is obligated to carry out the mission of family." As such the task of the housing ministry was "a great work of social justice."[10] His easy transitions from industry to the family, to property, created alliances between these various socioeconomic strands, binding them together into a unified system of belief. His eulogies to property reached a fever pitch in one intervention where he opined: "The ideal formula, the Christian formula, the revolutionary formula from the point of view of our very own revolution, is the stable and harmonious formula of property, which makes possible that so logical and human goal . . . that one's home is what one lives from."[11] Home-ownership had become enveloped in the dominant ideology of the regime. Invocations of Christian revolution, stability, and harmony created an ideo-logical through-line to other elements of Falangist belief. They tied together an economic tool—private property—with extant concepts of Catholic devotion, loyalty, and the family, a central pillar of the Franco regime.

Finally, Arrese created and popularized the idea of transforming *propri-etaries* from *proletarios*. The opposition between "proletarian" and "property owner" created a delineation between those who own and everyone else, who ostensibly must find housing through the rental market. Thus the urban poor, conspicuous in their absence, became the regime's others, in keeping with the regime's general intolerance toward the impoverished portions of society. Dur-ing a moment of virulent anticommunism both within Spain and the greater west, that opposition rendered much of the urban majority into enemy com-batants, their form of life antithetical to the Francoist project. The only way for them to gain inclusion within this analytic was through access to the pri-vate property market. Homeownership thus meant not only taking part within Spain's Christian revolution, but also taking on the guise of the good urban subject, compliant and yet imbued with personal initiative. The middle class—practically nonexistent during the early years of *franquismo*—was to be the bas-tion of this new society, the crucible in which this heady mix of cosmopolitan Catholicism and high culture might be born anew. Discrete domestic arenas then constituted greenfield sites for the making of a new urbane, capitalist society.

These concerns for cosmopolitanism and culture dovetailed with broader cultural imperatives and repressive ideologies. As Helen Graham and Jo La-banyi have documented, the regime elaborated a particular vision of class, which was disseminated through cultural artifacts, national policy, and puni-tive social norms. Here Franco articulated an idea of the nation as divided "into victors (the true Spain) and vanquished ('la anti-España') through political and economic repression, both of which turned the material practices of everyday life—the sheer task of survival—into politically charged instruments of resis-tance." While Franco espoused his position as a popular leader opposed to the avant-garde ideologies of his democratic predecessors, he vilified the poor for their poverty, misery, and potential insurgency, through the "demonization of the working class, seen as the epitome of an alien and threatening moder-nity."[12] Thus the categories Arrese propagates of prol and property owner reflect broader divisions that sought to cast out and punish a large segment of the population deemed threatening to the Francoist project.

In this light homeownership was a tool to distinguish the worthy urban subject from the popular, pauperized masses. For much of the urban population, this vision of stable domesticity and economic attainment was out of reach. During the bleak autarkic period, there was little employment and no housing. The working class struggled endlessly to survive. Even as the country opened up to outside investment, the capital city remained mired in poverty, which Franco himself regularly lamented. Expansive shantytowns continued to haunt the urban experience, evidenced in the classic work of fiction *Tiempo de silencio*.[13] The novel, often held up as evidence for *madrileño* life under Francoism, portrays a bleak city in which even the emergent middle classes must struggle for shelter. This urban landscape was the consequence of a model that privileged spectacular placemaking instead of comprehensive growth—luxury tourist developments instead of social housing and infrastructure, an *arc de triomf* rather than pavement and sewage. The gains from private ownership— mostly middle and upper class—were then channeled into reimagining central parts of the city deemed emblematic for an outside audience (see the previous chapter). At a stone's throw from the urban spectacle entrenched poverty continued to mire the vast majority of the city's population. Housing then became a means to blame the poor for their poverty. If the good urban subject was a homeowner, he who rented or lived in the misery of peripheral shanties must then be anachronistic to the project of modern Madrid. His poverty made him also deserving of humiliation and repressive rule.

When finally the regime had adequate means by which to address the housing problem in the 1960s and early 1970s, it either built enormous, soulless blocks at the very limits of the city or simply gave everyday urban dwellers the materials with which to build their own housing.[14] Thus contemporary peripheral neighborhoods throughout San Blas in the southeast, Villaverde in the south, or Aluche in the west are filled with squat, four-story apartment buildings arranged around dusty patios.[15] Castells writes in *City and the Grassroots:* "Workers found low-paying jobs but no housing." Those workers lived in shantytowns dispersed throughout the city. When housing did arrive, it was in "newly built estates [that] began to crumble from the moment they were occupied." Toward the end of the dictatorship, homeownership was now a possibility celebrated by many, but "people had little choice but to migrate, work ten hours a day for low wages, to commute for two hours, and buy expensive houses of poor quality in the middle of nowhere."[16] The poor were subjected to various iterations of dispossession: first they were essentially kicked off the land during bleak depression (and sometimes kicked out of Madrid during autarky because the city was so full), then they were exploited as disposable wage labor, and finally they were treated as a captive market for substandard, outrageously expensive housing. Homeownership did not then accord them entry into Franco's highly revered middle class. Instead, the *clase obrera* toiled long hours, with no hope or possibility of upward mobility or participation within a robust consumer economy. Their fates were sealed, bodies shunted into peripheral neighborhoods devoid of services.

In accessing property, moreover, peripheral populations could not then access Arrese's vision of advancement and middle-class comfort. As a generation of neighborhood activism revealed, these housing estates lacked many of the basic services that might allow residents the smallest modicum of urban comfort.[17] Far from the center of town, many areas had few transportation options. They lacked schools and even clean water, proper street paving, and electrification. The *colonia de barro,* mentioned in the last chapter, replaced the shanty, but life in the urban periphery remained bleak. While the extension of homeownership to the working classes meant they no longer dwelled in shanties, it did not then inaugurate a concomitant social mobility. Nor did it imply everyday people could take part in the spectacle and seduction of the central city. Without material access, the working and lower middle classes instead were separated physically from the *centro* and its many delights and pleasures. Wage labor and even homeownership did not imply an ability to consume or to move up the ladder of class status.

Many have used the lens of (post-)Fordism to analyze landscapes of production, consumption, and social reproduction.[18] What is often implicit in such analyses of industrialized relations is the worker as consumer, who is afforded social mobility through access to the marketplace of ideas, education, healthcare, and other goods and services. The factory owner pays the workers enough such that they might then be able to consume the product they produce, an idea central to Henry Ford's idea of factory production and wage labor. At the same time, the upper and middle classes had sizable tax bills that financed the robust provision of public services, such as schools and healthcare, but also roads, rail, and sewage systems. Madrid, however, had largely exiled industry in the service of construction; gone were the assembly lines, as the real estate industry became the motor of the urban economy. The state, meanwhile, privileged spectacle and repression over investment in public services. As such, members of the working classes were separated physically, ideologically, and materially from the gains of the late Franco era.

When Franco died, Madrid was a sweltering behemoth of a city. While people had housing, it was far from centers of employment, without schools or medical facilities, proper transportation systems, or even adequate water supplies. Democracy was supposed to rectify this bleak panorama, in which 54 percent of housing was substandard.[19] Yet for many their lives continued to unfold divorced from the modernization and possibility of the central city. We see this reality in two films from the 1980s that depict life at the city's peripheries. In Carlos Saura's 1981 *Deprisa, deprisa,* a group of youngsters live and play within decaying housing estates.[20] Their chief pleasure is heroin, which presaged the city's very serious epidemic of the 1980s and '90s. As they steal cars and rob banks, we see little evidence of Spain's new democratic future. At the edge of the city, their lives appear more connected to the dusty fields at the peri-urban fringe.

While much more exuberant and humorous in tone, Almodóvar's *¿Qué he hecho yo para merecer esto?* from 1984 portrays a similarly bleak landscape.[21] His protagonist, Gloria, lives in an enormous housing block, its exterior turned sooty gray from pollution. The interior of her house is cramped and dark. The children wander the litter-strewn exteriors of the estate. Madrid here is dingy and depressing. These portrayals dovetail with native interlocutors' recollections of urban life in the young democracy. Daniel is a young man who purchased a loft in the posh suburb of Pozuelo, in part because it was such an extreme and pleasant contrast to his youth in the Tetuán neighborhood. While the area has posh Franco-era flats along the Castellana, it is mostly known for narrow streets, small remnants of light industry, and many decrepit buildings in need of reform. During Daniel's childhood, the neighborhood was also ravaged by heroin usage. Many of his friends and acquaintances became consumed by the drug, which decimated large swathes of his urban experience.[22]

Images of dirt, decay, and drugs are far removed from the robust, potent social movements that gripped the city from the late 1960s until the early 1980s. Madrid's mobilizations during this time have become emblematic struggles over collective consumption and the amelioration of everyday urban life. Indeed, the absence of Fordist urbanism impelled citizens to fight against their conditions and demand improvements. The movements attracted a diverse array of urban dwellers, from the working poor to the middle classes, all of whom sought to improve the terms of contemporary urban life. But once the streets were paved, once streetlamps lit streetscapes in peripheral neighborhoods, and once shacks were replaced with secure housing, the movements dispersed. After many years of dictatorship, they were transformative, allowing citizens to enact their rights and make demands upon the state in a way that was previously impossible. Yet those demands didn't confront the dominant model of urbanism and left unchallenged the hegemony of private ownership. The efforts of many years of struggle were then channeled into state mechanisms of rule or institutionalized through an extensive network of neighborhood associations. As democracy took hold in the city, those associations were what remained to fight for peripheral areas of the city.

Madrid's recent cultural histories remind us that homeownership alone cannot transcend wider political economic conditions. Configured as a panacea that might catapult citizens into a modernizing project of prosperity, owner-occupation first served to punish the poor for their poverty and then to tie those same poor to the urban periphery.[23] There homeownership, for many of Madrid's subjects, did not then usher in some kind of harmonious middle-class existence. Nor did it undo the repression, humiliation, and violence of the dictatorship as it enacted its cruel vision upon urban society. The everyday urban comforts of modernity were dreamed for but long denied. As such, the stakes for Madrid's working and middle classes at the dawn of the democratic era were incredibly high. Democracy might mean not only the end of repression and silence, but also the comforts of class mobility and material consumption. Finally they might dwell in the city as equals.

Making Madrid's Middle Class

During the summer and fall of 2006, I lived in an elegant middle-class neighborhood full of tree-lined streets and stately apartment buildings, abutting the manicured lawns of the Parque del Oeste. I was working for an American university at the time; despite the origin of our students and their hefty tuition dollars, I was paid a Spanish salary. A newly minted graduate, I was making around 1,600 euros a month, or just over US$2,000. While this was a pittance in comparison to the wages of friends who had gone off to finance jobs in Manhattan or consulting posts in Los Angeles, my monthly income was actually significant in comparison to a young urban population composed mostly of *mileuristas,* the portmanteau used to describe people earning 1,000 euros a month. Aware of the abysmal state of Spanish wages, I was thus surprised whenever I walked the wide avenue near my house. A boulevard that connects the imperial Plaza de España with the Franco-era architecture of Moncloa, the calle Princesa is lined with trendy shops; during my tenure in the neighborhood, there were three Zara boutiques within two blocks from one another.[24] Bustling through the sidewalks, flocks of people, male and female, old and young (the university area is nearby), were always laden with purchases. Giant paper shopping bags announced to the world untold euros spent on new clothing and shoes, video games and sporting equipment. Yet such consumer goods were similar in price to, if not more expensive than, their American counterparts. Aware of the limitations of my salary (and perhaps yearning for a new Inditex wardrobe) I constantly wondered as to the provenance of these consumer euros, and more generally this insatiable appetite for consumption.

The *flaneur* spectacle of consumption was not confined to retail consumption alone; rather, it infiltrated all aspects of life, but was most acute within the housing and homeownership market. What I witnessed during my regular strolls was the realization of a particular modernity long denied. While many generations of politicians and planners had sought to make Madrid into a global, cosmopolitan capital awash in possibility, ordinary urban dwellers were often locked out of that vision. Even as portions of the center became more glamorous and tourist-friendly, the city's urban majority was kept at the periphery, unable to partake in consumer culture. Upward mobility was a fantasy. Soon, however, homeownership provided a vehicle that allowed for other types of consumption to take place. The mortgage became a tool that not only allowed participation within the marketplace, but also obviated the realities of an urban economy that had never benefited from Fordist structures of class and employment. Housing debt allowed people to participate in the consumer economy and achieve the illusion of upward mobility. Thus debt became a central tool in the making of citizenship.

Dreams of middle-class comfort propelled much of the Spanish boom. Attention to that period often highlights public investment, new credit opportunities, and various forms of European integration.[25] But the aspirations and experiences of everyday urban dwellers were also integral. The only way for Madrid's model of urbanism, reliant on homeownership and its spread, to function was to mint new homeowners. An assemblage of considerations transformed everyday *madrileños* into homeowners. To become fully modern, to make manifest these primordial dreams of cosmopolitan consumption, and to rid themselves of the bleak terror of previous penury and oppression meant to finally realize Arrese's staunch belief in the *propietario*. Membership within this particular moment of urbane European modernity required urban home-ownership. Looking to both archival and ethnographic materials, I argue that investment in the housing market served as a means to participate in the labor market, finance and protect certain forms of social reproduction, and finally produce European identity and subjectivities. At the same time, if homeowner-ship was the mechanism that might transform urban subjects into citizens, then debt was the tool that would then finance that transformation. This particular regime of dwelling in and reproducing the city relied intractably on spreading not only the homeownership model, but also new forms of credit and risk.

Market Citizenship

The last section traced the emergence of the figure of the homeowner, par-ticularly as articulated as the good Francoist subject. Here, however, the focus is on how homeownership became integral to a regime of *urban citizenship*. A number of debates across the social sciences grapple with the question of citizenship. While once wholly conceived as a national system that determined rights and responsibilities, more recent work has drawn attention to the ways in which it is imbricated within identity-based claims, transnational networks, and even global discourses on cosmopolitanism and belonging.[26] The work of James Holston is particularly instructive; he has argued for a notion of ur-ban citizenship that configures the local scale as the de facto arena for claims-making, which acknowledges, too, the experiential ontologies of belonging and the political responsibilities that membership within a community entails.[27] As Aihwa Ong has demonstrated, moreover, capitalist citizenship regimes produce "new modes of subject making," which is central to this inquiry.[28]

Key to subject making in Madrid was a form of urban citizenship predi-cated on a particular *market* or *financialized* regime of belonging, in which ac-cess and membership required participation within the marketplace. As stated in the last chapter, democracy and then Europeanization meant state reforms to increase market access, which also demanded new mechanisms for everyday individuals to also take part. While some explore the idea of *financial citizen-ship* as a means of promoting democracy, Adrienne Roberts advances an idea of *market citizenship*. Here ability to participate and reap the rewards of mem-bership relies on ability to take part in the market, which in turn produces inequities even while it is understood as benevolent provider.[29] She writes: "The market is discursively and materially constructed as the best, if not the only, means of assuring the well-being of all individuals."[30] Neoliberalization has thus "require(d) people to take active responsibility for financing key elements of their own welfare." The move to foster a culture of entrepreneurialism has meant lowering the threshold for "informational capital," allowing members of the working classes with little financial education to take part with ease.[31] The question of rights and recognition here become subsumed in one's identity as a financial subject, for whom the market will now provide creature comforts and material necessities previously associated with the welfare state and strict labor regulations. Thus the pension becomes the 401K, or in this case investment in real estate, and the unionized job is now work for commissions as a real estate agent. Such considerations are useful when untangling the relations between homeownership, mortgage debt, and urban membership within Madrid. As demonstrated in the remainder of this chapter, Madrid's urban citizenship in the era of Europeanized modernity relied on the extension and accumulation of debt as a means of financing and making manifest its demands.

Banking on Homeownership

When I lived in Madrid in the mid-2000s, I regularly chatted with my friend Raúl, an art historian and curator. We lived blocks away from each other in the bohemian neighborhood of Las Letras, which I had chosen after growing weary of the posh spectacle of Moncloa. There we would wander the narrow streets of our *barrio* after work or drink beers on the balcony of the small flat he shared with his Norwegian wife. Raúl bemoaned his housing situation. As someone making a fairly good living, he and his wife nonetheless could not afford to buy a house. Everywhere they looked, houses went for 250–350K euros, the 20 percent down payments far more than they could ever afford. Perhaps they could purchase a house in one of Madrid's far-flung suburbs, but even those exurban towns and villages were becoming increasingly expensive. Many of these locales were also engaged in the frenzied activity of construction and speculation, flooding the market with tens of thousands of new units. Yet their prices continued to surge, belying earlier belief that the liberalization of land would drive costs down. Indeed, rather than solve the problem of skyrocketing housing costs, deregulation of land and rapacious urbanization seemed only to make prices climb higher. Finding a place to rent was also no easy task. In the poorly regulated rental market, landlords were capricious, and rents were expensive. When the Franco regime disparaged renting through both policy and discourse, it instantiated a series of urban legends that continued to influence the housing market. Landlords were often hesitant to rent without charging exorbitant down payments or six-month security deposits. And yet throughout his immediate environment, Raúl saw many around him were proud home-owners. Many had purchased before the market had gone crazy. Completing his PhD in France, he hadn't been able to enter the property market before its euphoric rise; now he felt it was out of reach. Not owning a proper house, he often expressed to me, made him feel somehow inadequate. In a moment in which housing appeared abundant and acquisition so ubiquitous, how could this middle-class, educated professional not own his own home?

Across the democratic era, Spain had made it easier for someone like Raúl to access homeownership. Indeed, mortgages issued at 80 percent of the sales value were relatively new. Until the early 1980s mortgages were generally issued at around 50 percent of the value of the property, payable over a short period of time. Further, all mortgages were controlled by state entities, including the Banco de España and the Banco Hipotecario; savings and commercial banks played no role in housing acquisition, even if they were involved in speculation and construction. During dictatorship, the country essentially did not have a mortgage market; mortgages were small and under the direct purview of public administration. In 1981, however, the young democracy passed a new law to al-low mortgages at much higher percentages of the purchase price.

As part of the state's broader push to modernize the economy and integrate it within European markets, this legislation sought to bring "agility and secu-rity" to the emergent mortgage market, so that capital could more freely circu-late through society—often at the behest of the burgeoning real estate market. Public entities would soon have private competition as savings and commercial banks would now be able to underwrite mortgages. The law also allowed for variable interest rates and credit lending up to 80 percent of the purchase value of the home. While couched in terms of democratizing homeownership, new mortgage policy's greater economic goals were evident. Deregulation of the mortgage market was meant to "satisfy the endless demand of the industrial and commercial sectors," particularly so that they might compete on a global scale.[32] Policy ought to allow more people into the regime of homeownership because it represented an important asset in capital markets. Emphasis on homeowner-ship as a tool to encourage the circulation of money hinted toward the growing demand for deregulation in other areas of the economy, including land.

In the 1990s, as Spain prepared to enter the European Union, the country once again grappled with several national and multinational issues relating to investment and the flow of capital. Housing was still in short supply and credit didn't flow easily, despite these earlier efforts of deregulation.[33] Again the central state was concerned with making the Spanish housing market legible to the outside and compatible with the multinational edicts of the nascent Union. Thus, the country passed a series of laws in 1992 and 1998 that allowed for the securitization of mortgages. Securitization, however, only really became a central banking practice after 2001 and was driven primarily by "liquidity needs."[34]

Meanwhile, local and regional or savings banks began issuing mortgages. Securitization greatly expanded the ability of small financial entities to enter the mortgage market. *Cajas de ahorro*—local and regional savings banks—were state-sponsored and supervised, and their advisory boards and executive committees were composed of the local governing elite. Additionally, such entities had mandates to serve social ends. Their foundations funded public programs and international scholarships, art museums and cultural productions. As such they were an important arena for social welfare and urban reproduction, meant to serve everyday citizens. Within small towns and modest neighborhoods, the local *caja*—in contrast to large commercial investment banks such as Banco Santander or BBVA—was a stolid institution similar to the primary school or the church, ministering to the economic needs of the local population. Often the bank director was a pillar of the community, well versed in the modest finances of everyday neighbors. With millennial deregulation and the frenzy of housing construction, however, the director figure was thrust into the brave new world of international money markets. With the deregulation of mortgage markets and the introduction of securitization, these small savings banks entered into the competitive game of credit lending.[35]

What Raúl imagined when he contemplated buying a house was the traditional mortgage with 20 percent down payment. Yet it had become standard practice amidst the flurry of acquisition for banks to propose other forms of financing homeownership. While regional savings banks had begun to issue mortgages, often indiscriminately, several of the main investment banks also created new franchises to cater to more precarious populations. Banco Santander created the Unión de Creditos Inmobiliarios (UCI—Real Estate Credit Union), for example, which was dedicated exclusively to the provision of mortgages for people who might have trouble accessing homeownership through more traditional financial entities. Their customers, unable to find financing elsewhere, were often young people, single women, or immigrants. An entity like UCI combined personal loans and mortgages in order to facilitate the purchase and required potential homeowners to secure guarantors who might put up their own property as collateral.[36] What Raúl was unwilling to do was amass all the other bits of credit and debt that might cover that initial payment, and he did not have family to whom he could go for the guarantee. For others, however, new forms of debt accrual were simply mechanisms that aided their transformations into homeowners, necessary to live out their particular vision of themselves in this material world. Purchasing a house could often be cheaper initially than renting; the financial entity could arrange for a 100 percent mortgage, in which 80 percent was covered by a securitized mortgage, and the additional 20 percent as a personal loan. A young person could walk into his new home without ever seeing money flow out of his own pocket. But he was also clearly investing in his future. If prices were to continue rising, he would be lucky to get into the market as soon as possible.

The Homeowner Consumer

The visual economy of the moment portrayed homeownership as both aspirational and highly attainable. A relentless stream of real estate advertisements and news stories assaulted pedestrians as they passed through their neighborhoods, or readers who perused the pages of mainstream magazines. *20 minutos* is a free daily publication, mostly distributed at the entrance to the metro, thus reaching a broad swath of Madrid's public. When I lived in the city, I would swipe a copy on my morning commute, and read news stories that documented the city's urban transformation and the emergence of new neighborhoods at the peripheries. These short stories reported the rising prices of Madrid's real estate, the availability of new units for sale in some new suburban location, and the innovative credit products that entered the market. At the same time the reader was bombarded by stories of the triumph of the Spanish real estate and construction sector and the seemingly limitless growth of the economy, advertisements for mortgage and credit products, sunny vacations, and foreign automobiles lulled the audience into a stupor of consumption. Because of these innovations in the banking sector, evident in both advertisements and news stories themselves, this lifestyle was in reach, immediate, possible rather than purely aspirational.

Furthermore, this lifestyle was distinctively European, as questions of political, economic, and cultural membership within the Spanish polity became subsumed into the broader geopolitical moment. In the pages of *20 minutos,* for example, travel agencies offered not only exciting family vacations to the

Canary Islands or the Valencia coast, but also romantic getaways to Paris and Rome, or package deals in the Greek Islands. The contemporary reality of a borderless Europe made these once exotic locales suddenly close, brought into a visual economy of circulation and consumption. Additionally, while press from previous years had advertised deals on Spanish Seats, now the everyday consumer was offered a French Renault or a German Volkswagen. Europe meant the entrance into a globalized culture of consumption: international holidays, Italian clothing, American movies, McDonald's, Nike, and H&M all became common currency of pleasurable exchange. Placed in visual proximity to one another, these advertisements created a sentimental link between consumer goods, leisure activities, and the pleasure of homeownership.

Real estate advertisements often reflected this more global worldview, subtly proclaiming their consumers to be cosmopolitan, discerning, and well versed in international consumption. For example, an advertisement for Martinsa, a construction company, took up an entire page of *20 minutos* in a special section on SIMA, Madrid's annual real estate fair. The ad features a young woman beaming, her laptop open in front of her. While we cannot see a brand, we suspect she has the latest Apple MacBook, as we can espy its steely exterior and distinctive keyboard font. Clad in jeans, she sprawls on a clean, cream-colored couch, a far cry from the fusty, uncomfortable settees of previous generations. Her dress, her electronics, her interior style all establish her as a part of an international marketplace, her tastes clearly worldly, her lifestyle surely cosmopolitan. Above her floats the text, "Homes with unique personalities*," followed with "*yours." Below, a list of numerous suburban neighborhoods and vacation towns reveals the extent of her possibilities, flung across Spain. The young woman, who appears no more than thirty years old, can find a home "in the best locales, with all the luxurious details and tailored to your expectations." Here we see a promise of endless possibility: in this moment, one could choose not only where to live, but an entire lifestyle to go with such a decision. These notions of possibility and international cosmopolitanism mixed easily with messages of domesticity, hearth, and the home.

Such portrayals conjured up lifestyles that were in distinct contrast to previous forms of urban life. One now had a choice of where to live, rather than be condemned to dwell in substandard housing at the urban fringe. The available housing stock was bright and new, with modern features and contemporary plumbing. Fully integrated neighborhoods provided recreational areas and educational options. With the extension of rail lines to far-flung parts of

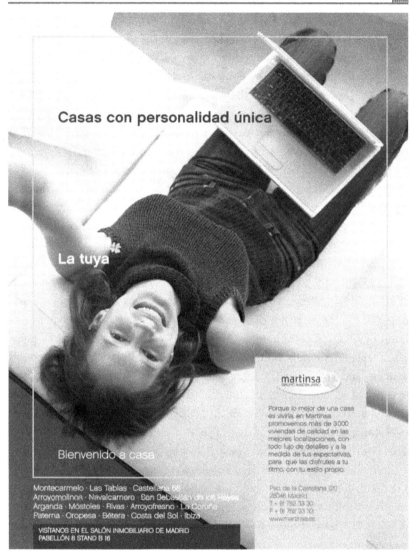

FIGURE 4.1. Advertisement for Martinsa. Source: *20 Minutos,* April 6, 2006, 13.

the metropolitan region, living in the suburbs was no longer a penance. The expanded metro also offered easy passage from peripheral Madrid neighborhoods to the center. Villaverde, once a *colonia de barro,* now had several metro stops where residents could be whisked away for a short ride to Puerta del Sol. But one now also had the ability to take part within an entire consumer economy, refashioning both the domestic sphere and the presentation of self however she saw fit. Where once there was misery and material lack, now there was possibility.

While homeownership was part of a constellation of practices portrayed as European, it also became the vehicle by which ordinary *madrileños* could live out the rest of this consumer fantasy. The wide windows of bank branches and real estate agencies—often several to a block—regularly advertised exciting promotions that came with a mortgage or the purchase of a house. Some banks would offer new furniture sets or exotic vacations to entice customers into their franchise, while others promised lines of personal credit with favorable terms. Many interlocutors relate how banks required them to take out a credit card when they signed their deed of sale. All of these offers, promotions, and invented requirements were tied into, and sometimes financed by, the acquisition of a mortgage. But they also allowed people to suddenly realize this vision of globalized consumption. As Hannah Clarke and Jane Zavisca point out in their discussion of housing and consumption, "Intensive consumption practices—and consumer spending—are required to transform the physical properties of a house into the cultural embodiment of a home."[37] Furnishing one's home becomes a means by which the homemaker expresses her cultural capital, integral to both the making of "home" and the presentation of self as part of Bourdieu's *habitus.* With new purchasing power, these everyday urbanites could now also join the swell of people along the calle Princesa. As the city rapidly transformed, people could also enjoy the pleasures of its modernity. Homeownership was thus a constitutive component of consumer citizenship as it allowed a host of other possibilities to become reality. To be the girl on her laptop, then, demanded the acquisition of property. Through that initial acquisition one might then acquire more, the designer furniture, the American footwear, the guise of the global denizen.

Domesticity, Gender, and the Millennial Man

Entry into homeownership relied on more than the public display of conspicuous consumption. It also worked through aspirations of family and the private sphere, and became a necessary component for domestic futures. Nestor,

Borja, and Iñaki are three interlocutors from working-class backgrounds who purchased homes in the Madrid metropolitan region's southern peripheries. None attended college, and while they each acquired a house for slightly different reasons, they all alluded to domestic aspirations as integral to their decision. Nestor, a young father of two from the southern working-class suburb of Fuenlabrada, detailed to me the ways in which purchasing a home was the only means, at nineteen, with which he could leave the family home. Earning a decent if not exorbitant living as a furniture restorer, Nestor had a steady girlfriend, a steady income, and a desire to no longer live with his parents. In Fuenlabrada ample new housing enticed young people. The ethos of the time stipulated that housing prices would only rise; Madrid's recent history impressed upon this young consumer that economic imperative. Homeownership, after all, was necessary for a particular realization of self and personhood. In a society in which young people, especially young men, leave home later and later, homeownership allowed for both independence and economic and financial self-sufficiency. Nestor regarded his decision as wise and mature; as his friends cavorted in bars and spent their earnings on package holidays and video games, this young man planned for a future replete with partner and children.

Borja is another working-class interlocutor from Madrid's suburban periphery. In relating his financial history to me, he spoke of dreaming, since childhood, about his future matrimonial home: "Always drawing my house, my family." Purchasing a home after many years of backbreaking manual work meant the realization of this primordial dream. Borja's financial history is closely linked to his sense of himself as a family man. This chapter opens with a quote from Iñaki, who evoked similar sentiments. He spoke of the necessity of the mortgage for an aspirational future of wedded bliss. There emerge clear links between mortgage credit, domesticity, and middle-class sensibilities. The mortgage was fundamental for the expression of status; Iñaki alludes to it as one part of a larger dream of stability and upward mobility, as essential as a partner with whom to share one's life. A family requires a house; a house requires a mortgage. The mortgage thus became that tool that mediated between the broader social structure of millennial Madrid and the individual.

Throughout my ethnographic encounters—in interviews, counseling sessions, assemblies, or protests—there was an elision between family, house, home, and, by extension, a mortgage. While many of the people I came across were single, their housing purchases also allowed them to think pragmatically and wistfully about an imagined future of domestic family life. The mortgage was that instrument that allowed them to live out the comforts of home.

Likewise, such parallel constructions, as Borja's quote above illustrates, make immediate the inextricable links between family and home, but also family and homeownership. For Iñaki, for example, striving for a particular vision of the good life included a partner and a house, but also a mortgage that would make such a lifestyle possible. Within the confines of estate agencies across the metropolitan region, young people were making the leap into adulthood. In so doing, they were finally able to live out Arrese's much earlier vision of domestic stability and private life. Thanks to deregulation in both the housing and mortgage markets, that vision could finally come to fruition.

These aspirations, meanwhile, perpetuated certain gendered tropes, revealing the ways in which homeownership became entwined with masculine identities. Indeed, to take part within the dominant, heteronormative, family-oriented culture of millennial Madrid demanded the purchase of a home. What was implicit in my conversations with these men is that they envisioned themselves as providers. The house was their responsibility as male wage-earners. Rather than enter into homeownership with a partner, these men saw it as a first step within a longer process of maturation. Borja makes this sequence evident—in his words, the house comes first, then the family. The acquisition of a house was necessary to then make possible the domestic fantasies that could develop within. This understanding, however, was in contrast to the social reality of millennial Madrid. During the dictatorship, Franco prescribed strict gender roles that confined women to the house. Those women who transgressed the borders between public and private were objects of shame and vilification.[38] During the democratic era, however, changing gender roles, economic necessity and restructuring, and the feminist movement all transformed the social landscape. Now women were active, vital members of the workforce—both main political parties, after all, featured numerous women within their highest ranks.[39] Indeed, to stay at home was a sign of elevated social class that most households could not afford. Yet in the domestic imaginaries of these young men, Spain's new sociological reality is rendered invisible, as they rely instead on antiquated notions of house and home. Their understandings of themselves in the world still adhere to traditional roles in which the male partner is breadwinner and provider.

The mortgage as a tool both to modernize and to preserve traditional gender divisions is of course a paradox. Integral to narratives of globalization and cosmopolitanism is the idea of gendered equity, at least in the arena of capitalist advancement and consumption. Gender mainstreaming has been central to

European Union policymaking and programming since the 1990s. The figure on the laptop is of course a woman—young, attractive, female, she would not have previously been able to choose this particular destiny. Instead it would have been chosen for her by male figures in her familial orbit. Entrenched gendered divisions continued to circulate—Spanish *machismo* is legendary, evident in the bravado of the bullfight and the posturing of politicians. But public life increasingly challenged these ideas and tropes. Indeed, in the pages of *20 minutos,* real estate advertisements featured either couples or single women, reflecting the emergence of a new client base. Single men, however, never appear as potential homebuyers. The new sociological panorama of purchasing power and shifting public identities could open new, sometimes confusing avenues for the construction of male subjectivities. Here again, the question of *habitus* is paramount in the construction of both popular culture and the market; the dispositions of working-class men, inherited from generations of traditional class and gender-based structures, were by no means extinguished and conditioned participation within the global moment.

In Almodovar's *Carne trémula*, two male protagonists experience very different fates. Victor emerges from poverty to win over the Italian beauty Elena. He does so by besting his rival for her affection, Javier Bardem's David. In the prelude to the movie, David has suffered an accident that renders him paralyzed from the waist down. Despite his injuries, he goes on to become a national and international star of Spain's handicapped basketball team, awarded endorsements from international brands. We see his image plastered across billboards advertising American athletic wear. Such allusions place him within the realm of a multinational Spain where he is a global star (hinting toward Bardem's own global fame a decade later). Yet it comes at the expense of his ability to walk, and, indeed, his virility as revealed in one graphic sex scene. Victor, however, remains a provider, taking care of his mother's estate upon her death. Almódovar also makes amply evident his masculine sexual prowess. Living amidst shacks, the urban remnants of Francoist Madrid, he is a figure still tied to the *castizo* Madrid, to traditional modes of living in the city, yet capable and able-bodied. He has not lost himself within the forest of international signs, still upright and capable.

Throughout the filmmaker's other works, characters bend those strict rules that once governed gender, sexuality, age, and the traditional family unit, presenting a colorful society of gay men, drag queens, alternative families, and nuns who buck the mandates of their habit. We cannot take Almódovar's

worlds as simulacra for contemporary life and the quotidian, yet they still reveal shifting mores and cultural appetites. Madrid was a city of rapid, startling
change, caught up in the emergent web of multinational expansion. Our globalized present provokes contradictory responses, including reactionary ethno-
nationalism and the rejection of gendered equality.[40] While virulent intolerance
and reactionary revanchism remain at bay, desire for tradition, hegemonic ideals of normalcy, and normative concepts of gender and the family lurk within
the dark reaches of my ethnographic encounters.

Homeownership thus can be seen in part as a tool to navigate the globalized
city. Borja, Iñaki, and Nestor all reveal visions of themselves in the traditional
role of male head of household. In Iñaki's analytic, the quest for a partner (female) is allied closely with the accrual of mortgage debt. To be a man in millennial Madrid within this portrayal of domesticity meant being a homeowner,
echoing my earlier discussion of Raúl. Somehow defective because he did not
own a home, Raúl felt less than a man as a result: he was unable to fully provide
for his pregnant wife and unborn son, neutered to the demands of the consumer marketplace. Similarly, Borja speaks of purchasing his home and then
furnishing it to provide for his young family. He created the small nest in which
his wife and child might live comfortably. His public role as a worker earning
a wage is closely related to his ability to provide and care for his family. The
mortgage, then, became the tool that mediated between a traditional past and
the millennial, exuberant present.

Stagnant Wages and the Spanish Dream

Within the symbiotic relationship between mortgage debt and domesticity,
homeownership provided crucial economic support that was otherwise absent.
Borja told me how the bank offered him seemingly endless lines of credit for the
realization of certain middle-class aspirations. Working blue-collar jobs from a
young age, he described the feelings of tremendous possibility during this moment of ebullient consumption. He had been with his girlfriend since he was
a teenager and had worked tirelessly since then to make manifest his domestic
desires. Now the bank would allow for the security of a new home, financing
an entirely new lifestyle that had previously appeared out of reach, belonging to
a different social class. Into the mortgage could be included credit to purchase
a new car and completely furnish the new house. These enticing trappings of a
middle-class lifestyle beckoned seductively to the young family man.

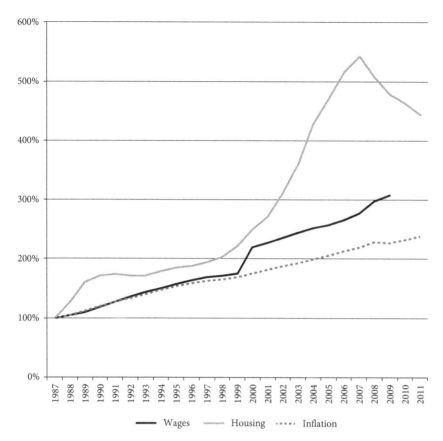

FIGURE 4.2. Evolution of housing prices relative to salaries and inflation. Source: Alfonso Sainz de Baranda, "¿Es la vivienda una buena inversión? Precio Vs. Valor." *Thinking Rich*, June 14, 2012. https://www.rankia.com/blog/thinkingrich/1320111-vivienda-buena-inversion-precio-vs-valor. Used with permission.

The climate of consumption that permeated Madrid during its boom years largely relied on credit to lubricate demand and stimulate exuberant spending. Entrance to the European Union inaugurated certain processes of globalization and the acquisition of cosmopolitanism. But it also meant the introduction of the euro, which forced prices to rise even as salaries remained the same. When the euro was introduced, it was equivalent to 160 pesetas. To simplify this equation, everything that had previously cost 100 pesetas—a cup of coffee, a *caña* of beer—was now one euro. The costs of goods and services thus immediately increased 60 percent. There was, however, no concomitant swell in salaries; López and Rodríguez, in fact, argue that real wages actually fell during this period.[41] We see in the above graph that salaries barely kept up with the rate of inflation. For the working class, salaries only increased slightly during that time. Yet the price of housing, and indeed many other consumer goods, only skyrocketed.

In addition to wage stagnation and rising prices, the employment market remained deeply unequal, particularly for young people seeking not just jobs but rather careers. An older generation of professionals had benefited from well-paid work with indefinite contracts.[42] The old protections built into these contracts meant these workers were difficult to fire. Dismissal would also require many years of high unemployment payments, which were calculated on the basis of length of service and monthly wage. Thus, the middle-aged middle class benefited from job security with healthy compensation. Not so their children, despite high levels of educational attainment. Instead these young people often found precarious employment with temporary contracts, low wages, and part-time hours—the *mileuristas* mentioned before. When I lived in Madrid following college, many of my friends and acquaintances found temporary work for little pay. At one point, as Spain teetered on the edge of crisis, a marketing company wanted to hire me; they were looking for someone who was fully bilingual to lead an international campaign but offered around 700 euros in salary. The expectation seemed clear that whomever they hired would live at home with parents, thus freed from the costs of room and board. The younger generation constituted a separate class, easily fired and without the large salaries of their older colleagues.

Against this backdrop of stagnant wages and a bifurcated labor market, real estate provided an obvious avenue for the accrual of wealth, becoming a mode of participation in the labor market.[43] On the one hand, the spectacular rise of Madrid's real estate market was everywhere in evidence: new housing estates bloomed like wildflowers along suburban highways, one's friends and family spoke urgently of the need to buy, neighbors purchased second homes in the sunny warmth of the Valencia coastline, and prices seemed to jump thousands of euros from one day to a next. This market promised astonishing rates of return in addition to easy entrance. Such low thresholds for participation are of course integral to establishing personal financial products as necessary components of social reproduction.[44] Commonsense understanding of the market's endless rise conspired with the liberal availability of credit, thus "blurr[ing] the boundaries between investment and consumption."[45] Housing also became the key investment strategy for everyday people in a country that lacked a strong investment culture.[46] The middle classes purchased second or even third homes with the intention of selling them later on to feather retirement nests and provide inheritances to children caught in the lackluster labor market.

Meanwhile, flipping properties, which many small-town speculators and large development companies pursued, promised untold riches. In the absence of well-paid work, urban speculation offered a promising avenue to make one's fortune. Iñaki, for example, told me in no uncertain terms that he purchased a townhouse far from Madrid to the southwest for the sole purposes of speculation. An ambitious young man, he had been involved in a variety of business deals and companies before he had reached thirty. Without a university education, he nonetheless convinced a master's program to admit him. Having accumulated an array of experiences in hospitality and finance, where he helped people with poor credit secure loans, he decided real estate was one more arena in which he could make money. He had witnessed others get rich through flipping. Once members of the working class, these peers could suddenly live lives of luxury through their masterful command of the property market.

The property market became a means of not only securing housing, but also professional advancement and the accrual of wealth in the absence of good waged employment in traditional sectors. As Madrid's reliance on housing and homeownership proved successful in fueling spectacular growth, the city increasingly relied on the construction industry to the detriment of other forms of economic activity. Madrid's long-ago embrace of construction presaged major shifts within the Spanish economy as a whole, which abandoned earlier industrial models of development and employment. The urbanization of the city and its peripheries through homeownership meant that the housing and construction industry pushed out traditional economic activity such as small-scale fabrication and manufacturing. Gone was salaried factory work on a regular schedule. Now the working classes laid bricks, installed plumbing, or welded the ghostly skeletons of future high-rise housing. Soon they abandoned that work to newly arrived immigrants such as Eduardo and Morton from Ecuador. Millennial Spaniards became real estate agents, small-time developers, or financial services professionals. Iñaki's boomtime biography is emblematic of the possibilities that were afforded a generation of young men and women.

Interlocutor José Antonio, a longtime militant in the United Left party and one of the founders of the PAH in Madrid, became a small-town construction baron with several employees. Professional and thus class mobility was now possible, as many jobs in the industry required little formal education. Many people also worked in auxiliary industries that had sprung up to support construction and real estate: Nestor worked as a furniture restorer, while Sofia, another Spanish interlocutor now in late middle age, had a decoration firm with her husband, providing the lavish interiors for new homes. The confluence of wage stagnation, increasingly precarious employment, rising prices, and the erosion of the traditional working-class base meant real estate was an attractive arena for investment, speculation, and also employment.

Mortgage debt also provided the vehicle through which to finance businesses, particularly as the economy began to crumble. Both José Antonio and Sofia were small-business owners, their homes paid off long ago. But as economic troubles started to set in, they were confronted with the reality of maintaining not only their small companies, but also the livelihoods of themselves and their employees. In the absence of loans to small businesses—which have only really entered the Spanish marketplace post-2008 as a means of stimulating the depressed economy—they refinanced their homes to keep their businesses afloat. José Antonio said, "I found myself without any means of income" and was thus forced to take out a small loan to "try to get out ahead." Similarly, Sofia found the business was no longer sustainable without an additional personal loan—in crisis, people no longer needed decorating services. Debt taken out against the house thus maintained participation in the labor market in a climate poorly equipped to aid small businesses.

Rather than signify middle-class status, homeownership became the sole means of attaining that status. Borja said to me, "I'm a blue-collar worker who wasn't able to live above my means. I'm a *mileurista* or a bit more, I learn for myself alone." But the introduction of easy credit signified that Borja's possibilities were now greatly expanded. The mortgage credit was an agile vehicle through which other consumption opportunities presented themselves, as bankers and financial officers encouraged introducing secondary credit products through the greater balance of the mortgage. Thus someone like Borja, who initially purchased his house with a mortgage of 100,000, saw that number grow to 180,000. Various car loans and credit for future remodels inflated his debt. We can think here about the idea of living above one's means. Since the crisis, politicians and bankers have chastised people in debt for living beyond their means, as if they were greedy scoundrels who had gamed the system. But if we look at Borja's story, that analysis tends to disintegrate. The bank—certainly expert within its field—told him his means were expanded; it had nothing to do with his salary and everything to do with the size of his line of credit. For each of his doubts, it had a soothing word to calm him into greater debt. In examining the single-family home market in France, Bourdieu describes the informational asymmetries that mark financial transactions between agents and bankers on the one hand, and the homebuyer on the other.[47] He determines such transactions are always prejudiced against the homebuyer, who will be duped by a variety of methods into acquiring a house, and thus a mortgage, that lies just slightly beyond his means. In the case of Madrid, proffered credit also took into account the steep upward curve of housing prices, inflated by banks and appraisers. Surging housing prices meant that Borja's 100,000-euro house with 180,000-euro mortgage would soon be worth 150,000 or even 200,000. This complicated financial arithmetic took his modest salary and multiplied it several times. Thus even if we assign him some guilt in provoking later disaster, certainly guilt must also lie with the bankers and politicians who insisted on his audacious though short-lived fortunes.

While advertisements assaulted the senses, the tentacles of the rapidly expanding real estate and banking sectors infiltrated people's daily lives. Borja described being offered all manner of products from his local bank branch. Similarly, José Antonio described how small-town culture came to be completely entwined with economic possibility facilitated by the banks. He wanted to purchase a new cargo van, discussing it with neighbors and friends in his small town in Madrid's hinterlands. The next thing he knew, the local bank director was on the phone, offering him all manner of financing opportunities so that he could get something more luxurious or larger than originally intended. While José Antonio demurred, in his retelling those provincial bankers appear as seductive gatekeepers, Sirens beckoning to seafarers with their promise of great wealth and possibility. The sociologist Quentin Ravelli conducted a series of interviews with bank branch managers.[48] Asked to describe their histories in the role, they revealed how the requirements of the job shifted over time. For many years, they were local figures akin to the neighborhood priest or doctor. They administered to the community's financial needs instead of its spirituality or health, but their role was essentially that of a benevolent community leader. With the advent of Europeanization, their role shifted. Over time they were encouraged to promote riskier forms of credit of expanding sizes to members of their community. They were now salesmen, dressing up complicated financial products in enticing terms. Many of the public acquiesced. In a moment in which salaries stymied economic possibility in light of rising prices, such easy credit flowed forth to finance economic demands and foment the new ethos of consumption. Thus wage stagnation was masked through a reliance on credit.

Such economic considerations perhaps point to the conditions of labor and employment under post-Fordism. But to ascribe their logics wholly to that economic temporality would bely the historical entanglements between wage labor and housing. In many analyses of neoliberal urbanism, financialization, securitization, and increased precarity replace a robust economy of secure wage labor. Absent the obligation to pay a premium on labor, firms can direct their assets into other circuits with the promise of more audacious returns. In turn, the mortgage becomes the means to finance social reproduction as expenses in education, healthcare, and retirement skyrocket. Using one's house as an ATM, as the saying goes, is about perpetuating the middle class in a moment of uncertainty. Yet this vision of (post-)Fordism in many locales remained elusive at best. I refer here to Fordism not only as that system of labor, as a mode of factory production with the assembly line. Rather, I consider Fordism more broadly as an organizing logic for an entire economy of politics and culture, as that system that allowed its working class to participate in the marketplace as consumers of the very goods they themselves produced. In millennial Madrid, these relations of indebtedness, tied to homeownership, instead *inaugurated* a consumer class and social mobility, albeit very briefly.

Here Madrid was catapulted into the global era of Europe; authoritarianism gave way almost immediately to neoliberalism. As wages stagnated, the mortgage became the tool to obviate that stagnation. Someone like Borja, a handyman who worked menial jobs since the age of sixteen, would once have lived in either a shanty or a soulless housing block, a concrete prison far from any goods or services. Life would most likely be nasty, brutish, and short, recalling the novelist Pio Baroja's dark *fin de siècle* dramas of Madrid's urban poverty. Borja would not be able to afford a social life or the physical trappings of the middle class. Yet for a brief moment he was able to enjoy the myriad benefits of urban consumer cosmopolitanism. Those benefits came not because of increased wages, improved educational attainment, or robust economic development, but rather because he had access to a mortgage. And that mortgage was a powerful tool that financed his brief upward ascent.

These myriad financial and cultural considerations configured homeownership, and more specifically mortgage debt, into a central component to millennial citizenship. Through private property, individuals could grow their wealth in a way unavailable through traditional wage labor or maintain floundering businesses afloat in the absence of more sophisticated banking practices. While it allowed for the realization of production, it also crucially furthered reproduction, financing old age or urban middle-class lifestyles. Finally, homeownership made manifest domestic aspirations for a new generation of young people eager to make their homes in the metropolis of possibility and promise.

Financing the Homeowner Citizen
Homeownership became the central mechanism to instantiate upward mobility and consumption and perpetuate social reproduction and economic growth, but it relied exclusively on new forms of credit and risk. Debt was disseminated throughout Spanish society and political economy, a common condition that permeated household economies, municipal governments, regional governance arrangements, and national treasuries. Borja, Iñaki, and Nestor were able to access large amounts of credit not because of the largesse of bankers or changing cultural imperatives, but rather through deliberate structural shifts that promoted lending. While ethnographic material has allowed me to paint a portrait of acquisition during this time, broader macroeconomic trends bear out my analysis.

During the period of the Spanish boom, household finances experienced marked changes that reveal an expansive prosperity born out of credit lending. The Banco de España launched its own survey efforts in 2002 to collect

TABLE 4.1. Household wealth versus debt, 2002–2011

	2002	*2005*	*2008*	*2011*
Median income (euros)	22,000	23,100	26,000	25,400
Median net worth (euros)	96,300	177,000	206,800	153,000
Median percentage of primary residence[a]	66.50	66.10	54.80	60.30
Median value of main residence (euros)	97,300	180,300	180,300	150,300
Indebtedness of population	43.60%	49.60%	50.10%	49.30%
Median ratio debt to household income[b]	73.3	99.3	104.7	107.0

Source: Bank of Spain.
[a] In total assets.
[b] In households with debt.

data Spaniards' household finances. Released every three years, the data demonstrate that during the 2000s, Spaniards saw their wealth grow as a result of rising property values. Yet indebtedness grew significantly, wages stayed largely stagnant, and inequality increased.[49]

Additionally, during this time investment in secondary real estate went up. The jump between 2002 and 2005 in terms of both median net wealth and median value of main residence is startling; wages are insignificantly higher three years later and cannot account for such a jump in prosperity. Meanwhile, households that did not own their primary residence, which accounted for less than 20 percent of households overall, saw little asset growth during this time. Yet those who owned were fortunate: their wealth almost doubled, as property values went up almost 100 percent. Such numbers demonstrate that homeownership was the only mechanism by which families could build equity during this time, even if only on paper. Furthermore, few households had investments outside of the real estate market; investments in stocks and bonds, mutual funds, etc., was practically nil, particularly among younger generations. Yet during this same period, households were clearly taking on debt to finance this system. Furthermore, the percentage of households with outstanding personal loans grew from 19.9 to 24.6 percent during the 2002 to 2005 period and then held steady to 2008; credit card debt, not recorded during 2002, also grew from 2.9 to 7.3 percent from 2005 to 2008. The data suggest that households grew increasingly comfortable with and reliant on debt to finance consumption; after the mortgage came the credit card. Widespread debt gave the illusion of prosperity and masked deepening inequalities. On paper, low-waged workers nonetheless appeared rich, their financial ledgers buoyed by readily available credit and inflated property markets.

Indebted Cosmopolitans

As Madrid's housing stock grew with the advent of new planning laws and the deregulation of land, consumer credit products flooded the market in order to expand the homeowner population. These products soon became constitutive components in the perpetuation of millennial subjects. Debt permeated many aspects of contemporary life, including gendered identities, new configurations of wage labor, social reproduction, and middle-class common sense. These various elements of belonging converged to form an emergent system of citizenship, in which debt was a necessary tool. This system was predicated not on political rights and responsibilities, but rather on consumption and participation within a marketplace of cosmopolitan urbanity. Indeed, rights and the traditional tenets of the welfare state were quickly subsumed into this system.

Indebted urban citizenship worked in harmony with a spatialized ideology of expansion. James Holston insists in *Insurgent Citizenship* on the ways in which citizenship operates through the urban scale, as the arena in which the relationship between self and society, individual and polity are mutually imbricated and constituted.[50] Indeed, in millennial Madrid, debt served as the mechanism by which that relationship was concretized. Its introduction, through a host of innovative products, crafted citizens readied for the demands of this enterprising city, as a site of consumption of goods and services, culture, leisure, and most importantly, homeownership. While debt was crucial for housing consumption, at the same time housing allowed an additional vehicle for debt to take hold, fomenting a host of other opportunities critical to membership within this imagined whole. Thus a vicious circle emerged, in which homeownership, debt, and citizenship were symbiotic, their interdependence encouraging people (and municipalities) to over-wager their hands.

Why might we consider such a system one of citizenship? Participation in almost every aspect of urban life required homeownership. Work and leisure, consumption and cultural expression, in addition to basic needs of housing and old age, all came to rely on investment in private property. But the perpetuation of the city, too, through investment in its building stock, also demanded the homeowner citizen, who might continue to take out loans both to finance his own urban survival and to further development of the built environment. The urbanism of homeownership, after all, sustains itself not only through large-scale investment, but also through the compliance of modest figures who buy into its promises and acquiesce to its fictions of endless expansion.

5 Debt Sentences

Homeownership was supposed to inaugurate a new age of prosperity and comfort for Betsy as she approached middle age. But she soon became consumed and unmade by her investment in exurban Madrid. She never actually got to live in her flat in Coslada. By the time it was finished in 2007, her mortgage payments had shot up exponentially; she worked all hours of the day in order to pay the swelling fees. Desperate to pay her mortgage, she could neither afford the monthly costs nor find the time for a move. She contemplated putting the house on the market, but suddenly no one seemed to be buying. The common sense of homeownership in Madrid—that both prices and demand always rise—now appeared to be a myth. Soon, the Spanish economy began to contract and she lost her job. Her brother returned to Peru and she had to face the monthly payments alone. What once promised a future of comfort and riches now seemed like a penance. Soon she realized she couldn't pay the monthly installments and entered into a deep depression. Shame consumed her. The banks cut her off financially, providing no relief: she had passed onto a credit blacklist that prohibited a host of transactions. Betsy, like many I would come across, thought of herself as a *muerta civil*—a civil dead. While metaphorical, Betsy's death was still violent and painful.

Homeownership for both immigrant and native members of the working class—people like Betsy and Borja, Yvette and Iñaki—relied intractably on the accrual of debt. Debt was ubiquitous throughout Madrid, where it made manifest modest aspirations of domestic bliss and outsized desires for urban cosmopolitanism. It united personal bank balances and municipal coffers, small businesses and multinational corporations. For many everyday citizens, it briefly accorded the illusion of wealth, class, and status. Soon, however, home-ownership's debts would prove unsustainable. Indeed, as a wealth of scholar-ship on neoliberalism, debt, and finance reveals, the risks associated with this overleveraged situation were borne almost wholly by individual citizens, many of humble means.

When we owe far more than we actually have, we don't necessarily think of ourselves as broke. Most people I know carry debt, sometimes tallying into the hundreds of thousands. Mortgages, expensive education, youthful and not-so-youthful misadventures with credit cards, or some unholy combination of all of the above mean some of their balance is in the red. They do not, however, think of themselves as destitute. We view many of these debts as savvy financial decisions that emerge in response to low interest rates, the potential personal and financial return of a graduate degree, a steady rise in property values, and an opportunity to accrue equity through ownership. What happens when we go from indebted to broke to completely underwater? What does dispossession do to the family, the household, and the self?

This chapter explores the lived experiences of dispossession, of lives under the tyranny of debt. Homeownership, it reveals, produces new forms of vulner-ability and exclusion through its singular forms of dispossession. In the case of Madrid, rather than further economic prosperity and social incorporation, the city's long dominant housing system instead created deep fissures that coursed along lines of ethnic difference, gender, and class. Homeownership, long an engine of growth, became in economic crisis an engine for precarity and in-creased vulnerability, further marginalizing already precarious populations. Its violent dispossessions were suddenly laid bare, confined not to the economic sphere alone, but rather implicated throughout familial structures and social relations, gender roles, and personal identity.

The Dispossessed

In Madrid the mortgage wrested years of equity from modest urban dwellers who founds themselves mired in debt. In January of 2007 the Euro Interbank Offered Rate—Euribor for short—went up significantly. Over 90 percent of mortgages in Spain use the Euribor as reference. Suddenly mortgage payments across the country began to rise, a situation that would only worsen as the rate continued to climb over the next year and a half. In this same moment, the economy was slowing; years of frenzied construction were finally coming to a halt. With the implosion of Lehman Brothers in September 2008, Spain's long decline began in earnest, as droves of people began to lose their jobs. Immigrants employed in precarious work were the first to lose jobs and then homes. Members of the working class soon found themselves in similar positions. Mortgage debt suddenly, sometimes tragically, became a problem.

Indebtedness is a financial situation, evoking, too, social relations and kinship ties. But it is also a sentiment, a feeling that then influences one's orientation to the world at large. As I listened to people describe their situations of financial precarity during assemblies in 2013, the analytic of civil death began to emerge. Throughout the spaces of the Plataforma de Afectados por la Hipoteca (PAH–Platform for People Affected by Mortgages), the antiforeclosures and evictions collective whose origins are discussed in the next two chapters, people regularly described this new poverty as *muerte civil*—civil death. I wanted to uncover it as an affective category to understand the layered meanings behind this provocative turn of phrase. In the process of foreclosure they found themselves dead to society at large. This condition determined their place in the world, while also hinting at a loss. An evocative descriptor for financial exclusion, civil death imbricates participation in daily life while also insisting on an ending, a death. Yet even while they spoke of themselves as relegated to this tragic category, the civil dead were still condemned to dwell in the city, to eke out survival at the margins of their former lives. Dispossession thus produced new, tenuous modes of inhabiting both the city and the self.

In Spain, once a person enters into arrears she becomes a *morosa*, on a credit blacklist that prohibits a whole host of economic activities and exchanges.[1] She cannot take out a credit card, a new cellphone line, or a small loan. Further, in the absence of personal bankruptcy laws, she cannot wipe her slate clean, and the debt can also pass down to children in the event of death. Mortgage law, too, dictates that even after foreclosure and bank repossession people owe the outstanding balance. This bleak financial terrain conspires with social processes to configure the debtor as a *muerto civil*, experiencing civil death in the act of foreclosure.

Civil death, at first blush, is a colloquial term people use to denote financial delinquency.[2] Yet as I spent more time with people going through foreclosure, I came to realize it contained a rich, though tragic inner life that hinted at an agonized ontology of dispossession. As Elyachar writes, "Dispossession is more than an economic process. It strips individuals of their political identity and their psychic well-being as well."[3] The ubiquity of indebtedness in financing housing and the broader landscape of social reproduction allows for dispossession to take place.[4] In Madrid dispossession gave rise to a condition that was not merely an economic marker. Rather by hinting at the demise of a civil life, *afectadas* were conjuring up an entire landscape of ruin that conjoined the public sphere, the private space of the home, and everyday domestic economies. Civil death is of course a category of domination that emerges out of "signs of social value," articulated through social structures that accord privileges and cultural capital to some and enact domination of others.[5] As such, it is a product of what Bourdieu terms "symbolic violence," a form of violence not of blows and fists, but rather of a social order of stratification and inequality. The status of *moroso* is one conferred by the state, having responded to the dictates of the bank, which lends legitimacy to processes of dispossession. In conferring that status, the state provokes a cascade of consequences, financial and otherwise.

Here personal, atomized emotions and experiences interact with broader trends of financial and sociospatial inequality to create forms of exclusion. If the detective relies on forensic analysis to untangle the physiological causes of someone's demise, here I rely on ethnographic insights to make sense of this metaphorical death. I also rely on an archive of forms produced by the PAH that detail eviction cases; several vignettes from this archive will complement the experiences of interlocutors and draw out the experiences of life under debt's dispossessions.

Physical and Psychic Isolation

The metaphoric death of myriad homebuyers was not a sudden event. Rather, it was an agonizing process that dragged its victim through ever more greater depths of despair. The door to consumption did not close immediately and suddenly; rather, it was preceded by slow decline, anxiety, and increasing isolation. With the rise of the Euribor, people faced ever-greater difficulty to make mortgage payments. Betsy recalled how her life became consumed with work in order to pay the rapidly expanding payments on a house she never came to occupy. She described it as a "vicious circle of work," in which she worked evenings and weekends, always with her mind on her monthly payments. In a rather prescient description of homeownership, Bourdieu writes: it "tends to become the exclusive focus of all (material and psychological) investments."[6] What he hints at is the all-consuming nature of homeownership, which demands endless work in myriad forms. It also reveals the home to be a site not of refuge but of concentrated effort, made evident during financial crisis when work becomes even more burdensome because of the great terror of the home's potential loss. Rather than become a nice place to escape the demands of work and the city, Betsy's house had consumed her being, demanding physical and emotional toil to keep her from ruin.

The work that went into maintaining the monthly payments, meanwhile, was not only all-consuming. It also furthered isolated people. Outside of work, Betsy had little time for anything other than sleep. Here again we see the fallacy of equating homeownership with greater integration or inclusion. Rather than provide stability and middle-class comforts, owning a home instead demanded endless labor so as to stay afloat, as *afectadas* barely scraped together the money for monthly installments. For someone like Betsy, homeownership precluded participation in civil society because it demanded she work all the time. Here again Bourdieu is instructive, as he describes how homeownership confines the individual and her aspirations to the domestic sphere, thus preventing her engagement in a social milieu beyond the home. The struggle and politics of public space and public life are thus avoided, "which always had to be carried on in the face of the temptation to retreat to the domestic sphere."[7]

Isolation took on other forms that were not purely physical and pervaded many people's experiences with financial decline. Interlocutors overwhelmingly described their early days of financial difficulties as laden with a profound sense of being completely alone. Here their isolation was psychological rather than physical. They perceived others around them living happy and full lives without a care in the world, while they carried with them an unimaginable secret. They could not conceive that others, too, were experiencing such hardship; they alone carried the weight of ruin. Such sentiments emerge from the hardened boundaries that dictate matters of domestic economies must be hidden from the outside world, such that questions of personal finance "are *consumed in private,* typically in the nuclear family unit," and, as such, "people are reluctant to discuss personal finance outside the family circle."[8] One interlocutor alluded to the concrete separation between public and private, stating, "You never talk to people about your mortgage and what you owe, never; talking about money is the ugliest thing that can happen in the world, you could talk about your [financial] excess, but about what you owe, never!" Money and its myriad problems are discreet issues best left to the privacy of home, to hushed conversations with bankers, or furtive words exchanged only with family members. We do not air such laundry in public; to do so would be vulgar or crass, trespassing sacred social rules that condemn such topics to the confines of the domestic sphere. Such rules do boundary work to separate public and private, such that they require we suffer economic hardship alone.

Isolation is internalized, used to turn the debtor against herself. In his famous treatise on suicide, Durkheim explores financial crises and their effect on the psyche. He writes: "Something like a declassification occurs which suddenly casts certain individuals into a lower state than their previous one." That declassification is at once violent and brutal, and requires immense self-discipline to weather, even as the self and her orientation to the world are entirely transformed. Such a sudden change in circumstance means "they are not adjusted to the condition forced on them, and its very prospect is intolerable; hence the suffering which detaches them from a reduced existence even before they have made a trial of it." Durkheim's language here evokes the ideas of the financially ruined subject as removed from the polity; society cannot adequately respond to her needs and instead places upon her a series of new demands, including, as he writes, "belt-tightening."[9] Indeed, as people like Betsy sunk into financial despair, political discourse demanded self-constraint, economizing measures, and restraint from usual avaricious tendencies. The wider political economy of austerity here projected delinquency and deviancy onto the new urban poor. Politicians spoke callously of tightening belt buckles and scrimping on luxuries while mortgage debtors literally starved.[10] At the same time, mortgage debtors also found they were in excess to the urban polity: jobs had dried up and services were slashed.

The ability to make monthly payments soon became impossible with the loss of work, which further isolated people. While work had been all-consuming, it at least provided contact with other people. Upon loss of employment, that one social outlet was no longer available, and people like Betsy and Mabel found themselves confined to a home that was steadily consuming their entire worlds. The conditions of immigrant employment, meanwhile, condemned them to further precarity. Many immigrants found work in informal situations, as subcontracted employees or home help kept off the books. As Mabel noted, employers skirted the law, neglecting to contribute social security and other forms of taxes in an effort to keep payroll as lean as possible. The multiple irregularities and shortcuts that plagued immigrant employment meant that with its loss, many foreign-born workers could not then claim state benefits. Loss of work meant complete economic ruin. Thus many immigrant homebuyers found themselves confined to their houses, with neither work nor any kind of income.

Intense sensations of failure, rampant through the civil dead, emerge out of hegemonic logics of debt that occlude processes of dispossession. The links between debt and morality, which haunt talk of domestic finances but also national bank balances, transform the debtor's inability to pay into an ethical breach.[11] Rendering the debtor as an immoral subject serves to cast her from society, setting her adrift in a sea of economic ruin made by her own hand.[12] She is excised from the political whole, treated as aberration. So, too, must she bear all the risk and responsibilities of her financial situation. The bank that lent the money is more or less absolved, its wager almost wholly without risk. Such an arrangement insists we see the debtor as a victim of her own poor financial decision-making while doing little to interrogate the situated economic, political, and cultural conditions that would have made such a decision rational in the first place. The devolution of risk combined with the moral valences of debt obscure the work of dispossession. Thus neoliberal understanding of indebtedness distort the way in which foreclosure and civil death are embedded features of political economy.[13] Civil death is thus a disavowal of the very dispossession that produces it as a category.

Immigrant Shame

Excluded from economic systems, soon to lose their homes, interlocutors speak intensely of all-consuming shame and guilt. Everyone I have spoken to regarding their mortgage problems narrates the first period of their struggle in terms of shame, guilt, and emotional collapse. The physical and mental toil of maintaining oneself afloat financially came with incredible psychological expenditure. At the same time, because of the ways in which society configures debt and default, people found themselves ravaged by shame from the self-perception of failure. For immigrants, this shame is located within a landscape that prescribes forward progress. The typical success story of the foreigner, who overcomes hardship in her new land to triumph over adversity, gaining citizenship and respect from both her community and society at large, circulates throughout many environments in which immigration is a substantive facet of contemporary life. We see these ideas within the advertising images discussed in the first chapter. Following the tenets set out for them by the world at large, immigrants performed the rituals and duties that might confer legitimacy. People such as

Mabel and Betsy, Yvette and Aida, meticulously stayed within the bounds of legality to prove they were "good" immigrants, willing and able to contribute meaningfully and productively to civil society. Thus when they fell behind on payments, they were inundated with shame: they had failed to live out normative visions of immigrant life, perverting the imagined, triumphant narrative of settlement and success with its attendant registers of integration and inclusion.

One was supposed to be able to get ahead through hard work and long hours. Popular and academic debates throughout many parts of the world insist hard work is key to escaping poverty. Prevailing antipoverty discourse in the United States, for example, ascribes laziness and listlessness to the unemployed. Such notions were echoed in Madrid, where politicians bemoaned the specter of the lazy immigrant, here to leech off the largesse of the Spanish state. Meanwhile anti-immigrant sentiment renders newcomers into threats—we need only recall Donald Trump's vicious rants that portray Mexican immigrants as violent thugs intent on rape and murder. While such portraits are seen as the exception, they filter into everyday policy and practice. Hard work, diligent saving, and the performance of a range of activities are means of dispelling with such characterizations. Immigrants were thus keen to disprove this myth, an idea that reverberated throughout many testimonies: hard work was the only means to get ahead and prove to yourself and society at large your worth as a productive member. As mentioned in the first chapter, Mabel's described her early time in Spain, when she was able to settle "without making any mistake as a citizen." Homeownership was one of the rewards that one reaped from that hard work; it was supposed to be refuge and comfort. For immigrants, in addition to working-class interlocutors, their lives had consisted of constant hustle, of scrimping and saving, of backbreaking labor. Yet what if hard work is not enough? What if it doesn't prevent you from finding yourself in the unemployment line? Shame comes, then, because you are now redundant to the system despite desperate attempts at access. What that implies for the self in its death, then, is that you are now that delinquent, that deviant specter of otherness who cannot compete.

Internalized concepts of shame were enhanced by the demands of the crisis-ridden city, as daily illegalities—small acts of skirting the law—became not uncommon as a means of survival.[14] Morton, for example, described his journey daily to the center of Madrid from the far-flung suburb of Fuenlabrada. He would show me a one-euro coin—his budget for the day. Unable to afford the train and metro fares, hoping to stretch his exceptionally modest finances, he jumped turnstiles to evade fares as he traveled from his home to his bank branch in the capital city and from there to an assembly or protest. He hoped daily to not get caught—he would of course not be able to afford the penalty fine for his misdeed. He understood his daily acts of transgression as necessary for survival and to stave off total ruin. Nonetheless, each time he slipped covertly through the plexi-glass barriers as they silently made way for a fare-paying commuter, his guilt would mount. Even as he raged at the city that had wrested from him domestic bliss and upward mobility, he feared proving correct the assumptions of immigrants as deviants and criminals. He also knew that as an immigrant he would draw more attention from the police for a minor infraction. Such small transgressions contribute to the shame of poverty. Engaging in acts deemed outside the law become the only way to be able to live in the city, despite previous hard work. He has shown himself to be unworthy of membership, outside of formal systems and alone because of his own failings. The perception of the self as criminal of course dovetails with extant environments that ascribe criminality to poverty. As a wealth of debates has established, the poor are increasingly penalized and illegalized, and prisons and jails have replaced the poorhouse as warehouses for populations made excess.[15] The turn toward petty illegalities thus shored up understandings civil death's punishment as legitimate, articulated through connections to dominant ideologies and practices of poverty.

The Death of the Self

Immigrants alone did not face such situations of isolation, shame, and despair. Borja, reflecting on his financial decline, stated, "From loneliness and being alone, living alone, I didn't want to see friends. You feel ashamed." Feelings of shame here translate immediately into thoughts of his social circle, from which he felt increasingly alienated. Writing on displacement, gentrification, and logics of property, Ananya Roy has recently articulated a notion of banishment, integral to dispossession.[16] While she speaks of literal removal, of forced exile to "city's end," we see in Borja's experiences another form of banishment, this time from sociality and civility. His internal emotions and experiences, brought about by indebtedness, translate into external actions of avoidance and self-exile. Indeed, debt also produces its own sensations of carceral confinement through the internalization of culpability.[17] Such confinement is not physical, but rather produced through the psychological and affective interpretations of oneself as a debtor, alluding to the biopolitical management of life under debt.[18]

The intersections of social stigma, colloquial idioms, and state punishment conspire such that the debtor understands dispossession's brutality as rational, the product of her own deviance.

Banishment is here a form of denied personhood: shame and alienation entwine and reinforce one another, colluding to separate Borja from his previous life not through physical removal but rather through silent interior suffering. Shame, a deeply personal, individualized sensation, thus contributes to the broader social milieu. Here we can see how the financial self is embedded within a terrain of social life, revealed only upon its banishment.

Borja, too, was wrested from previous visions of European cosmopolitanism. The life he had been living suddenly proved to be a lie, and he found that he was instead worse off than previous generations. Homeownership was supposed to better his stock in life. Throughout his childhood and early adulthood, the promise of upward mobility animated his milieu. A generation removed from the Franco era, Borja and his contemporaries were supposed to lead lives that were vastly improved from those of their parents and grandparents. While his grandparents, rural to urban migrants from Spain's devastated peripheries, faced hunger and repression, he was to have a life of comfort and material pleasure. Yet crisis revealed the illusion of his success. Instead he, too, faced precarity, lack, and even the specter of hunger. Progress, once everywhere in evidence, suddenly came to a halt.

These transformations of economic circumstances—of relative comfort into material lack and uncertainty—also provided a radical transformation of the self. Many people's narratives of their civil death reveal a profound estrangement. In addition to an estrangement from their former environments—work, social life, family—they also experience an estrangement from themselves. They no longer recognize the emotions coursing through their bodies or the thoughts, often violent, that come suddenly and jarringly to mind. In assemblies and counseling sessions, many *afectadas* discuss thoughts of suicide. As they attempted to get out from under the weight of financial collapse, their anguish provoked emotional chasms and detachments from the world at large that made actual death an available alternative.[19] Or at least that is one explanation. Part of that response, however, seemed born from an inability to describe precisely the emotional turmoil of civil death. Suicide, to me, seems like an easily available idiom to describe a complicated constellation of emotions. It conveys urgency and horror, desperation and exhaustion. Yet the reality of estrangement seems more complicated, fraught with economic ruin and the foreclosure of an imagined and longed-for future. It is a profound alienation that implicates social life, finances, past and future, all shot through with intense shame. Bourdieu, writing on physicality, alights on "embarrassment" as "the experience par excellence of the 'alienated body.'"[20] This isolation is not just about being cut off from friends or family. Rather, it is isolation from one's own self; it is to occupy a familiar body made alien through circumstances seemingly outside of one's control, the psychological terror of being completely estranged from the self.

In his discussion of shame, guilt, and violence, James Gilligan argues shame is the "death of the self."[21] Mortification after all carries within it *mort,* the Latin root for death. Pointing to the broad vocabulary that describes feelings of shame, he argues that it is an essential estrangement from both oneself and one's environment, the negation of both internal and external love. Much of Gilligan's analysis emerges from his work with violent offenders; he argues their own self-inflicted death is one means by which they can overcome and transcend their shame. While society and the state designate the category of civil death, here the internal classification of shame readies the soul for sacrifice. Shame is an "emotion that makes us most want to disappear," "that individuates, that isolates, that differentiates the self" more so than any other sentiment.[22] Finally, shame is that affect "which makes us conform to our cultural environment."[23] As such, it becomes a boundary that encloses us within the whole. When we feel this emotion, therefore, we are no longer constitutive of that whole, outside and other. Shame is thus a means of policing boundaries that delineate and confine the whole from the constitutive outside.

The aggressive strategies of banks attempting to secure repayment by any means necessary only exacerbate situations of shame. Dozens of incidents of harassment and abuse litter people's experiences with nonpayment. When payments suddenly rose, and people found they were unable to make ends meet, they often attempted to negotiate with the bank. In many instances, before the PAH had formed to aid in such negotiations, the bank refused to even hear their pleas. Calm, rational attempts to lower monthly payments were met either with stonewalling or with the offer of additional financial products. Personal loans might allow the person to meet the immediate cost of the mortgage but would increase the size of the overall debt. But at some point the *afectada* would come to the end of her grace period, or the additional loan would run out, and she would once again find herself with little option other than to cease payment altogether.

Then the abuse would commence. The bank would call her day and night, at any hour, demanding she make her payments. If she was a single mother, the voice on the other line might convince her that if she did not make payments, the state would take away her children. If she was an immigrant, they might threaten deportation or internment camps for undocumented populations. The emotional abuse was relentless, terrifying, and exacerbated the already consuming conditions of guilt, shame, and fear. Some people described bank officers even threatening to visit children's schools to report financial difficulties to teachers and fellow parents. Thus internal suffering was deepened and intensified by the unsavory strategies of the banking industry, which had only recently wooed this clientele. Here the enticing seductor suddenly turned toxic. Such behavior enforced feelings of shame and separation. The bank painted the debtor as criminal, complicit, and evil. Again the *afectada* saw her financial hardship transformed into a sign of incompetency and disgrace. Her feelings of shame and guilt were thus amplified by the personalized predation of the financial industry.

While legitimated through a host of institutions, civil death is also a process of the dispossession of the self. Within the context of chattel slavery, the historian Orlando Patterson denotes that enslaved subjects passed through a process of social death. That process meant the slave was wrested violently from his milieu and rendered into a nonbeing, "desocialized and depersonalized."[24] The logic here is one of subjugation to the authority of the master, a holistic system that demanded the institutionalization of marginality. Similarly, Giorgio Agamben writes of "bare life," by which the individual becomes that being who might be killed with impunity, the *homo sacer*.[25] In both cases, the individual is fundamentally dispossessed of her own personhood. Civil death evokes similar patterns of exclusion and exceptionalism. The debtor is alienated from society through institutionalized, state-sanctioned dispossession, which delineates her as outside and other.

Familial Ruin

Civil death is also a means of splintering and punishing extended networks of family and friends. While its earliest manifestations are perhaps individualized, it can soon become a common symptom among an entire collective. Through both formal and informal mechanisms, extended families became implicated in ruin. The financial industry took advantage of dependence on familial structures that compose modern life; within the ranks of the working class—immigrant or otherwise—traditional social relations came to be mediated through banking and finance. Deemed high-risk clients, immigrants, young families, and single women, for example, were often required by their banks to procure a cosigner who would guarantee their loans, as mentioned in the previous chapter.[26] Typically, a family member served in such capacity. While previously people lived at home with their parents, now those parents acted as *avales,* guaranteeing the loans of their children with their homes or salaries. The reliance on *avales* was rampant among immigrants, many of whom used family members as a means of accessing homeownership.[27]

While guaranteeing a loan would have disastrous consequences, family members readily agreed to do so in the moment of purchase as it was a naturalized extension of support for their kin. Betsy described involving her father in the folly of her mortgage: she said, "of course he said yes. It's your father or mother," alluding to the emotional binds that conspire to aid financial decisions. While seemingly a rational economic transaction, the purchase of a home also imbricates sentiments, imaginaries, and the dreams parents have for their children. In writing on student debt, Caitlin Zaloom elaborates the idea of *social speculation,* a shift from more traditional forms of social reproduction toward one that is reliant on debt. What is crucial in that shift is an imaginary buttressed by kinship ties of a prosperous and fruitful future. In her ethnographic work Zaloom explores the lengths parents will go to financing college, which activates notions of parental responsibility to realize youthful aspirations. In the case of mortgages, families drew upon similar imaginaries of upward mobility and familial obligations in order to make homeownership manifest.[28] At times, however, securing an *aval* might have been little more than a technicality, and a sister or brother would suffice. In the moment of purchase, no one—parent or child, sister or brother—imagines default, and thus this formal agreement of financial responsibility was rendered insignificant, a signature on a piece of paper. Yet the consequences for financial guarantee meant financial ruin could spread throughout the family; the contagion of the mortgage soon became the contagion of financial ruin. People were drawing family members into a web of financial responsibility in which any and all assets could be confiscated. Extended networks were thus implicated in default and subsequent demise, as the banks would then pursue the assets of whomever acted as *aval.* Thus individual debtors carried with them the anxiety of not only their own potential ruin, but also the ruin they might bring to those who had formally supported their entry into homeownership.

The financialization of kinship ties destroy families, as the punitive conditions of debt splinter throughout extended networks. One woman who became a committed activist came to the PAH because she had acted as the *aval* for her son. When he lost the house, he ceased to speak to his mother. Perhaps his shame was too great, or perhaps he lashed out with resentment at her for having abetted his ill-fated decision to buy a home. Now, however, mother and son had not spoken for years, and she subsequently lost her house to the bank. Her neighbors would whisper about her as she passed them in the hall: one chastised her for going to the salon to have her hair done instead of using her scant resources to help pay off an outstanding debt to the condo association. She felt the shame, isolation, and alienation of debt without ever actually having taken out a loan herself. The decision to help a loved one became disastrous. Nearing old age, she now saw a once comfortable future rife with uncertainty and poverty. Her only mistake was to act on maternal responsibility in assisting the dreams of a loved one.

The more informal arrangements of everyday survival also strain family ties. Mired in financial woes, adults come to rely on their immediate families for monetary support. Throughout my interviews, interlocutors spoke to me about the help they received from their families, which while crucial to their survival was also the source of additional and crushing shame. As adults, they had long been living on their own, no longer reliant on anyone but themselves. The act of explaining their situations to parents or siblings was traumatic, as they had to admit externally the extent of what they perceived to be their massive failings. Financial ruin was thus infantilizing because it transformed them once again into dependents reliant on family handouts to stay afloat. Sofia said to me, "This crisis also consumes your family." When her business failed and she and her husband had exhausted all other economic resources, they had to turn to their adult siblings. In the twilight of their middle age, they were keenly aware of the financial strain they placed on those around them. They were unable to find any kind of work, but felt the familial tensions of economic dependence.

The widespread effects of the crisis also mean such novel forms of dependency create additional pressure. At first families helped, perhaps thinking it was a temporary situation until loved ones got back on their feet. But the subtle pull of economic depression is insidious, reducing pensions and placing other family members on unemployment. Because the crisis was so extensive, even those who didn't face foreclosure or unemployment felt its devastation through slashed salaries or reduced hours. For the *afectada,* as her family begins to more directly feel the effects of crisis, her guilt becomes exacerbated; she is one more drain to finances. Such situations reach their crescendo when eviction takes place, and family members become dispersed throughout the homes of relatives, straining the system further. The *oikos* is suddenly evident, as intimacy and familial love translate into financial obligation and distress. Families here might split up, such that mother and daughter might live with one set of relatives and father and son with another. Financial devastation thus might also give rise to literal separation not because of the end of a relationship, but rather because of the straining of all resources.

The Foreclosure of Masculinity

This landscape of rupture and ruin, meanwhile, is profoundly gendered, furthering structural violences that are unduly prejudicial to women. With the onset of foreclosure, male subjectivities often undergo great transformation. Men saw their roles in society pass through their own process of foreclosure, as they were rendered useless and marginalized. Homeownership, as demonstrated in the third chapter, was a means of demonstrating their capabilities as wage earners and providers. In addition to allowing for a host of opportunities tied to the European moment, the home was also crucial for men to think about their domestic futures. In that imaginary, they saw themselves as living lives of comfort, able to create a happy nest for partners and children. Their public role as a wage earner—which would soon disappear during crisis—was then tied to their role as the domestic head of household. Such thoughts resonate with our established gender norms that dictate men must take on the public role of provider, earning the keep that will then allow the rest of the nuclear family to live in comfort. While women maintain that domestic space, men are expected to uphold this bargain through hard work and an earnest wage. Even as women have flooded the workforce, such ideals continue to permeate popular understandings of gender, domesticity, public, and private. Such understandings haunted my interviews with men who set off to make their fortunes so as to provide for a rich and fulfilling family life. Making their way in the world, proving themselves as men, imbricated domestic dreams of hearth, home, and a partner to keep those spaces sacred.

In his analysis of the rural bachelors' balls in France, Bourdieu reveals how urban capitalist society has left behind many male youths, who no longer see a place for themselves within immediate society. Unwilling to take up the mantle of urban living, no longer good matches for their young female counterparts, the bachelors of the ball are alienated and adrift, the imagined futures of yore no longer available.[29] Homeownership was the device that allowed the former male peasant to participate in the booming marketplace of millennial Madrid. Without homeownership, many male members of the working class were dispossessed of their place in the world. Men like Borja or Iñaki thus experienced an alienation from their masculine identities. Their sense of themselves as productive male individuals within a financialized society was taken from them through both the loss of the job and the subsequent loss of the home. Borja describes his descent into loneliness and shame in ways that hint at a profound loss of identity. An active member of the working class since adolescence, when he found himself without employment for the first time in his life he thought it was because of "my own thing," that is, something wrong with him. He understood his economic troubles as evidence of his own inadequacy as a man, as a worker, intertwined concepts that made up his sense of self. Yet his failure to provide implicated not only himself, but also his wife and young child. His own inadequacy reverberated through the small confines of his domestic life. Iñaki, meanwhile, described his civil death in terms of violent social and economic repression. While previously he had endless possibility, now "it's whatever thing you want to do. You're fucked and they continue to stomp on you. There's no way to have success to then pay. They demand you immediately pay with something you don't and can't have." There is physicality in his words that reveal the ways in which psychic wounds enact themselves upon the body. Here we see the embodied nature of debt, as it becomes a physical sensation of being ground down—the financial system a literal weight shoving him into the earth. Material lack and indebtedness translate into material situations of bodily oppression. He feels completely beholden to forces beyond his control, neutered and dominated by the machinations of financial capital.

Indeed, both informants' narrations reflect a sense that they have lost control over their lives; with economic crisis they no longer are masters of their own destiny. In losing identity and control, many of these men appear unmoored, their roles as earners and caretakers gone with the crisis, and their failures externalized as they are felt throughout the family. What remains is a sense of uselessness: Iñaki felt there was nothing he could ever possibly do to remove the great weight of defeat from his shoulders. With the onset of crisis, he had no agency; civil death signaled the foreclosure of opportunity, choice, and possibility. The doors to his future were shut, as this political economy of financialization and extraction beat him into submission. Indeed, in his reference to being "stepped on," he articulates the physicality of his own situation, as he has been literally removed from society, swallowed into the earth by the early grave of metaphorical death. Without the ability to consume, he is in turn consumed.

Such experiences were evident in the haunted visages of men who would pass through the PAH. Women would also appear enthralled to the terrifying specter of foreclosure and eviction, but they often expressed a desire to fight back. Their male partners would in turn be cowed by the system. During one assembly in the northern neighborhood of Tetuán, a well-to-do family sought help in preventing an imminent eviction. They bore the outward signs of the upper middle class; their clothing was pristine, with discreet designer labels, and their bearing still hinted at generations of comfort. They also carried with them their eviction notice. The bank had repossessed their stately flat near the Castellana boulevard. Mounting business debts, recent unemployment, and the exhaustion of a decent inheritance had left them unable to pay, and so the mortgage had entered into arrears. They cast about for ideas, until finally they decided, with the date of the eviction looming, to seek activist help. As the assembly incited them to fight, the middle-aged father was reticent. He didn't want his neighbors or friends to find out about his financial woes. To the outside world, he was still a successful member of his class, and no eviction could shake his steadfast refusal to reveal to the world his ruin. While his wife and daughter were inclined to fight, his refusal meant they quietly turned the keys over to the bank, avoiding any public spectacle of hardship. Activists helped them negotiate the terms of their departure. The women continued to come to assemblies and help out others in the neighborhood. The man wanted nothing more to do with the activists or the anti-evictions cause. They remained reminders of his misfortune, his inability to fulfill his role as the male head of household.

Gendered Violences

> In my house there were a lot of arguments. I wasn't able to understand that I was hurting my wife, too. A call from my wife [to the police] because she felt I'd been violent because I have a temper. I'm a man . . . nothing more.
>
> *Borja. Ciempozuelos.*

Such situations of desperation, in which economic agency and thus identity have been forcibly removed, can then go on to provoke both subtle and covert violence. Isolated socially, their identities undergoing serious transformation, while suffering under the weight of economic ruin and internalized guilt and shame, people respond to the structural violence of the capitalist system with acts of actual violence, which is borne out through emotions, psychologies, and the body. The covert violence of dispossession reverberates through actual instances of domestic discord, including physical harm. Borja, in the throes of economic distress, began to argue with his wife. At a certain point, his behavior turned verbally abusive, and his wife called the police. She was issued an order of protection, and he was forced to live outside the family home. As he slowly lost his sense of control over the domestic arena following a series of unfortunate events, the abuse reached a crescendo. His wife had gone through a brutal childbirth that had greatly depleted her physically and emotionally. Economic difficulties only exacerbated her depression and caused her husband to experience his own emotional decline. His private sphere was now a site of despair, the future murky. Once he had dreamed of his house as the site for a host of aspirations. Now it was as if a noose had been laid around his neck: Borja felt completely powerless to alter impending civil death. Robust and stocky, he would several years later describe to me his descent into violence as also marked by a loss of control, as he no longer could keep his emotions or physical presence in check.

Violence, in Gilligan's analytic, is entwined intimately with shame, as a means of temporarily overcoming that shame. It is a means of claiming honor, albeit briefly. Yet the emergence of violence represents the perversion of control: while the rest of his world crumbled, Borja attempted to maintain his influence over hearth and home, violence erupting as consequence. The body of his wife, in moments of deep and abiding frustration, became the target for his anger and desperation. But Borja's was not a singular case. Instances of domestic abuse run rampant throughout many households experiencing eviction. In the epoque of financial crisis, in which many men feel the profound loss agency and thus identity, violence against women can be one means of exerting control, a tragic performance of elusive masculine domination.

Mother, two daughters, and a 9 year old grandson. Currently, the daughters' partners also live there. One of the daughters is 8 months pregnant. The child goes to school in the area. The mother and one of the daughters are victims of domestic violence, for which the mother's husband and the older daughter's partner are in jail.

—PAH eviction information form for family in the Vallecas neighborhood, with an eviction date for September 17, 2012[30]

While Borja's story demonstrates the kinds of overt, immediate violence that can spring forth in situations of precarity, the familial effects of crisis shored up gendered divisions through more covert means. Throughout both interviews and participant observation, I came to realize the tremendous weight women carried through processes of foreclosure and evictions. This weight was not only financial. Rather, many were already single mothers, while others found themselves abandoned by male partners once crisis set in. Many women were immigrants who had already experienced crushing violence back home, past histories that had already furthered gendered inequity. Those who were still married were often far more active than their male counterparts, striving to solve their mortgage problems alongside those of their new community of *afectadas*. Violence haunted many of their experiences, whether the gendered violence in the home, the slow violence of abandonment, or the political violence of previous lives under repressive regimes.

For example, Carolina, an educated and well-to-do Argentine woman in her late fifties, came to Madrid in the mid-1990s following the military dictatorship. In an educated enclave in the north of Argentina, she had experienced the haunting violence of the murderous military *junta*, which had disappeared her husband and many of her friends. Desperate to escape memories of brutal loss and provide improved opportunities for her daughters, she migrated to Madrid. Mabel and Margarita also made that journey, eager to leave behind the dire conditions of Peru and Ecuador and anxious to provide for young children. All three women have had to face the dual violence of the authoritarian state as it inflicts brutality and the *longue duree* of gendered social reproduction. Finding themselves alone with other mouths to feed, Mabel, Margarita, and Carolina took steps to ensure for their future and that of their children. As sole earners in their households, these three women thought little about depending on others, instead creating opportunities for themselves in their adopted homelands. Purchasing a home was a means of making that future a bit brighter, obtaining some small patrimony to leave behind to their children. Thus migrations were marked by violence—the audacious violence of dictatorship, the covert violence of dispossession that impels exile, and the social violence of gendered division. Soon, however, the violence of eviction would infect their daily realities.

> [Name redacted] Second child, studying high school and is a good student. As a result of this situation he attempted suicide.
> [Husband and wife] are going to start divorce proceedings.
> —PAH eviction information form for Spanish couple; Arganzuela neighborhood; eviction scheduled May 30, 2012, postponed until July 27, 2012

Elena, Yvette, and Jane, meanwhile, saw their marriages collapse under the weight of foreclosure. For Elena, the covert violence of dispossession was accompanied by brutal physical violence, as her Dominican husband took out his rage upon her. As Salwa Ismail details in her study of the everyday in Cairo, male youth enact gendered control over female bodies as a means of performing hegemonic masculinity.[31] Poor, peripheral to the dominant project of Egyptian masculinity, these youths find other outlets to assert control. Foreclosure marginalizes masculine identities, thus forcing its victims to find opportunities for the performance of hegemonic male identity. Here women become convenient subjects of domination through a host of both overt and subtle tactics. Such situations also recall Ananya Roy's discussion of the fictitious man-eating tiger of advanced capitalism, a mythic beast that has sapped the energies and wage-earning capabilities of men who dwell at Calcutta's peri-urban fringe.[32] Sometimes departure is the only form of liberation from this marginalization. Yvette and Jane, however, experienced the slow defeat of abandonment. As familial economic struggles worsened, Jane's husband retreated into himself, crushed by the blow of unemployment. Thus husbands succumbed to uselessness, ultimately leaving the family home, the former site of domestic bliss now a container for discord. As their husbands left, sometimes quietly into the night, these women were left to keep their families afloat, caring for young children both economically and emotionally. In Yvette's case, her husband slunk off, returning to Ecuador. There he moved into a small house she owns; his new girlfriend moved in shortly thereafter.

The violence of such situations emerges not from physical blows, but rather from increasingly marginalized masculinities faced with a relinquishment of responsibility. Male absence implies women must not only earn a wage, feed, clothe, and care for the children, and struggle to make mortgage payments, but also experience the slow extractive process of foreclosure and resulting civil death alone. Male absence exacerbates the crushing isolation, cutting women off from companionship and social ties, perpetrating and exacerbating the violence of isolation. Further, she must now deal with the shame of both economic defeat and the collapse of a marriage. Shame here multiplies, becoming more intimate and invasive. Literature on crisis, austerity, and eviction often highlights the undue burden placed on women.[33] As Elvin Wyly had demonstrated through quantitative analysis, this trend is seen across populations struggling under the emergent risks of neoliberalism. My ethnographic analysis in this section reveals some of the intimate dimensions that can help explain such trends. Women, caught amid the wreckage of crisis, are often faced with the prospect of soldiering on alone. They bear the brunt of domestic responsibilities, ensuring social reproduction even under great duress, and often with numerous dependents. In the event of financial tragedy, women simply carry more than their share.

> I'm a single woman with 5 children in my care. Well, my story is very sad because the father of my child—the other owner of the house—abandoned me, leaving me to care for my children and the debts. I didn't have enough for even my children's food.
> —PAH eviction information form for single mother, Carabanchel neighborhood. Five children ages 17, 11, 7, 6, and 5 months. Eviction set for June 6, 2012.

Madrid's landscape is now littered with both empty homes and broken families. Foreclosure and eviction have hollowed housing and households, battering bodies and souls in the process. During 2012, for example, two-thirds of the households that came through the PAH in Madrid with eviction notices were immigrant; one-third were single women, half with children in their care. A 2013 survey concluded divorce or separation accounts for 15 percent of failure to pay.[34] In many instances, women are unduly burdened with both financial and familial obligations. In the wake of absent husbands, they must take on all responsibility for urban survival. Often, family finances were firmly the domains of men; Elena, for example, had no idea her mortgage was in arrears until she received the eviction order. Thus many women must suddenly gain financial literacy as they attempt to keep ruin at bay.

When these subjects—both male and female—evoke their *muerte civil*, they speak to a condition that goes beyond an inability to take part in economic life, evoking instead a mental, physical, and emotional state that implicates a plurality of tragic outcomes. Because financialization has so thoroughly pen-etrated the modest livelihoods of urban denizens, losing one's ability to take part in the marketplace triggers a host of other consequences. Civil death fun-damentally calls into question one's place in society, excising her from the gen-eral polity through not only financial ruin, but also familial rupture, gendered violence, and a profound loss of identity. When homeownership, constitutive to Spanish citizenship, collapses, it renders the owner on the outside, excess to the imagined whole.

The Materiality of Dispossession

> He works in the Metro for four hours a day, she is unemployed, with five minors in her care (13, 10, 4, 2, and 7 months) and the smallest has recur-ring respiratory infections because of the poor state of the unit—they have a City Hall report on its inhabitability
>
> *—PAH eviction information form for a Nigerian-Spanish family; Villaverde Alto; eviction scheduled March 27, 2012, was suspended the day before.*

Civil death is not merely a psychic or economic condition. Rather, material consequences inflect this experience, producing their own necro-geographies of exclusion. The ghostly city of the civil dead was one once foreign to me by space and time. As a young college graduate in Madrid, I knew the city as it wanted to be portrayed. It was the *Gran Madrid* of Franco, the European capital of Tierno Galván, first mayor of the democratic era. I traversed stately boule-vards of the Salamanca and Moncloa neighborhoods and the charming alleys of the historic center. My friends and acquaintances also dwelled largely within this city of privilege, taking in and taking part of its cosmopolitan spectacle. We lived in elegant homes near convenient metro stops on tree-lined streets.

When I returned to Madrid to carry out fieldwork, I discovered another city. The entire metropolis had of course descended into crisis. Yet those sites of spectacle still contained their glamour and prestige, even if they were slightly dingier with fewer patrons. Now, however, I traversed the margins and inter-stices, far-flung neighborhoods mired in poverty, the deserted refuse of urban decadence, and the mundane spaces of everyday survival. The peripheries were now the province of the civil dead, possessed of their own distinct forms and qualities.[35] Indeed, civil death is not only a process of subjectification; rather it is a sociospatial condition rife with forms of exclusion. Here subjecthood and space are entwined dialectically and materiality to produce the terrain of civil death.

Within Spain, discussions of urban poverty often focus on exclusion as its primary variable. *Inequality*, a term rampant throughout literature on similar issues within a variety of geographies, remains associated almost wholly with income. *Exclusion*, however, speaks to social conditions in addition to economic factors, and often appears in conversations on housing. That term also emerges frequently in reference to immigrants, and while immigrant social exclusion is high in Madrid, it is not necessarily accompanied by spatial segregation.[36] There is no precise definition to exclusion as it appears in the literature; Martínez del Olmo and Leal Maldonado use overcrowding and housing conditions as indicators. What is useful, however, is the manner in which the term brings together questions of the domestic sphere with larger considerations of social status, economy, and location. If inequality exists within the domain of personal finances and income, then exclusion implicates situated questions of bias, social interaction, possibility, and place. My discussion seeks to evoke this term's multiplicity, bringing to the fore the quality of the urban experience, location, potential segregation, economic hardship, and the increasing association between race and place—what Loïc Wacquant terms territorial stigma.[37] What I draw out is homeownership's dispossessions even before the onset of urban crisis. Rather than offering a means of inclusion into the polity, homeownership instead accelerated exclusion and deprived immigrant homebuyers of urban experiences of sociality.

The Illusion of Choice

The discourse surrounding immigrant homeownership emphasized choice and possibility. Instead, however, homeownership increased isolation and exclusion for immigrants. Reflecting liberal ideals of rationality and free will, homeownership appeared to offer a horizon of near limitless opportunity, reflected in advertisements analyzed in the first chapter. Immigrants were promised the house of their dreams, easily in reach through the power of debt. Yet the reality of homeownership and the process by which one attained that supposed dream were in fact limited, laden not with endless choice but rather with the harsh demands of an overvalued real estate market. Many homebuyers were able to access brand-new units that seemingly met the needs of the cosmopolitan citizen. The neighborhoods created under the 1997 General Plan contain tens of thousands of new units, destined to thrust their populaces into the future.

Here star architects built cutting-edge developments meant to house the city's burgeoning population. Yet many of these new units were located far out on the central plateau, glimmering housing estates that were in many ways modern ghost towns. Additionally, these areas were not yet fully serviced by public transportation and lacked the vibrant street life that made many parts of the city so popular.

Immigrants, however, largely bought in old peripheral areas of the city, in units that had been abandoned by their native counterparts. In this decision, they were presented little choice. Trusting their real estate agents to lead them to the best deals and offers, many immigrant interlocutors describe the process of purchasing a home as one dominated not by choice but by harried urgency. Agents would show them units in areas that were often foreign to them; one interlocutor from Colombia, Maria Dolores, describes her move to the Carabanchel neighborhood, at the very southwestern edge of the city, as one motivated wholly by anxiety. She related to me one spring afternoon, "They would look for a house for you and tell you that you have buy this one right now because if not, then the bank won't give you a loan, then you have to sign immediately." Rather than select the area in which they were going to live, in proximity to work or friends, immigrants like Maria Dolores describe simply going where they were led, induced to purchase because real estate agents presented it as the only option.

The areas in which these purchases took place contain conditions that promote sociospatial segregation and financial hardship. The housing stock in areas such as Carabanchel or Tetuán is old and in need of rehabilitation, often without elevators in midrise housing blocks. As city hall funneled money into revamping the historic center, it often left areas on the periphery to decay and fall apart. While the then-president of the Madrid Community planned a massive extension of the metro, the transportation options to many of the peripheral working-class neighborhoods remained limited. A neighborhood like Villaverde, the most southern area of the city, was only accessible via commuter train or a very lengthy bus ride. An old village incorporated into the metropolis under Franco, that area now has a metro stop on its old main street, yet that one stop services a sprawling neighborhood. Even in the center of the city, there were certain areas of degradation and exclusion. Along several old streets in the Lavapiés neighborhood, old six-story apartment buildings seemed to sink into the earth. Their innards were often kept upright through hastily erected steel beams. There were often PAH cases of families that had purchased units only to find that they required tens of thousands of euros to make them legally habitable.

Despite expanding public transportation infrastructure, many areas remain poorly serviced, particularly those in traditionally working-class neighborhoods. Several times during my fieldwork I went with Elena, a middle-aged Spanish single mother once married to a Dominican, and her two adolescent children to her house in the Puente de Vallecas neighborhood. A traditional area of working-class solidarity, the neighborhood is a rabbit's warren of narrow streets and uneven blocks of housing and commerce—its local bars still charge a euro for a glass of wine and a tapa. Many of the transit stops are located along the lengthy avenue that runs all the way from the old Atocha station through a posh neighborhood near the Retiro park, under the M30 ring road, through Puente de Vallecas and out to the impoverished hinterland. Yet Vallecas sprawls throughout a large area now delineated by various highways and byways, train lines and factories (one area is called Entrevías, or Between Lines, to reflect a location shoehorned between train tracks and national highways). Elena worked in the northern neighborhood Pio XII, where her children went to a nearby school. She would leave work to collect them and then take an extensive metro ride home, in which they would change trains twice. Upon arrival to Puente de Vallecas, she would marshal her children for their kilometer walk to the house. They would arrive at their street, a block full of small individual structures, many in disrepair. Their house is two-storied, squat, old, and badly in need of repair. Its dark interior contains a garage area on the ground floor, with three tiny bedrooms and a small shared area in the upstairs. The flat was musty and damp, its walls covered in blossoming mold spots. Homeownership has thus fixed her in place while demanding mobility.

Immigrants often bought into areas that had housed the urban poor under Franco. Neighborhoods like Villaverde, Tetuán, and Carabanchel were once the warehouses for the city's excess, where poor day laborers struggled to make ends meet while living in substandard shanties. In that era, the emergent entrepreneurial oligarchy of the late dictatorship controlled consumption and production in these areas, extracting high rents from the poor in desperate search for housing. When the Franco regime finally was able to address the housing question, it put up squat, shoddily crafted low-rise apartment blocks. Sprawling neighborhoods at the periphery are characterized by these extensive, orderly forests of brick and concrete, usually oriented around communal patios. One summer afternoon I navigated my way to Aida Quinatoa's house at the edge of the San Blas neighborhood. Her place was far from any subway stop, on the first floor of a squat building, sibling to a host of identical edifices. I climbed the dark stairs to her modest flat. A tiny kitchen featured antiquated appliances. Several small rooms circled a dark, narrow hallway. The unit was in a bad state of disrepair, with holes in the sheetrock. This domestic scene was not one of upward mobility; rather it was a modest diorama of everyday survival within a hostile city. What has changed since the regime in a neighborhood such as San Blas is the scale and scope of extractive capitalism and the tools that make that process possible; its logic is more or less continuous. These neighborhoods, long sites of arrival for industrious workers, are place of struggle, as the poor attempt to maintain their foothold within the city.

Indeed, newer forms of exclusion inflected the housing experience, despite a decrease in segregation. In Martínez del Olmo and Leal Maldonado's study, they note the elevated percentage of overcrowding among Ecuadorian immigrants—higher than for any other collective. Overcrowding also contributes quantitatively to segregation. Yet as people settle, gain stability and a job, they are able to leave behind temporary housing arrangements for more permanent solutions, including ownership. With the demands of the temperamental housing market, however, immigrants buying homes during the boom often had little choice. Thus they were shunted into neighborhoods far and wide. Some, too, bought farther and farther afield; hence areas dozens and even hundreds of kilometers from the city saw an increase in ethnic diversity during this time.[38] Thus exclusion took on other forms: people had to travel great distances to work, they lived far from friends and colleagues, they were not able to take part in associational and community life, and they saw their social capital decrease.

A map of Madrid's evictions cases reveals the vast majority of the city's foreclosures have taken place outside of the M30, the ring road that engulfs the "central almond" of the city.[39] Within that ring, foreclosures have been concentrated in both the old, degraded part of the historic center, or in the Tetuán neighborhood in the north. In the Center, properties are largely clustered along the old streets of Lavapiés, an area in which many buildings were in terrible condition. City Hall's statistics reveal that in 2001 only 10,600 out of almost 19,000 units in that neighborhood were in "good" condition, while the remaining 8,000+ units were mostly in "bad" or "deficient" condition.[40]

Rather than access the glittering beacons of Madrid's new modernity, Latin Americans instead were allowed to consume the detritus, that which was left

over in the modernizing project. While the products that allowed for their participation were new and novel, they were not accorded the same access as native
counterparts, occupying those sites left behind by an emergent middle class.
Maps reveal foreclosures have taken place in areas such as Carabanchel, on the
southwestern shore of the Manzanares River, or Puente de Vallecas. Narrow
streets are littered with foreclosures, often along blocks that lie far from the
closest transit lines and major avenues. As old parts of the city, largely constructed through the sweat equity of previous residents, many of these neighborhoods are characterized by low housing blocks made of brick or concrete.
The units in these blocks are small, crowded together; in Carabanchel, for example, almost 60 percent of units are between 40 and 75 square meters according to data from city hall. Many of these properties sold for hundreds of thousands of euros in 2004–8, the height of the boom, but are now worth a fraction
of their former prices. That neighborhood also became increasingly diverse.
In 2005 the district's population was around 18 percent foreigner; by 2010 that
percentage had jumped 5 points to just over 23 percent. The majority of the
housing stock was constructed between 1950 and 1980. In 2001 around 80 percent of buildings, meanwhile, didn't have elevators and, while not in deleterious
conditions, still lacked amenities and updated infrastructure.[41] Despite these
conditions, prices rose steeply during the boom, forcing new homebuyers to
take out inflated mortgages for old, overvalued properties. We see evidence of
this bubble in two Carabanchel cases of eviction from October 2012, in which
mortgages were issued at 245,000 and 326,000 euros each for small, old apartments. Homeownership, then, meant immigrants were in many cases replacing
working-class Spaniards, buying up their refuse as they scaled the sociospatial
ladder.

Civil death must be understood against a landscape in which homeownership was a means of further inscribing difference. Differentiation operated
through spatial terms, abetted by public imaginaries around safety, security,
and stigma. I mentioned above my experiences living in Lavapiés, which has
long occupied a curious location within popular cognitive maps of the city, as
a site of both alternative, cool lifestyles, and danger, otherness, and filth, both
moral and physical.[42] Immigrants certainly feed into that imaginary, bolstering
notions of the neighborhood as both multicultural and cosmopolitan, and in-
civil and unsafe. Carabanchel, too, has been characterized in the popular imagination as a site of territorial stigma and insecurity.[43] Its peripheral location has
been concretized theoretically, defining it, too, as a site of marginalization and

scarcity. Historical associations bolster its danger in the popular urban imagination, as it was home to an infamous prison built by civil war prisoners in the bleak post-bellum years. Following its abandonment, the panopticon style structure became a squat, which was then demolished in 2008.

Entry into homeownership, moreover, instantiated processes of dispossession. While immigrants often used subprime loans to purchase overvalued housing, they faced another dispossessive impulse of the housing market. Only offered far-flung units, Madrid's immigrants were thus deprived of the delights of the central city, shunted outward. In order to take part in urban social life, they had to travel great distances in order to work and play. Before the dispossession of foreclosure and eviction, they already faced removal from distinct parts of the city. Buying a home meant the loss of other pleasures and a demand for increased mobility.

If dispossession is removal or banishment, how else might we understand immigrant homeownership? While many immigrants bought into the outer neighborhoods of the city, others acquired homes farther and farther afield. As the market was reaching its peak in 2006 and 2007, the pages of *Latino* advertised houses not only in neighborhoods such as Carabanchel and San Blas, but also in distant suburbs, some located outside the Madrid Community. For example, on May 25, 2007, a small ad sought to entice homebuyers to Hormigos in Toledo, with the promise of homes for as little at 85,000 euros. With allusions to flexible financing and no money down, the small yellow image hoped to attract immigrants to a development in a tiny town located almost 100 kilometers away. Likewise, on December 14 of that same year, CAP Inmobiliaria announced the high quality of units located in another far-flung *toledano* town. Offering the attractive possibility of payments as low at 120 euros/month (which would probably balloon shortly thereafter), the units were one kilometer from the train station; what the ad neglects to mention, however, is that trains to Madrid run only once a day. On March 7, 2008—the final days of excess—a small image offered single-family dwellings in a small town in Segovia for upwards of 183,000 euros.

During my time with the PAH, I often spoke with people who had purchased in places far out on the plateau. The isolation, great distance, and distinct lack of urban amenities would have deterred me from such a decision. But the thirst to own was all-consuming, as many of my interviews bear out. As prices rose to astronomical levels in the city, even in old degraded areas, the newest customers were desperate to own for its promise of permanence. Illescas in Toledo, for example, may lie beyond the bounds of the Madrid Community, but there the young Ecuadorian family could buy a place far larger than what they could afford in the city. Such a decision, moreover, was influenced by notions that such places would soon become lively hubs as more people were pushed out of urban centers. The Podunk town would lure the masses with its beautiful new housing developments offering the latest amenities; the old adage, if you build it, they will come, here proved rationale for planning, execution, and consumption. Rather than interpret insane housing prices as a sign of overvaluation and imminent demise, Betsy, for example, understood herself as a pioneer, exploiting an opportunity others would soon discover. Thus dispossession worked in concert with aspiration to produce a landscape that also revalued the urban detritus as a means of pushing immigrants outward.

The civil dead are often spatially dispersed, requiring time, an extra budget for transportation purposes, and the energy to travel great distances in the pursuit of employment. If homeownership was largely coterminus with citizenship, then it was a system that privileged economic participation above all others forms of inclusion and membership, precluding leisure, sociability, or the flourishing of a metropolitan multicultural sensibility. While there was an illusion of choice and opportunity, the reality was one of increased sociospatial exclusion and financial hardship, as homeownership promoted the outward dispersal of immigrant bodies to those sites deemed peripheral.

Collapse

> Ask any economist: broke is made of how you feel. The credit crunch didn't happen because people woke up any poorer than they'd been the day before; it happened because people woke up scared. . . . Broke can lead people to places they would never have imagined. It can nudge a law-abiding citizen onto that blurred crumbling edge where a dozen kinds of crime feel like they're only an arm's reach away . . . until all that's left is teeth and claws and terror.[44]

In Tana French's *Broken Harbor,* a young Irish family is consumed by their debts to the point of violence and even death. Having moved to a new exurban development at the very edge of the sea, where Dublin's sprawl meets rolling green hills, the Spains have taken out mortgage and personal loans to finance what was once a promising middle-class existence. Foreclosure and its attendant forms of financial risk soon wreck the family. Their last name, of course, hints towards a wider geography of mortgage failures, one that connects a multiplicity of locales ravaged by debt and dispossession. Financial ruin through the vehicle of homeownership was widespread following the 2008 crisis, evident in the novel. I introduce this fictional account because its subjective, material, and interpersonal violence recalls similar processes in mortgaged Madrid, where homeownership soon proved to further exclusion and vulnerability. What's striking about the quote above is that French writes of emotional and mental life, while also evoking the urban milieu in which the abandonment of reason transpires. That crumbling edge is both the debtor's inner state and the decaying and rotten landscape of urban peripheries rife with foreclosure and eviction.

Civil death is a condition that implicates both space and time. It requires its sufferers to traverse vast territories of a city that has been made strange to them. The category also isolates people, cutting them off through shame, violence, and the intense work required to stave off complete destitution. Dispossession, after all, is a process that is tied to possession, which privileges the individual.[45] What kinds of claims can they then make upon this city, upon a polity that has rendered them excess and outside? How can they find one another amidst alienation and despair? Those are two of the great challenges for organizing. People who feel unbound from time and space are not then easily capable of radically reinvesting in their urban futures.

The category of civil death also reveals some of the paradoxes of homeownership. First, rather than promoting inclusion into society, ownership instead meant greater exclusion and vulnerability for both immigrants and Madrid's working and middle classes. The period of easy riches and European cosmopolitanism it was thought to inaugurate was short-lived, and the common sense of homeownership soon appeared to be a myth. In the end, both Yvette and Borja found themselves worse off than prior to their acquisition of a home. What appeared to be transformative for the better instead condemned them further to the urban margins.

Homeownership's collapse reveals its centrality in crafting urban subjectivies and perpetuating identities. To be tied to a particular place through the stolidity of the home meant not only investment in the city but also sociality and self-worth. It meant embodying masculinist fantasies and ensuring economic self-reliance. It reinforced one's public role while also securing a private life.

Yet that division between public and private was revealed to be porous with the advent of civil death. The insidious invasion of economic despair into the space of the home then meant the concomitant erasure of one's public life. Terror and ruin in the private sphere wrested sufferers from the pleasure of every day urban life. Rather than remain distinct arenas, public and private are entwined and given life through myriad variables. Dispossession, then, is not merely an economic process of banishment. Rather, it is the deprivation of social, familial, and gendered relations of urban existence, condemning everyday urban dwellers to the constitutive outside where they must dwell stripped and alone.

6   Immigrant Capital

We said, "No," because of the experiences we had in Ecuador. Alone they'll eat us. If we're many people, that won't happen. If we're many people, [we'll get things done.]"

Aida Quinatoa, Activist

In the afternoon heat of June 2017, I made my way to the house of Aida Quina-toa. We were going to conduct an oral history, parts of which are included here. Aida, Indigenous Quechua from Ecuador, had worked on and off as a house-cleaner since arriving in Madrid in 2000. She went to the Centro Hipotecario del Inmigrante (CHI–Mortgage Center for the Immigrant) to look for a place to rent with her husband in 2004. CHI immediately suggested they purchase instead. They found a first-floor unit at the edge of a park in the San Blas neigh-borhood in the west of the city. The area had been incorporated into Madrid in 1949 as part of Franco's quest to create the *Gran Madrid*. Once dotted with small shacks, single-story buildings, and livestock, the area was still far from public transportation and lacked many amenities. Aida's house, located in a squat, aging four-story brick building, identical to its neighbors on either side, had been built as part of Franco's Emergency Social Plan in the late 1950s. Sev-eral tiny rooms crowd around a miniscule entryway, and the kitchen is badly in need of an update. What might have been modern in 1958 now feels squalid and cramped. Aida and her husband purchased the apartment, no more than forty square meters, for 150,000 euros. They used a combination of mortgage, personal loans, and cash. The debt had grown to over 200,000 euros by 2007, the year Aida began organizing against the spate of foreclosures and evictions that was threatening her community.

When I knocked on the door that day, a tall young man welcomed me in-side. As we exchanged pleasantries, I was struck by his accent, which I couldn't place—it was neither Spanish nor Ecuadorian. As Aida bustled in she explained: Carlos was a visitor originally from Chile, now pursuing his studies in the UK. He and a friend were in town for the weekend, staying with Aida and her husband. Aida had never met them before. The two young men were Mapuche—the Indigenous group native to Chile and Argentina—and through a network of Indigenous activists they had connected with Aida. Prior to assuming her role as cleaning woman, immigrant, and homeowner, Aida was an active and important figure in the Indigenous movement in Ecuador during the 1990s. Her hospitality toward Carlos and Quique was one small act of solidarity that spoke of a particular orientation toward the world in which one shares resources, knowledge, and strength with those who might need it.

The following story reveals how Indigenous pasts have shaped Madrid's indignant present, contributing to the potent right to housing movement. I argue that traditions of solidarity and political action emerging out of Indigenous organizing influenced immigrant responses to the mortgage crisis. Additionally, recent experiences with migration, marginalization, and racialization forged a politics of resistance, in which Andean immigrants refused the terms of their civil death. In doing so, Madrid's Andean community was the first able to translate civil death into civil disobedience, sparking the subsequent anti-evictions movement.

In this case, immigrants refused to abide by the terms of dispossession. When immigrants don't conform entirely to dominant systems, they are often perceived as a threat, signaling their failure to integrate. Here we can recall the earlier discussion regarding the *padrón municipal,* in which politicians read nefarious motives and cultural incompatibility into immigrant refusal to register with the local government.[1] Notions of incommensurability haunt migration debates as they address questions of housing and work, leisure and religious custom.[2] Policymakers in Madrid implied that members of the first and second generation refused the social norms of their adopted homeland rather than becoming "proper" citizens. Of course, another story can be told here—that immigrant living conditions and routines were shaped in part by everyday hostilities and structural inequities, thus illuminating the paradoxes and hypocrisies of liberal democracy that espouses tolerance on the one hand and reifies difference on the other. Here refusal can emerge from a host of causes—daily survival, perceptions of unjust systems of rule, intolerance. It is also predicated on a sophisticated geographic imaginary that is given life through experiences of migration. Refusal can shed light on the violences and predations of hegemonic systems; further, it can be fruitful in advancing radical causes. In the case of Madrid, Andean refusal instantiated a potent movement against homeownership.

The Spatial Politics of Migration

Since the start of the Spanish crisis, hundreds of thousands of families have experienced foreclosure and eviction. During my fieldwork in 2012–14, almost 200 evictions took place daily throughout the country. This landscape of devastation and loss gave rise to the Plataforma de Afectados por la Hipoteca. By 2012, when I began fieldwork in Madrid, the PAH had over fifty chapters throughout the peninsula and the Balearic and Canary islands. It evinced a sophisticated political message that reimagined domestic financial crisis as part of a wider geography of boom and bust. The collective located personal financial ruin within a coercive political economy. Foreclosure constituted a political situation that demanded a political response, and was thus a public, rather than domestic, problem. Rather than accept the terms of civil death, the PAH instead transformed its experiences into political claims.

In the analytic of the PAH, the mortgage defaulter is not a delinquent debtor in arrears, but rather an *afectada*, located within a specific political economy and armed with situated expertise. Through assemblies and protests, actions and counseling sessions, the collective produced an alternative common sense that gives structure and meaning to the *afectada* against the punitive moralities of indebtedness. She carries with her the burden of experience, but also the burden of being forced into a particular economic choice that appeared more than rational in the moment, yet has brought dire consequences thereafter. Much of the rest of society has told her that she is a personal failure: banks call incessantly demanding repayment, neighbors might exchange disapproving glances in hallways, and debt collectors visit her children's school. In this translation, therefore, she goes from failure to expert, retaining her autonomy yet charged with knowledge. Those experiences that inscribed failure now constitute the genesis for her ability to fight back, providing the raw material for her education.

The PAH has been the most emblematic collective to emerge out of recent Spanish social protest, capturing international attention from activists, NGOs, academics, and progressive policymakers. Its prominence, its capacity to organize large groups of people, its legal successes, and the subsequent political

careers of many of its most visible participants has made it an important touch-
stone for struggles over housing throughout the globe. The foundational role of
immigrants in both its origins and its sustenance remains largely unacknowl-
edged in narratives of its success.[3] The standard story of its birth concerns a
collection of activists in Barcelona who were organized around the question
of housing affordability. Many of these activists had been involved in V de
Vivienda, a collective that drew attention to the massive imbalances in the
political economy of Spanish housing—high prices and low salaries, particularly for young people.[4] In their retelling, they observed the housing problem
begin to shift toward the end of 2008: the question was no longer about affordability, but about the looming threat of eviction. The national movement
against evictions, however, has a diversity of origins, including traditions of
mutual aid, squatting, and autonomous struggles, all important precursors to
the emergence of contemporary housing struggles.[5] In this account, however, I
draw attention to the pioneering role of Andean immigrants. In late 2007 and
early 2008 Ecuadorians in Madrid organized around the issue of foreclosures
and evictions. In December 2008 several hundred Ecuadorian immigrants held
Spain's first anti-evictions protest.

Before the formal creation of the PAH in Barcelona, the Latin American
community in Madrid was denouncing dispossession through mortgage debt.[6]
On December 20, 2008, they walked north from the headquarters of the Bank
of Spain, to the criminal courts in Plaza Castilla, and then headed southwest to
the Constitutional Courts in Moncloa. Their itinerary of protest on December
20, 2008, made explicit the connections between banking and finance, statecraft and legislation, and the pernicious role of the justice and legal system;
the political economy of housing was laid bare. They had already drawn together various strands of cultural common sense, banking and finance policy,
and fraudulent practice to reveal the extent of their damnation. These early
pioneers translated their individual civil deaths into collective action, providing
a blueprint for the later movement to follow. Indeed, Aida explicitly rejected
death as a metaphor. When they began to organize, someone suggested they go
as a platform for people "hanged" by their mortgages. She said, "How can you
say hanged?" She agreed when others proposed "affected," locating their experiences within a broader landscape of political economic crisis. Yet how did their
alternative understanding emerge? How did everyday individuals transcend
experiences of civil death? How did they channel those experiences into resistance and disobedience?

For the immigrant, the crisis is not a new feeling; many have lived in crisis since they were born.

—Alex Pallete, advertising executive. "Cuál crisis?, preguntan nuestros lectores." *Latino*, October 17, 2008, 9

I argue that the experience of migration itself contributes to political subjectivity and later action. Immigrants could relate to and see their mortgage problems in a different light, which in turn conditioned responses and contributed to future activism. In the case of Madrid, migration and status as an immigrant often inflected and deepened the myriad experiences of civil death. Yet they also fostered a political thinking and embodied forms of knowledge that made dissent legible. For people like Aida, Eduardo, Betsy, and Morton, situations of political uncertainty, violence, and crisis had prompted migration. Long before the Spanish boom, many had already lived the deeply painful experience of economic ruin. That condition, suddenly thrust upon the Spanish public, was one that was already known to them. Each immigrant history contained at least one loss—of house and home, of children left with grandparents, of previous social lives abandoned for the sake of a small slice of economic advancement. They were aware of crisis's intimate nature: it not only transformed governments and public expenditure, but also infected the small scale of the household, the family, and the reproduction of daily life. Macro changes in the government, the onset of economic crisis, and the proliferation of debts all demanded wrenching personal decisions. As such, Andeans in Madrid were personally familiar with the intimate ties that bind together politics, the economy, and the domestic arrangements of home.

As described in the first chapter, the decision to migrate was often painful, the opportunity for potential economic gains weighed against the loss of immediate contact with family and friends. Migration was not a process entered into lightly, instead made necessary by entrenched economic need and political violence. In addition to contemplating a new life abroad, immigrants mourned the changes in their homeland: loss of previous systems of government, earlier economic possibility, and shifting modes of everyday life. Evolving geopolitical forces altered both national political economies and myriad modest households littered throughout the urban and rural spaces of Latin America in profound ways.[7] It is within this landscape of economic and political decadence that immigrant interlocutors situate their trajectories. Betsy left behind her beloved mother, while Yvette and her husband had to place their two children with their grandparents. Mounting debts forced Aida to abandon her burgeoning activism with the Indigenous movement and her deep ties to that community. Personal failings had not brought despair to their families; rather, corruption, greed, and the brutality of the capitalist system provoked punishment of the most vulnerable. Dispossession occurred not because of innate qualities of incompetence, but rather through extractive processes that were unduly prejudicial to certain communities. Migration as a strategy for increased prosperity emerged as the personal solution to a political economic problem.

Upon arrival in Spain, immigrants continued to observe the intense links between the macro and the micro. Madrid was a boomtown in which they could take part, a flourishing frontier where one could make new fortunes. Parts of these new fortunes—albeit modest—were always kept aside to send back home. The Latin American population in Madrid was assiduous in destining some portion of their monthly wages to communities in Peru and Ecuador.[8] The pages of *Latino* were plastered with advertisements for money wiring services. Alongside promotions for calling cards and cheap trans-Atlantic flights, remittances constituted another practice that maintained intimate contact between home and abroad, Madrid and Quito, San Blas and the highlands near Cayambe. While a phone call allowed someone like Yvette to keep up to date on family back home, her monthly money transfers meant she could contribute to the creature comforts of her children and loved ones, even from thousands of miles away.

Remittances have become ubiquitous features in contemporary geographies of migration that reflect the flows of both money and people from one point on the globe to another. While Madrid's politicians bemoaned the unchecked outpouring of money to various parts of the globe, intense flows of cash not only reconfigured domestic relationships; they also provided the crude materials for the entire transformation of urban and rural landscapes. Since the 1990s, households throughout Ecuador have become heavily reliant on remittances, which in turn completely changed its economic, social, and cultural geography. As small bits of money flowed from modest bank accounts in Madrid to household economies in places like Quito, growing urban and rural wealth allowed families once ravaged by crisis to slowly improve their situations, often through investment in the city itself. A globalizing real estate market abetted this urban investment, promoting the development of new homes and suburbs on the peri-urban fringes of many Andean cities. Margarita and Yvette, for example, both purchased properties back in Quito as they saw their fortunes rise in Madrid. The pages of *Latino* make evident this spatial system: real estate agencies promoted housing not only in Madrid and Spain, but also in places of origin, offering immigrants easy opportunities to purchase units back home.[9] Marina D'Or holiday village was a famous development that sought to expand tourist offerings in the northern Valencia region at the height of the boom. As it inaugurated thousands of new units in Castellón, Spain, it also advertised a new, similar development in Guayaquil, Ecuador.[10] The "vacation city" would soon be available for purchase in the country of origin, contributing to immigrant fantasies of comfortable futures. In this case, the developer was clearly taking advantage of a burgeoning market, as many immigrants used their gains in Spain to invest in the built environment back home.

On a research trip to Ecuador in July 2017, friends and I drove north out of Quito on our way to the rainforest. I was staying in the heart of the city, in the bohemian Guápulo neighborhood, which hosts cute cafés and Parisian patisseries. To get to the edge of the city took almost two hours. New roads, built through remittances, oil dollars, and international development funds, were still clogged with traffic. We coursed through the ever-expanding suburban landscape, past informal settlements and planned bedroom communities. Local restaurants serving ceviche and roast pork sat alongside McDonald's and KFC. At the very edges of the city we passed several gated developments that closely mimicked American suburban sprawl. Two-story brick houses lined straight roads. Each house had a garage and driveway. Renderings of pleasant, modern suburban life were splashed across billboards advertising these new homes. Two neighboring communities were named "Alcazar de Toledo," and "Alcazar de Segovia," evoking Spanish imperial pasts even as they promised modern, efficient presents.[11] Built with money that had flowed from Spain, these twenty-first-century *alcazares* offered aspirational middle-class comfort to a new generation of urban dwellers.[12]

Remittance landscapes, to use a term coined by architectural historian Sarah Lopez, bring into intimate contact very different sites that are nonetheless connected by the transnational movements of itinerant laboring bodies.[13] She theorizes these landscapes as connected spaces despite their literal geographic separation. Juxtaposition and connection allow us to see parts of rural Mexico as entwined with metropolitan spaces of the United States, as Lopez draws out in her work. Here the built environment—the houses and churches constructed sometimes by community members themselves with money from abroad—acts as an evidentiary archive, bearing witness to the movement of people and capital. Fixed in place, these structures make visible subaltern flows of capital, labor, and care. Throughout many locations, the powerful and wealthy dictate the form and arrangement of many of our built environments, from Versailles to New York's Hudson Yards. As such, modest remittance spaces attest to the power of transnational migration as a tool for development and the accumulation of wealth, revealing myriad forms of capital—social, political, economic—of actors often theorized as beyond the scope of politics and placemaking. In Marina D'Or Guayaquil or Quito's Alcazar de Toledo, for example, we can apprehend an architectural history from below, not of grand castles and cathedrals but rather of everyday space and its substance. They also help us to see anew the question of development. Often within that project such postcolonial sites are rendered in need of western expertise and money.[14] If their inhabitants are visible, they are docile subjects who might benefit from the west's aid, rather than actors who transform these geographies through their own agency.[15] Yet such mundane landscapes—local leisure sites and exurban single-family homes—reveal instead how remittances, and the individuals who both send and receive such flows of cash, are instead agile forces that produce forms of development beyond hegemonic international institutions.[16]

The relationship between Spain and Ecuador in this respect has been especially intense, inflecting, too, large-scale urbanism. As one of the biggest receptors of Ecuadorian migration, Spain represented an important font of remittance money, which flowed back to Ecuador in increasing amounts. But Ecuadorians in Madrid also produced new relations of exchange between the two countries.[17] The presence of a large Ecuadorian population within Spain meant the two countries deepened their diplomatic ties, in part so that Spain might aid in development projects. In regards to urbanism, Ecuadorian planners and policymakers observed Madrid's rapid urbanization and sought to emulate it. Ambitious new *quiteño* infrastructure projects relied on Spanish expertise. Specifically, the engineers and planners responsible for Madrid's subway expansion have consulted on a new project to create a metro line in the Andean capital, a complicated undertaking in a hilly city nestled in an immense mountainous valley. Finally, as Spanish banks have recovered from the crisis, they have increasingly invested in Latin American projects, including in Ecuador. Thus both massive urban projects and modest dwelling spaces are testaments to migrations between the metropole and the post-colony, in addition to various modes of development that circulate through forms of mutual aid and multinational cooperation.

Transnational landscapes not only bear witness to the historical circulations of people, money, and domestic aspirations. They also force their inhabitants to constantly reckon with those trends. As such, they foster a particular geographic thinking that allows ordinary people to see the intense links between urban transformation and personal circumstance. If we recall immigrants' decisions to enter into homeownership, we see evidence of that thinking. Mabel, for example, purchased a house in Spain with the knowledge its price would rise. When she wanted to return to Peru, she could sell her house and reap great rewards. Those rewards, in turn, would finance a very comfortable life back home. She also decided to purchase real estate in Peru, meanwhile, which further reveals a calculative reasoning of risk and reward. This mode of geographic thinking connected the larger political economic moment with her aspirations in both Spain and back home in Peru. It allowed her to anticipate a future at a far remove from her immediate reality. Such thinking did not dissipate in crisis. Links between familial duties and relationships, economic advancement, and international geographies of migration have given many in these communities an awareness of the ways in which everyday domesticities and personal lives are highly circumscribed within much broader trends and movements. While many, too, felt the intense sting of isolation, shame, and guilt, their lived histories served to contextualize and make sense of personal ruin as situated within complex political economies.

Meanwhile, the experience of being an immigrant in Madrid exposed them to the racialized vagrancies of capitalism. In moving to Spain, many immigrants replaced one peripheral identity—poor, often Indigenous—for another—that of immigrant. In the first chapter, I introduced the stories of Mabel and Yvette. Mabel knew upon arrival that her employers should pay social security but wouldn't. Similarly, Yvette knew her employers wanted someone without papers whom they could pay less and make to work longer hours. Both situations embedded these women in particular political economic landscapes in which race and gender were salient features enabling the extraction of value from labor, experiences not precisely new, as Suzana Sawyer elaborates: "The ways in which [racialized] bodies have historically been distributed and managed in Ecuador is intimately linked, and indeed has enabled, the accumulation of capital."[18] Mabel and Yvette thus situate their immediate circumstances within a broader context of economic success and its others. Coming from societies highly stratified by race and class, these women saw how Madrid perpetuated the same hierarchical categories, even while questions of race were largely disavowed. Their status as other, outsiders, accorded them fewer rights and little protection. Homeownership of course was supposed to be a bulwark against these predations. And yet, soon it revealed itself to be another means of managing bodies, of accumulation by dispossession, and of furthering and even punishing difference. The daily illegalities proximate to immigrant experiences—whether experiences of racism and harassment or employment irregularities—also reminded them of the state's general indifference if not out-right hostility. In light of rampant vulnerability and potential fraud, the govern-ment might turn a blind eye to the plight of a few immigrant families.

Within trajectories of sociospatial transformation, immigrant women also emerge as resilient actors who have had to weather many tribulations. Follow-ing the decision to migrate to Spain, they found a city that was awash in both possibility and urban anxieties of difference. Work was difficult and sometimes backbreaking, as in Mabel's case, where an employment injury required spi-nal surgery. They often moved numerous times, sometimes within the span of a single year. Aida, for example, had taken up residence in various homes throughout the city's periphery, always searching for something more perma-nent. While Andeans created a community in Madrid, they also painstakingly maintained ties with family back home. Placed against a longer history of strug-gle, their mortgage problems became but one more challenge. In conjunction with previous histories of crisis and loss, immigrants from Ecuador and Peru could thus comprehend their mortgage situations in terms that differed from those of their Spanish counterparts, which I return to later on in this chapter.

Indigenous Histories, Indignant Futures

While these facets of immigrant life fostered alternative understandings of crisis and corruption, Indigenous traditions were key in promoting a politics of resistance. Alternative forms of common sense were not enough to spark a movement. Rather there also had to be the impetus for action. Here is where a small group of Ecuadorian activists at the Coordinadora Nacional de Ecuato-rianos en España (CONADEE–National Coordinator of Ecuadorians in Spain) played a singular role. Prior to arriving in Madrid, where they organized to gain rights and recognition for the Andean community in the city, they had ex-perience in the Indigenous struggles of their native homeland. Aida's personal history illustrates how the threads of the Indigenous movement came to be entwined with the problem of homeownership in Madrid. While Aida was one of several people involved in the early days of anti-evictions activism, her narrative in particular reveals the influence of indigenous struggles on responses to urban crisis.

Aida is a seasoned activist. At the start of the crisis, she was the president of the CONADEE. In this position, she was a tireless advocate and saw her role as facilitating mutual understanding. She was keen to introduce Spaniards to the richness of her culture, including the history of struggle that mark Indigenous communities such as her own. She is soft-spoken with a vocabulary bereft of the political language used by many of the visible faces who dominate Spain's activist circles. However, she carries with her intimate knowledge of resistance and success borne out of dogged determination and collectivization. In 2008 she witnessed as members of her community increasingly found themselves out of work; their employers were firing people left and right, often without paying back wages and certainly without severance. As the construction industry contracted, immigrants were the first to feel the sting of crisis. But soon Aida noticed another trend plaguing her community: the loss of a job soon meant the loss of the home, as people began to face foreclosure and the imminent threat of eviction. The CONADEE set up an advisory office where Ecuadorians could come for counsel on the problems they were facing with the onset of crisis. "At first," one interlocutor related, "it was going to do a bit of everything. But in the end there was a torrential flood of mortgage [problems]." While the immediate issue of mortgages was perhaps far removed from Indigenous struggles around land and rights, it harkened back to similar processes of wealth, power, control, and extraction.

In bearing witness to the mortgage struggles of her community, Aida saw collectivization as one means of egress. Years later she related to me, "I've never seen any place on earth nor throughout history where getting a bunch of people together [to organize] doesn't achieve something." This urge to seek out strength in the collective recalled her previous modes of both communal life and the activism required for its reproduction. Aida grew up in an Indigenous community in rural Ecuador. Her family was one of several that worked the land through the system of *huasipungo*—colonial territories ceded to Indigenous people in the rural Andean region, yet owned by local members of the elite.[19] This life was far removed from any town or village, let alone the Ecuadorian capital of Quito. Theirs was a rural existence marked largely by subsistence. She and her brothers and sisters were expected to take part in working the land. She went to a school that was two hours away by bus; when not commuting or in classes she took part in the work of the community, the *minga*, a term that refers to the sharing and solidarity of rural Indigenous life.[20] While each family tills its plot in a kind of patronage, beholden to the owner, they see resources as belonging to the community. On weekends and in the evenings, however, the community gets together to help one another out. Sometimes this means help-ing a neighbor raise his house. In other moments it implies aiding another fam-ily with their harvest. No money changes hands; what is expected is that if you ever find yourself in the situation of needing some extra help, the community will come to your rescue. Aida described the *minga* as "the solidarity of lending a hand." The scant resources afforded these families were to be shared in order to improve the communal good rather than hoarded for the use of the indi-vidual. She was always aware of the struggles over land and rights that haunted her home; their very occupation of land and the livelihood it begot was a direct legacy of brutal imperial relations. Theirs was a precarious existence that always required negotiation and quiet forms of resistance.

The system of kinship and resource management in which Aida grew up also displays a different orientation to land and territory. The designation of separate plots for each family is largely arbitrary. Rather land is something to be cared for so that it might bear resources. Those resources are then collec-tive.[21] If we think back to the kinds of ideologies that animated Spain's land-use reforms of the 1990s, we can see a clear opposition between land as a com-monly held resource and land as something to be partitioned and divvied up. In the latter paradigm, the emphasis is on the individual and his amelioration— the *iniciativa privada* of the Franco regime translated for the global era. In the former, however, any scant piece of good is held commonly for the benefit of the collective.

Indeed, Aida's recollections of rural life in the Andes hint at both the im-portance of community and indigenous ideologies of *territorio*. Indigenous communities in the Andes evince a belief in "the 'traditional' values of reci-procity and rotating leadership."[22] Here local communal structures manage resources and carry out decision-making. That decision-making as it relates to resources and effects on community members "required the participation of the majority."[23] Such processes of what we might in the west label as de-liberate, participatory democracy are particularly important in decisions over *territorio*. In her work on Indigenous uprisings against multinational oil cor-porations, Sawyer engages in ethnographic analysis to elaborate Indigenous notions of that concept. She argues it is a recent category that has grown out of the politicization of Indigenous issues since the 1970s. Despite its relatively recent emergence, *territorio* is nonetheless important as an analytical frame for indigenous claims and communal life. Sawyer writes *territorio* "referred to an ancestral space of indigenous sociality," against the idea of *tierra* (land) or *propiedad* (property).[24] The latter two concepts were connected to colonial allotments, and served as counterparts for the more expansive *territorio*. If *tierra* was about a landowning elite, remnants from a colonial époque that continued to influence the present, *territorio* encompassed a host of collective concerns about subsistence, identity, resource managements, historical relations, and solidarity. That category imbricates both physical place, but also these forms of communitarian identity, livelihoods, and social relations. As such, it refuses representation within the cadastral map, a political tool for elite manipulation.

Aida told me this story within the dark confines of her small house. On the other side of a thin wall, her two new Mapuche friends dozed after a late night partaking of Madrid's famous nightlife. As she described to me the *minga*, I bore witness to her acts of sharing and solidarity. Her home was a space to be shared with others, particularly from the wider Indigenous community. When I arrived at her house, she immediately offered me food from a pot that had been simmering on the stove. While its contents were modest, she insisted in sharing her resources with me, in part as a social gesture to make me feel at home. Within this context, one's problems are not the domain of the individual or the family. Rather they are communal, belonging to all members. Thus all members should come together to help those in need.

At thirteen, Aida left home for the capital city, sent by her family to seek out better educational opportunities. When she made her trek from the Andes to the city in search of education, Aida sought this same kind of community in Quito. She went to live in a neighborhood in the south of the city. There, she found people with similar ideologies around solidarity and sharing at the local parish. Until this point, she had never really known anything about religion, the church, Jesus Christ. But she "found something there" that resonated with her, and so she began to study catechism. Of course she then found that this church was greatly influenced by liberation theology, a part of the greater network of churches throughout Latin America that advocated emancipation. She saw clearly the strength of networks of resistance and action as a means of sharing and disseminating information.

While she was involved in her church, she attended university. She was always very active. As she tells it, one day people at the university suggested she attend a meeting for Indigenous people around the issue of the 500th anniversary of Columbus's arrival in America. She went to the meeting, where she was named general secretary even though she had little idea of what that would entail. But she also began to see herself as a member of an entire community made up of all Indigenous peoples, and she wanted, with them, to discover their history and what had happened over many centuries of colonization. She soon came to learn that 600,000 of her ancestors had been slaughtered, and that she and many of her compatriots were very likely products of rape and violence. The Cross, which she had only just discovered, now came to symbolize colonization, oppression, and pillage. She wanted others to learn about this history but also to fight against it and claim rights and recognition. They began to organize for an Indigenous uprising.

Indeed, Aida came of age in a historic moment for Indigenous communities across Ecuador, Bolivia, Peru, and Colombia. Starting in the 1970s communities across the region began to organize around the question of land rights, recognition, and ongoing exploitation that had a lengthy colonial history.[25] In 1972 activists in the highland created Awakening of Ecuadorian Indigenous People, with the help of international NGOs and the local Catholic Church, "to fight racial discrimination and recuperate or fortify indigenous cultures."[26] This activism, which was in contact with and received support from institutions both within Ecuador and internationally, continued to grow through the following decades. During those years, a number of confederations emerged to perpetuate this struggle and seek support for the cause of Indigenous identity, rights, and recognition. In 1990 these activists, in collaboration with their counterparts in other parts of Latin America, staged the first Indigenous uprising in anticipation of the quincentennial of Columbus's "discovery" of America.

By the time Aida became involved, the Indigenous movement had begun to elaborate sophisticated repertoires of action and activism that took on forms of structural adjustment, deregulation, and privatization in addition to the struggle for rights and recognition. Here they targeted the ecological degradation promised by oil drilling and the pro-corporate ceding of large land holdings to multinational enterprise. Sawyer argues in her book *Crude Chronicles* that "neoliberal economic reforms" created the "conditions of possibility for a disruptive indigenous movement."[27] This reality is one of the paradoxes of neoliberalism within a variety of contexts including millennial Madrid. At the same time that it creates new forms of extraction and domination, it also can open up possibilities for solidarity, sharing, and alternative forms of production.

Neoliberalism and the tools and ideologies it advances can be used against it-self.[28] The Indigenous movement addressed historical conditions of exclusion, but also the contemporary manifestations of colonial domination through the guise of the market. Resisting that market, drawing out its contradictions and silences, is precisely how this movement gained traction and attention.

Indigenous uprisings, however, also sought to demand rights and representation for this community. In this struggle, some Indigenous people like Aida were experiencing political awaking, now discovering their painful histories as products of colonial rape. But they were also confronting their immediate present. As Aida described to me, part of the uprisings were meant to bring into evidence the contemporary conditions of *indio* life, which didn't necessarily conform to the rural peasant imaginary that predominated Ecuador's orientation to the Indigenous question. Indians didn't just come from the rural farmlands far away from cities and villages. There was also the urban population. But that urban population saw exclusion in more vivid terms. Living in the cities, they were shunted into the peripheries, unable to access the city center. Thus the uprising, too, sought to make their presence known in the city, confronting the white centers of power. Here the strategy was to make visible the problem for others, in addition to making others uncomfortable. Discomfort, coming into close contact with that which makes one uneasy, is a powerful tool for effecting social change. This discomfort comes from a kind of recognition. In that moment, we see that which makes us uncomfortable, in this case pointing out that discomfort and our own complicity in its production. We cannot ignore it as previously we had done. Thus it forces people to acknowledge their culpability in creating situations of risk and exclusion.

Aida impressed upon me the fact that she had learned and continues to learn by doing, "along the way." The lesson here from the Indigenous struggles was that one had to act, and in acting, one came to learn, to know, to gain expertise. Here collective education might make activists, as people gain information on their current situations. The Indigenous uprisings weren't simply about the demands being set forth by the thousands of participants. Rather they also sought to educate the public and members of their own collective about the contemporary situations of Indigenous communities and the historical trajectories that produced landscapes of exclusion. Collectivization is thus also a means of education, as it informs a broad swath of people who might then learn together. Here again the emphasis is on communal knowledge and information, in the absence of specific representatives who might possess authority.

Authority only resides in the collective, which might then elect spokespeople to articulate its claims and causes.

Aida's trajectory also displays a commitment to a kind of intellectual and activist promiscuity. By this I mean endless experimentation that also marks her journey through life. After rural life, she turned to liberation theology. After the church, she embraced student activism. And then she came to be a leader in the Indigenous movement. Throughout, she and her compatriots experimented with different techniques, and she learned from them in the process. Further, rather than target one institution alone, the movement identified a plethora of arenas in which to advance their struggle. They took to the streets and marched from rural communities to the center of the city. They put up blockades to protest resource extraction in the rainforest. As the movement developed and deepened, they created political parties and ran for election. There was no adherence to one ideological style of activism or even line of protest. The stakes were too high. They had to effect change however possible. Their arsenal of resistance refuses to follow one tactic alone, but rather demands insertion into all aspects of life. As such, the Indigenous movement targeted various centers of power, including the courts, the government, and the church.

The Indigenous movement made incredible gains throughout the 1990s and early 2000s precisely because of its eclecticism and promiscuity. The various groups that made up the movement targeted a variety of issues through numerous tactics. At times they filed lawsuits and deployed legal maneuvers, while at others they called out the law as a tool for colonial oppression. In Ecuador the movement is perhaps best known for demanding plurinational statehood, even if the ideas of nation, nationhood, and nationalism are all entwined with and emerge out of western trajectories of power and thought. Meanwhile, it sought support and sustenance from a number of organizations within Ecuador and throughout the world. One source of support at times, as mentioned above, was the local Catholic Church, even though it was clearly an institution of domination and imperial power. Yet the movement for the most part refused to dwell only in these contradictions, instead pushing forward on a variety of tactical fronts.

When Aida left Ecuador in 2000, the Indigenous movement had achieved many goals. It had also begun to organize around the issue of electoral politics. In 1995 an Indigenous political party formed to channel these myriad demands and strategies into an official body that might enter into national government. Aida's departure from Spain was difficult in large part because she was part of a movement that had only recently gained political power and convincingly advanced its cause within numerous arenas. Yet the economic crisis in Ecuador had devastated her household, leaving her with large debts. Spain beckoned as a site where she might be able to accrue a little capital before returning home to continue this struggle. The lessons of the Indigenous movement, however, were manifold, and would prove useful nearly a decade later.

From Civil Death to Civil Disobedience

In 2008 Aida was struggling to make her own monthly payments. Cognizant of banks' unwavering stance against negotiation, Aida decided to organize through the CONADEE. Initially, anxiety about her financial future and a desire for more information prompted her to act. She knew little about the contents of the mortgage she had signed, and so she consulted with others in the organization, who were horrified to see the terms. Aware that others had found themselves in the same situation, she began to mobilize.

The Andean community in Madrid was already particularly well organized. As one of the most established immigrant groups in the Community, Madrid's Andean population was ripe for financial penetration. Close knit with myriad civil society associations, the community featured strong social networks and intercommunication. Years of organized settlement had established small but potent immigrant enclaves (a May 2005 article in *Latino* declared Pueblo Nuevo to be "un Quito Chiquito"—a little Quito). The success and endurance of *Latino,* which had a weekly circulation of 140,000 editions in March 2007, attests to the size and social capital of this population. Financial entities leveraged such ties to disseminate credit products throughout the collective via a number of mechanisms. Formal mechanisms included financial entities geared toward immigrants such the CHI, which is how Aida found her house. That business was a conduit between immigrant households and Spanish banks, facilitating the extension of credit from the latter to the former. This formal entity, however, relied on informal ties, as they employed numerous immigrants to act as ambassadors within their communities. Working for modest commissions, enterprising individuals would convince friends and acquaintances to purchase property and introduce potential clients to financial agents who were more than happy to help.

Over the course of less than a decade, Andeans in the millennial metropolis had established their presence in the city. Burgeoning businesses catered to immigrant publics. Soon Latin American grocery stores and restaurants dotted residential areas, serving traditional Andean dishes of *aji de gallina* and *seco de chivo*. Mainstream stores including El Corte Inglés—Spain's most important department store, run by a family with close ties to Franco—also stocked Latin American spices and condiments on their shelves (though often at a shocking markup). During the weekends, families would make pilgrimages from peripheral neighborhoods to the Casa de Campo park, where they claimed large stretches for barbeques and soccer. There they chatted of children, family back home, and their recent housing purchases. Local parks in San Blas and Carabanchel also saw their soccer pitches overwhelmed with immigrants, who used these public spaces as sites of sociality and exchange. Such sites were also targets for the penetration of credit: outfits such as CHI saw them as potent frontiers for the spread of mortgage credit, and so sent their ambassadors to attend regular soccer matches to spread the gospel of the *hipoteca*.[29]

With the advent of crisis, those ties also proved to be a means of sharing information and collectivizing mortgage problems. Having lived through recent economic shock, the Andean community, via its numerous associations, soccer fields, and barbeques, began immediately in 2008 to discuss the crisis. The strong tradition of associational life proved key in fomenting dissent. Andean associations had emerged throughout Spain to address the needs and conditions of their communities, newly settled far from home. As such, they worked on a range of issues, providing both advice on logistical problems related to settlement—legal papers or adequate housing—and programs to introduce outsiders to Andean culture and maintain a sense of community far from home. As employment began to decline and mortgage payments went up, these associations took on the problem of economic instability as one more issue that troubled their constituents. Mortgages, foreclosures, and evictions were simply new components in the constellation of practices and problems that contributed to the Andean experience in Madrid.

Immediately after the economy began to tumble, the Andean community in Spain began to organize around the issue of mortgages. On January 11, 2008, *Latino* ran a small item claiming immigrants were "energizing" the real estate market. On April 4 of that same year, however, the paper ran another small item, this time titled "Inform yourself about debts and mortgages." By June a small group of immigrants had begun to meet to discuss their mortgage problems. Calling themselves the Unión de Proprietarios de Viviendas Familiares Hipotecadas Impagables (The Union of Homeowners with Un-Payable

Mortgages), this group sprung out of one of Madrid's numerous associations, the Asociación América-España Solidaridad y Cooperación (The Association for American-Spanish Solidarity and Cooperation). By October, the CONADEE began their own meetings, looking to consolidate efforts among a number of different groups.

In October, the CONADEE placed large announcements in *Latino*, inviting anyone interested to participate in an open meeting to address "what to do about mortgages." The meeting was designed to put together "a proposal from immigrants." What is interesting in this framing is that it immediately positions immigrants as political actors. Aida said to me years later, "They think we immigrants don't have experience, that we don't know anything, that they're the intellectuals . . . the ones who change the world. [I saw my mortgage problem] and said, 'No more.'" Drawing on her past experiences with activism, she decided to organize with the knowledge that her community in Madrid might be able to confront this problem collectively. The meeting was intended to attract and speak to the immigrant community, but also to offer the immigrant community as a source of wisdom and potential solution. Immigrants here emerge as potential experts in navigating the early days of crisis. In placing an ad in an immigrant newspaper, moreover, the CONADEE didn't have to use such language—migrant subjectivity and collectivity were implicit because of the ad's venue. The group's use of language thus subtly insisted on this community as agents rather than passive subjects victim to mounting financial collapse.

Furthermore, the language used in these advertisements, as in Aida's retelling of her recent history, subverts the typical narrative of isolation, shame, and guilt. For the CONADEE, mortgage debt was a collective problem that demanded a response from the community. At the first hint of economic ruin, their inclination was to learn more, to educate themselves and the community, and to elaborate strategies that would allow people to overcome the problem. Already in these ads, moreover, the group used the language of *afectado por la hipoteca*. The meeting announcement in the June 18 edition of *Latino* deployed the term "*afectado*," instead of the perhaps more evocative "victim." In doing so, they oriented the problem of mortgage debt into particular terms. Rather than dwell on the individual, atomized experience of personal financial ruin, they instead insisted on a relational situation. Aida recalled telling her bank, "I'm not to blame, you guys did this, so go fuck yourselves." She wasn't going to pay any more to a financial entity that had placed her in this mess. As people *affected* by a mortgage, they located their personal problem within a broader

FIGURE 6.1. Advertisement for first mortgage-related protest. Source: *Latino,* Dec. 12, 2007.

terrain of political economic questions. There is here a subversion of the common understanding of individual economic collapse, which inscribes onto the debtor full responsibility for her own misfortune. Instead, it insists on the problems of the household as part of a broader web that implicates the public and its institutions.

The CONADEE also sought out and found support from a number of different local institutions. An early connection between the group and Nacho Murgui, president of the Federación Regional de Asociaciones de Vecinos de Madrid (FRAVM—The Regional Federation of Madrid Neighborhood Associations), meant that the group could now count on help from one of the most established grassroots institutions in the city. The FRAVM grew out of the neighborhood struggles of the 1960s and 1970s, providing an organizational umbrella for local groups across the Madrid region. They often provided a link to the municipal and regional governments and drew attention to the various issues that plagued peripheral urban areas and modest housing estates. Evictions and foreclosures appeared to be the latest problem facing working-class and immigrant areas of the region. The group went on to gather support from the various trade unions in the city, which donated space so that the CONADEE could host its first meeting. Held in the auditorium of the Unión General de Trabajadores

(UGT—General Workers Union), one of Spain's largest mainstream unions, the meeting drew over 1,500 people.

That first meeting insisted on the public nature of private ruin. As an association with deep ties throughout the city's Ecuadorian population, the CONADEE was in a unique position to accumulate disparate stories, placing them like puzzle pieces to assemble the broader whole. Daily, mortgaged Ecuadorians flooded the offices of the association, searching for aid from the small team of activists and lawyers. With little formal training in mortgage law, this ragtag group attended to those in need as best they could. As such, however, they had a strategic advantage: they could see that the mortgage problem was widespread. It was not a question of a few isolated debtors, but rather an epidemic sweeping the community. Something so extensive must be an issue not of private homes and personal finance, but rather of public policy and practice. Within early meetings, people were thus encouraged to make public their mortgage situations. Collectivization was also necessary because of their status as immigrants. Aida was intimately familiar with the ways in which the majority ignores the concerns and conditions of someone differentiated by race, class, and migratory history. She had learned from the Indigenous movement that the only way to confront hegemonic power is through collective organizing. As a marginalized figure in her native Ecuador and then her adopted Spain, Aida knew her voice would only matter if it might be accompanied by numerous others. Thus from that first glimmer of trouble, she responded to a collective problem, negating its individual consequences.

Collectivizing the problem demanded they know its specific nature. Aida related to me, "The first thing is to know what we've signed. And with that [knowledge we can] put forward proposals and have a discussion." When a house passes into foreclosure, the household receives what is commonly referred to as the *tocho*, or the "brick." The *tocho* is a thick stack of papers, similar in heft and height to a brick. It contains every single piece of documentation related to the mortgage, from the initial contract, to deeds of sale, to the complicated financial terms of payments. Confronted with massive reams of paper, early activists decided the only way to deal with this onslaught of paperwork was to sit down and begin to uncover the pieces of each individual mortgage. But the tocho only told one side of the story. It did not contain the intimate details of each family's decision to purchase a house, nor did it include the various seductions of bankers, real estate agents, and public notaries who had encouraged that decision.[30] Each *afectada* had her own financial history that might be placed into a larger constellation of ruin. In piecing together histories of financialization, predatory lending, and domestic desires, these narrations took on the quality of testimony. Years of labor, consumption, and migration came to be summarized as part of a bearing witness to fraud. Within this context, an individual testimony was one way to discover the depth and breadth of the issue; sharing personal narratives of ruin served to untangle the mess of complicated and opaque financial geographies. In these early meetings, therefore, they alighted on the public testimony of private ruin as a key means of piecing together the clues of financial devastation. Public narrations thus became a way of analyzing what exactly they had signed so as to move forward.

> Some thought they were guarantors, but they didn't know what they were signing. The real estate agency just wanted more guarantors. People you didn't know. There were always people available to enter as guarantors.
> —Yvette. Ecuadorian. Single mother. Activist. Afectada.

The public testimony was key in making opaque financial histories legible. Emotional turmoil is an intimate partner to the process of foreclosure. But so is confusion. People are thrust into the great puzzle of their financialized lives as it is mediated through the financial industry and the state. The more-or-less straightforward piece to this puzzle is the sequence of events that leads from nonpayment to foreclosure and eviction. But in a landscape that had come to be dominated by guarantors, co-ownership schemes, personal loans, and other sundry financial innovations, chaos ruled. Scott, in writing on contemporary techniques of rule, argues the state seeks to create legibility as a means of governing broad territories.[31] But the targeted and successful deployment of *illegibility* can also serve to manage and control. The complexities of financialization become a biopolitical tool to manage and order populations.[32] Here individuals are exhausted not just by their own civil death, but also by the mountains of paperwork that describe financial arrangements incomprehensible to the layperson. The impenetrability of the system was a means of suspending individual debtors within uncertainty. One interlocutor, describing the complicated details of her situation, in which her mortgage had been bundled and sold to a German company, sighed, "I can't even pronounce the name of the company that owns my mortgage!"

Repeated testimonies served to order and make sense of the insidious details of banking practices. Within mortgage contracts, they found how petty informal practices inflected the inner workings of multinational finance capital. For example, a mortgage loan emitted by Banco Santander would be inflated artificially based on a sum designated by the appraiser. Hired by the bank, the appraising company would reach a figure that greatly exceeded the value of the home as it was written down in the deed of sale. The cash difference between mortgage size and recorded price would allow the seller to walk away with a hefty sum of black money beyond the reach of *Hacienda*. In the act of sale, innovative credit products, here in the form of a securitized mortgage, would abet the circulation of capital through the covert channels of the informal economy. The person taking on the mortgage would assume in this act all risk.

A common and perhaps more insidious practice that abetted immigrant property acquisition, however, was the practice of crossed guarantors or chained guarantors, a key component of those mortgages facilitated by CHI. Here two or more households would act as guarantors for one another's loans, creating a complex web or chain of debt and responsibility. If one household got behind on its monthly payments, the entire house of cards would collapse. CHI made it a requirement for their clients to guarantee others' mortgages simultaneously, often demanding that households that had no previous contact now enter into a complex financial relationship. Thus Aida, her mortgage guaranteed by a family she had never met, also served as the *aval* for another household. CHI insisted this was an act of solidarity, leveraging notions of communal responsibility. Immigrant financial services also advertised for guarantors within the pages of *Latino,* promising small amounts of money in exchange. Thus, the pages of the newspaper were rife with the kind of possibility I have described, but also significant and insidious forms of fraud.

Immigrant homeowners—and indeed many Spaniards—were also wholly unaware of Spanish mortgage law. In Spain the overwhelming majority of mortgages are recourse loans that allow the bank to pursue all assets up to the value of the mortgage even after repossession. If there were no other assets, the debt would be passed down to children upon death. Only by renouncing their inheritance could potential heirs avoid that fate. As they pored over the contents of their mortgages, these early pioneers discovered mortgage debt would equal the complete erosion of not only personal finances, but also the family and the community. Ruination was inevitable in the face of inaction. In discovering eviction meant not only homelessness but also lifelong debt, they also began to elaborate two courses of action that would prove central to the later tactics of the PAH. Their struggle must address both the inequities of the housing system and the broader capitalist system, shot through with fraud that perpetuated inequalities.

> I found a ton of people with the same problem! I thought I was the only one! But I found a ton, and some were worse off than I am!
>   —Yvette.

The testimony, however, served another key end: the *afectada* transformed herself from *muerta civil* into expert, from someone cowed by the system to an empowered individual ready to take it on. The emphasis on individual testimonies in the face of uncertainty and opacity sought simply to pull apart this complicated web. Learning to narrate one's own financial history, which continues to be a central facet within the PAH, became a means of gaining mastery over the situation. Through repetition, people also gained control over recent pasts in which they had been configured bit players in the larger drama of their financial universe. Learning the constitutive pieces on the puzzle, these nascent activists help to make sense of a confusing process, rendering it into their own language of the everyday. Their expertise relies upon both lived experiences of vulnerability—against the state's quantified data—and intimate knowledge of complicated processes of extraction. In writing down or orating their stories of loss, *afectadas* are called upon to create a coherent narrative that can be made legible in black ink and inscribed on paper. They might then present that narrative as one concrete piece of evidence, part of a larger web of artifacts that document a system designed against them.

For example, Margarita sought help with her mortgage problem after she had lost her job and her house was under threat of repossession. Approaching fifty, from a fairly middle-class Ecuadorian family, she had moved to Spain around the turn of the millennium, fed up with the political battles that embroiled her homeland. She worked at a large multinational pharmaceutical company; despite her decent salary, she was offered a garbage mortgage for a small fourth-floor walkup with two bedrooms. Perceiving it to be within her economic reach, she made the investment and subsequently injected a considerable amount of cash in monthly payments. She also remodeled the flat to her liking. Yet with the loss of employment, she faced foreclosure. Margarita began to attend each assembly, taking notes, incorporating new information, finding in the lull of repetition an emergent sense of order. She talked to the various lawyers who assist the PAH. By the time I met her in early 2013, she had a mastery of her financial history in addition to extensive knowledge of mortgage law, greater than many lawyers.[33]

Margarita began to lead assemblies and counseling sessions. At the start of each meeting, she would take the assembled *afectadas* through the steps of eviction, demonstrating with precision the order that makes up a process experienced as irrational. People would pepper her with questions as they attempted to sort out their own situations. In moments of calm, she banged on the keyboard of the old computer in the PAH office, modifying forms for people to take to their banks or the courts. She would sit with people to read their mortgage documents, untangling incredibly messy, jargon-filled contracts laden with fraud. From her, I too learned expertise. I became acquainted with some of the common tricks inserted into mortgages. More important still, she revealed to me that expertise was here a matter of dogged determination, constancy, and indefatigability. It required long hours, many journeys from one place to the next, patience in talking with people who had experienced and continued to experience great trauma, and sharing intimate personal details.

These itinerate journeys through the intricate maze of homeownership can serve to discipline. But they can also open up and uncover. In learning this system, in spreading wisdom and knowledge, *afectadas* destabilize the system and the work of economics. First, they present to the world an alternative expertise. The mastery they gain in these endless journeys, both physical and psychic, allows them to hone their narratives of vulnerability. Within those narratives, they can now draw in the work of the state and the banks, implicating them in their ruin. In reciting her financial history, a woman such as Margarita garners sympathy. As the problem of evictions ravaged the city, this group gained a broad audience that paid attention to these stories. In public fora, Aida or Margarita's expertise is appealing because it is emotive and affective, rendered into the simple language of the everyday. In a country in which most people have been touched by crisis, these stories both make sense and resonate.

Collectivizing the problem, demonstrating how it emerged within a situated political economy, these civil dead channeled their fear and sorrow, guilt and shame, into anger, rage, and action. Betsy, who went to the first meetings in 2008 and 2009, stated, "I see the same life in a different way." In relating her story, she revealed how becoming part of this collective completely changed her understanding of the problem. While the problem itself did not changed, the ways she related to and made sense of it underwent a profound transformation.

As she sunk into depression, without work, she saw her inability to pay as a symptom of her own moral failings. Yet she was gripped by the fear of what might come after, bereft of job, house, savings. Now, however, she understood herself as a victim of a complicated process of extraction and punishment, in which her hard work has translated into ill-gotten gains for an inhumane system. But instead of resigning herself to her victimhood, she maintained agency and *she was not alone*: "You start to believe in yourself, in the struggle. This struggle is like an ant against an elephant. But if we're a million ants. . . . We have to be a million ants." She has regained her sense of self, which is now tied inextricably to her struggle, to fighting against the conditions of her damnation.

> Since we have that bad habit of organizing . . .
> —Eduardo. Indigenous. Ecuadorian. Afectado por la Hipoteca.

Faced with the brutalities of an extractive political economy, this loose alliance of immigrants, broadly organized under the umbrella of the CONADEE, decided to broadcast their rage and frustration. After years in which the banks had wooed them so persuasively, immigrants suffering through unemployment and eviction now found their economic futures had also gone through processes of foreclosure. Situating their experiences within a cycle of boom and bust, they uncovered massive amounts of fraud that had conspired to put them in great risk. This fraud fell firmly within the purview of the state, which had relaxed regulations and allowed new credit products to flood the market. Once hidden beneath the winks and smiles of bankers and the averted gaze of public notaries, fraud was now everywhere in evidence, demanding denunciation. Implicating the state within this massive house of cards, immigrant activists sought to make visible the conditions that had led to their ruin, demanding in the process a response from the state that would stave off destitution.

Aida once told me she would talk to anyone, anywhere, about her situation. In telling her story, she hoped it would somehow find an appropriate response, someone who would listen adequately and respond in kind. Further, by telling that story far and wide, to journalists, academics, fellow activists, politicians, and whoever else crossed her path, her tale of corruption and deceit would spread, bringing it visibility and notoriety. The desire to make public and thus visible animated early anti-mortgage actions. It is in this context that Barcelona activists began to see clearly the problem of mortgages. Aida, Eduardo, and Rafael Mayoral—now high up in PODEMOS, then a young lawyer who worked for the CONADEE—made trips around Spain to talk to members of the Ecuadorian community.

The CONADEE sought to bring the public's attention to the mortgage crisis. The itinerary for the protest against evictions in 2008 reveals their sophisticated thinking. The issue of mortgages was not merely a housing problem or a financial situation. Rather, it wove together state policy and practice, the role of the courts, the oversight of the Bank of Spain, and the continued indifference of the central government. The system they confronted was not merely money or mortgage markets. Instead, it constitutes a complex web in which public systems and private enterprise conspire to dispossess marginalized communities, sometimes in the name of expansion, more recently in the name of crisis. Housing is located within this web, not as a separate system but rather entangled in the production of urban space and value. Years later, a young activist with years of militancy in the Communist Party related to me how the PAH had taught her to be more patient, to listen to others even if they spoke differently. She went on, "[An immigrant *afectado*] is explaining better than I could, and he doesn't know who Milton Friedman is, nor does he need to. He also knows a lot, and knows how to organize himself and others." Indeed, what Aida and Eduardo enunciated in their early forays into housing activism was sophisticated political economic understanding of crisis and its effects even if that understanding was not enunciated in the academic or activist lexicons of the Spanish left. Here emerged an analysis of their situation that saw clearly the marriage between state power and financial capital.

Taking to the street to make known situations of ruin, these early victims largely went unheard; the government paid them little heed, and the banks turned them away. In these early actions through 2009 and 2010, they attempted to gain attention, displaying their predicaments and demands openly. On several instances, they met with high-up officials from the PSOE—then the ruling party—and the Banco de España, but to no avail. Their agitation in the streets and in meetings largely got them nowhere. Aida told her story again and again because she hoped at some point it would stop being a sorry tale of a modest immigrant and take on the weight of universality, inspiring indignation. As she marched down the Castellana, her cries were met largely with indifference, from the public at large, from state officials, from bank executives. In the eyes of these various civil society and political actors, foreclosure and eviction were immigrant problems that required little if any intervention.

In my interviews with other activists who were involved during this period, their frustration continues to bubble to the surface as they recall years of activity in which their pleas went unheard. In that moment, immigrants were expendable, now made excess by the shrinking economy. While necessary in the years of promising expansion, as the political economic landscape shifted, they were easily tossed aside. Evictions were just collateral damage that required no meaningful inquiry.

As activists who have long been involved in this particular struggle explained to me, these early contestations sought to untangle the intricate, historical relation between finance and the state that had led to ruin. Rather than simply address contemporary conditions of economic exclusion, they hoped to "look for those who were responsible and sue them," as Eduardo explained to me. While they were exasperated by individual cases, they were motivated to uncover the extent of state-sanctioned fraud, corruption, and theft on a massive scale. Eduardo described to me any early instance of debt forgiveness, when an immigrant family successfully discharged their mortgage debt. They had incurred that debt with BBVA, but when they went to sign the papers, the name of some other entity appeared now to be in possession of the property. What was this entity and why was it suddenly involved in what was a straightforward transaction between a client and his bank? As Eduardo and others began to investigate, they realized it was a subsidiary of BBVA, which had created a fund that to aid securitization. For Eduardo this was a moment of "opening the medicine cabinet," when he suddenly saw a glimpse of the elaborate scaffolding that kept the system upright. The struggle that would follow was meant to "confront the essence of the capitalist system." In this way it was a continuation of earlier struggles in Ecuador, in which modest communities resisted the domination of resource extraction and dispossession. While the enemy had changed guises, the battlefield now different in texture and color, the terms of engagement had remained essentially the same.

As the first victims of the crisis, immigrants had another distinct advantage. As recent participants within the Spanish culture of property, they were not burdened with the weight of its history. For Borja and Iñaki, for example, homeownership was integral to family and sentiments of hearth and home. It was bound up in cultural imaginaries of domesticity and heteronormative gender roles. It also allowed them to realize dreams of middle-class lifestyles, which had previously been beyond the reach of modest households. For many immigrants, however, homeownership was a means to secure housing and a tool to accrue wealth, mostly for the benefit of families back home. Home-ownership was a vehicle that might allow more resources to flow back to their country of origin to be shared among the community. Most, too, wished to return to their countries of origin—homeownership didn't necessarily imply permanence. Thus the loss of homeownership meant different ends to different populations.

Who Speaks?

To plan a legal demonstration in Spain, organizers must go to the regional government authorities with a map of the planned route to get approval so as to avoid steep fines. A small group presented their itinerary for their 2008 protest, to be held on the last day of fall. When the government representative saw their extensive itinerary, she looked at them skeptically and said, "This is way too long for someone to walk in an afternoon!" Eduardo responded, "This, this is a little walk, this is nothing. We're used to walking for days from the rural Andes to get to the center of Quito."

These early seeds of resistance, which firmly located the debtor within a particular politicized terrain, are thus embedded within a genealogy of struggle against oppression. The repertoires of resistance that are now taken for granted developed out of very specific spatial conditions that imbricated past contestations with more recent struggles for visibility and legitimation. Intimate, highly personal histories of migration contributed to an innate understanding of the world that transcended civil death, inscribing personal economic ruin within a landscape of coercion, persuasion, and fraud. By dismissing shame and guilt, early Ecuadorian organizers developed strategies that would fundamentally alter policy and politics.

In the annals of contemporary Spanish social struggles and movements, however, this immigrant history goes untold. Instead, narratives point to the activism of the right to housing movement in Barcelona, led by Ada Colau, as the genesis for today's housing struggles. Indeed, the PAH was founded in Barcelona in 2009; two years later the various groups that had been collaborating in Madrid against foreclosures and evictions would decide to become the PAH Madrid. Colau would remain the public face of the movement until she abandoned her role as spokesperson in 2014 in order to move into electoral politics. Incredibly well spoken, she has appeared throughout the world as an advocate for the movement and the broader right to housing, even while she herself has never had a mortgage. Compared to Aida, Ada was an easily digestible, media-friendly face to present to the public. Her role as spokesperson signaled a shift in the social diagnosis of the crisis broadly and the mortgage problem more specifically.

Who speaks? Who has authority? How to maintain agency in the face of oppression? Such questions remain central to both the PAH's development and social movements more generally. The subsequent efflorescence of action and contestation is defined in part by the elaboration of new forms of inclusive politics, in which once marginal voices have found prominence and power. Yet these tendencies to silence, erase, and disrupt continue to haunt even the most progressive movements as they fight to define their tactics and meanings. As I describe in the next chapter, the tactics of resistance first elaborated in immigrant spaces in San Blas and Ciudad Lineal, in the CONADEE headquarters on Hermanos Garcia Noblejas, have resonated intensely with the public at large. Thus in the collapse of homeownership, born out of ideas of integration and inclusion, immigrants managed to carve out spaces in civil society in which they have garnered broad support and shifted popular consensus.

Finally, this history of death and disobedience demands we confront the nature of the latter and its availability to the public at large. Most defaulters went quietly into the night. For those people, civil death is absolute, without transcendence. The success of early Andean activism displays the importance of strong community leaders who can act as conduits for the rage, fear, and anxiety of everyday citizens. It also insists on the role of associational life as a means of establishing ties and building bridges throughout civil society. Ultimately, too, it demonstrates how activism begets more activism, even in wildly different times and places. Fortress Europe, despite its allusions to modernity, progress, and cosmopolitanism, did not guarantee rights, recognition, or even a much-improved quality of life. Nor did it eliminate activism and popular education. Experiencing and observing vulnerability and suffering within their community, people like Aida and Eduardo resorted to the one tool they knew to be proven within their arsenal. Dissent was there, immediate and available.

7   Waking the Civil Dead

As the Spanish crisis deepened and lengthened from the late aughts into the early 2010s, more everyday people experienced its effects. While immigrants were the first to feel the crisis, soon native working-class laborers lost their jobs, while members of the middle class saw their wages slashed and hours shortened. The central state, under the purview of the Socialist Party, made increasingly large cuts to public programs while also passing policy that made it easier to carry out evictions. Young people, fresh from university, couldn't even find internships. As precarity spread, so too did the threat of eviction. The gaping maw of the crisis was all encompassing.

By 2011 the city had lived through almost four years of crisis, and it was beginning to show the effects of disinvestment and slashed municipal budgets. Ghostly half-built ruins marked its peripheral neighborhoods, while vast amounts of housing stock went empty. Homeless people were now a constant presence haunting the center, where they often took up positions under the elegant arches of the Plaza Mayor for their nightly rest. The municipal, regional, and national governments did little to ease the pain of everyday urbanites. Instead, European mandates on austerity dictated all aspects of policy, resulting in ever-greater poverty. In response to the precarious urban landscapes, thousands of people took to the streets one morning in May, converging in the Puerta del Sol, Madrid's central plaza.

While 15M—named after the date of its first massive protest on May 15, 2011—would go on to elaborate a series of demands, its chief rallying cry was that of *indignación*.[1] This emotion was directed at political parties and the government, the financial system, the deepening economic crisis, and the increasing precarity of all areas of everyday life. After a month-long occupation, outrage was then channeled into myriad projects. The sudden politicization of thousands of people gave rise to a rich ecology of assemblies, platforms, experimental collectives, and newly squatted social centers. It also fed into a global repertoire of protests that connected—via technology, ambulant activists, and popular imagination—discrete sites in the degraded centers of Madrid or Barcelona with spatial counterparts in Cairo's Tahrir Square, New York's Zucotti Park, and Istanbul's Gezi Park. Those who took to the streets often defied unifying categories: young and old, the professional and working classes, the institutional left and unruly anarchists all came together in the space of the square.

Housing was a central concern to many who came to and stayed in the square. Wandering around the makeshift village of pallets and tarpaulins in June 2011, I saw numerous signs demanding the right to housing and denouncing the specter of debt as it threatened thousands of households. As shown in the last chapter, this moment provided healthy fuel for the PAH Madrid, which soon saw its numbers increase exponentially. This convergence led to a flourishing social movement that has transformed the relation between the city and its citizens. What has been remarkable about the PAH in relation to other social movements in Spain is the enduring diversity of its participants. The marriage of immigrant activism, traditional working-class politics, and a radical politics of *indignación* has encouraged a proliferation of tactics that in turn draw multiple publics into the folds of this movement. But the PAH also confronts the many sides of the problem of mortgages and evictions, including debt, the right to housing, and the fraud and corruption of the financial system. To unmake a hegemonic system activists must attack from all sides.

The PAH Madrid transformed homeownership into a potent terrain for activism and new networks of solidarity. Because homeownership brings together myriad systems, concerns, and everyday sensibilities, it can become an important site for social struggles that advance radical causes. Its financial dimensions, attachments to forms of state violence, and entanglements with justice and the law mean it can dispossess people. Those same facets, however, mean it can also be contested and unmade. As a regime for dispossession, homeownership paradoxically opens generative spaces for resistance and disobedience. In the case of Spain, immigrants were key in articulating not only the problem of evictions and a housing system that gave rise to such predation, but also in constructing a robust arsenal of resistance. The struggle against homeowner-ship provided a vehicle both to contest the system and offer robust alterna-tives to logics of producing and dwelling in the city. Finally, while the PAH responded to the devastation wrought by homeownership, it gave people back a different kind of ownership: that of their own lives and destinies. If *muerte civil* transferred possession of the self into the hands of economic ruin, civil disobe-dience provided avenues for the civil dead to reclaim themselves.

Assembling the Affected

In Madrid much of the public at large ignored the issue of immigrants experi-encing foreclosure. While they found sustenance, support, and even physical space from the FRAVM, the mortgage problem continued to be peripheral de-spite the early marriage between grassroots organizing and more institutional-ized activism. In interviews with Ecuadorian organizers whose early efforts in 2008–10 went largely ignored, they reveal how they welcomed any support—institutional or otherwise—if it would help to redress the rampant vulnerability their community faced. Having experienced numerous exclusions within civic arenas of leisure and work, activists could not rely on popular organizing alone: no one listened to the agitation of a few thousand Ecuadorian immigrants when they took to the streets to protest in the late aughts. Institutional support allowed them a means to build ties. Furthermore, existing housing movements in the city shunned them; Eduardo described meeting with squatting activists, in which the radical *okupas* accused them of perpetuating the capitalist system because their goal was to maintain their status as homeowners. Yet, as Eduardo made clear to me throughout my fieldwork, immigrant agitation and investi-gation sought fundamentally to confront and dismantle the existing capitalist order. Their struggle placed homeownership within a larger landscape of ac-cumulation by dispossession.

Yet Ecuadorians were not alone as early victims of the crisis. In urban spaces throughout the peninsula, families were beginning to feel the crush of economic decline. Many working-class towns throughout Madrid's periphery began to suffer; as previous sites of industry and suburban expansion, their growth had been predicated on the spread of credit and debt through home-ownership during the democratic era. José Antonio is a gregarious man then in his late thirties, husband and family man with a long history of militancy in leftist causes. In particular, he has been an active member of the United Left

(IU—Izquierda Unida), where he had met Rafael Mayoral, the CONADEE lawyer. He had used his home to guarantee a loan to keep a business afloat (see chap. 3). Yet the debts soon became unbearable. He decided one morning, as the pile of unpaid bills grew, that he would no longer pay the balance on his mortgage. He was outraged the bank was demanding repayment when he had to give his workers severance as the business collapsed. He related to me late one wintery afternoon, as we sat in the local offices for the IU in the center of Madrid: "My case is one of conscience. I went down to the bank and said, 'I'm not gonna pay my mortgage anymore.' The banker says, 'But there's money in your current account!' I tell him, 'Well, give me the money and then I will cease to pay the mortgage!' He said, 'You can't do that to me.' To which I respond, 'I can! I can!'" A resident of a small working-class town at the very edge of Madrid's periphery, he soon made contacts with others in a similar predicament.

José Antonio's militancy in the United Left introduced him to José Coy. A large, middle-aged bear of a man, Coy lived in Murcía, on Spain's southern coastline. Faced with eviction and thus a lifetime of debt, Coy began an itinerant journey throughout the country in an attempt to publicize his issue and gain support. In José Antonio's retelling, Coy traveled through the country with little more than one shirt and a pair of pants, hardly any money to his name, relying on the kindness of contacts and friends. He arrived in Meco, another small town in the far-flung outer reaches of the *madrileño* periphery, where he told his story to José Antonio. Like Coy, José Antonio is a large personality; a massive smile usually bisects his face. He often refuses to be quiet, even in the middle of an assembly. His early activism in what would become the PAH was crucial, serving as link between the concerns of the unemployed working class and the Ecuadorian activism of the CONADEE, through his relationship with Rafael Mayoral. Such coincidences of people, place, and time, like strangers on a train, have the capacity to set off a chain of events that can prove transformative.

Traditions of working-class activism inflect these contemporary events. Coy and José Antonio (in addition to Nacho Murgui and staff members at the FRAVM) have long histories as militant organizers. I once asked Murgui when he became an activist. He looked at me skeptically and began telling me about an action he had organized at nine years old with other children in his neighborhood. For him there was no onset of his activism; it was imbued in his sense of self, inherited from an earlier generation that had sought to collectivize their struggles during the neighborhood movements. The ability to organize was once a privilege denied under Franco, and so leftist worked clandestinely to imagine a more radical future. That institutional and historical memory has translated into militancy among portions of the working class. As we see in Aida's trajectory, urban histories, tied to situated questions of place and politics contribute to the making of contemporary activist repertoires and engagement.[2] The PAH's birth in Madrid was predicated on an early alliance between immigrant communities and working-class activism. Within a convergence that took place between disparate groups that sometimes make for uneasy bedfellows, what was at stake was maintaining one's home, preventing complete financial disaster, and finally denouncing the political economy that had conspired to produce such ruin. The direct and early confrontation with the ties that bound together the state and the financial industry was key in elaborating strategies of action that might untangle the deleterious effects of this complicated web. Furthermore, the circulation of people and ideas allowed this political project to gain momentum. By meeting face to face, Aida, Eduardo, José Antonio, and Coy, for example, could not only share their stories but also brainstorm lines of action. In early 2011 the PAH Madrid was born, uniting various activist trajectories into one common whole.

The early immigrant techniques of activism and resistance elaborated during the first terrifying days of the crisis became potent means of building alliances and spreading solidarity. In particular, the assembly became a space to wake the civil dead. The open assembly was a tactic that had originated in the efforts of the CONADEE as a means of sharing information, but it soon became the key site for both the convergence and the construction of solidarity among diverse populations. For most of 2013 and 2014, the PAH held its assemblies in the Centro Social Seco, a squatted social center that tended to the needs of the working-class Adelfas and Puente de Vallecas neighborhoods. It emerged out of neighborhood struggles in the late 1980s and 1990s. Wedged into the end of a narrow street that runs along the M30, the building showed wear and tear, its large rooms sparse save for rows of plastic chairs. There was always a sense of going to some outer limit during the journey to Seco. To get there, I would either take a bus and walk along a tributary of the M30 highway and then through a barren park or take the metro and then traverse streets of low buildings, devoid of the lush foliage of the nearby Pacifico neighborhood. I would get to Seco, which occupied the far corner of the Adelfas neighborhood, abutting the barren park, only to be confronted by sociability and liveliness in contrast to my journey thus far. People milled about on the street outside, smoking hand-rolled cigarettes and gossiping, attempting to capture the attention of one of the lawyers, or perhaps talking to someone from the media. The informal assembly outside—a site of chatter and laughter, skirmishes and tears—presaged the general meetings that would go on in the dark basement of Seco, one large space into which dozens of people would crowd.

> I went on a Wednesday. There were a lot of people, chaos. I thought it was going to be a personalized interview. A lot of foreigners.
> —Sofia, Afectada, Spaniard.

Within Seco, the sense of madness and mayhem upon descending the staircase was overwhelming. All interlocutors describe their initial attendance at a general assembly as consumed by chaos. Perhaps expecting an orderly site of counsel and support, instead they found a sea of people, each with a similar problem to their own. No one greets you or asks your name as you descend the staircase. You must simply listen as people tell their tales, ask for help, offer advice, and share their victories. The press of bodies around you is incredibly diverse: Ecuadorians, Senegalese, Romanians, Bulgarians, Spaniards, and Moroccans sit and stand throughout the space, at times engaging in hushed conversations at the edge of the scrum and cry. The assembly never starts on time; those tasked with its moderation are also chattering at the front, determining who will take on which part of the evening. Others straggle in late. Some cry with anxiety, clutching an eviction order in their hands. They are whisked away to speak to a member of *acogida,* the team of sociologists, psychologists, and social workers that administers to those urgent cases that need immediate attention. This chaotic space, however, bears some of the legacy of the Indigenous movement, which also encouraged spaces of learning by doing. Here one might find education in the same moment as action and resistance. Collective empowerment and the accrual of knowledge act symbiotically.

The frenzy of this space, however, insists on the importance of constant activity and experimentation. As soon as a newcomer enters the space of the collective, she is assaulted with the message that she alone must act if she wants help. The collective is not a charity, but rather a site for exchange in which activity is paramount where *afectadas* practice a "politics of possibility."[3] The chaotic space of the assembly is evidence of this philosophy: the movement of people, the chatter of conversations, the comings and goings, the interruptions, all impress on the observer a sense of active doing rather than passive reception. As people share their stories, make connections, and talk strategy, the effect can be overwhelming. But it also offers a microcosm of the PAH's repertoire, which involves agitation and constant engagement throughout a plurality of arenas. To be heard, to take part, the individual must acclimate to this riotous environment to cut through the chaos.

For native Spaniards seeking help in the early days of the PAH Madrid, entrance into the assembly was at times jarring. Spanish *afectada* interlocutors almost uniformly described the shock of the unfamiliar, as they entered a room full of people quite different from themselves. The first impression was to feel alien, estranged from those around them who—despite their migratory histories and official documentation—had the same problem. That entry into the assembly then becomes an important moment of confrontation. This confrontation is not between assembly and *afectada,* but rather between the *afectada* and her deep-seated prejudices. Joséfina, a middle-aged bohemian, entered a hot, stuffy room full of hundreds of immigrants and immediately fled, because "it's that little [social] education you have. That you're Spanish, with a degree. I went home with those prejudices. [This was] a situation for immigrants who had worked construction."

Listening to testimonies laden with anguish, however, forces people to realize their commonalities. During Iñaki's first visit, he had expected legal advice and counseling. Instead, he found an "avalanche" of people. He was the only Spaniard, which made him feel isolated: "So many foreigners. You think, what's up, this doesn't happen to Spaniards? Or rather native Spaniards? This doesn't happen to them? You feel kind of isolated. However, I saw that even though I didn't find my place there, within all that disorganization, it was the only option I had." He listened to the testimonies people gave that day and found it remarkable how similar they were to his own. Similarly, Elena told me how she asked for the "native section" upon her entrance into the PAH, at which point someone turned to her and said, "Don't worry, you're at home right here." Within such a phrase, there is an insistence on egalitarianism and tolerance. The assembly is a shared home for all those suffering through this predicament, regardless of race or previous class status. But it's also a demand for the newcomer to recognize that her home is here, amidst the chaos and diversity, besides other people who might appear different.

In this milieu of chaotic encounter, the personal testimony is a key device. Whoever is facilitating an assembly begins the evening with her own testimony, revealing how she is affected by mortgages and at what point she finds herself within foreclosure proceedings. If she has won the battle against her bank, then she is held up as evidence of the effectiveness of social struggle. Her testimony thus serves as example for the public at large: she can now speak knowledgeably about her situation. Often, too, she might be an immigrant, thus revealing immigrants to be equals and even examples within this struggle. Anyone within the public who wants help from the PAH must tell her story in front of the assembly. Often these are tortured narratives that take the public through many years of financial and domestic life. But it also helps the individual gain mastery over her own situation. If this was once a technique to attempt to understand the extent of mortgage-related fraud, now it is also a means of empowerment, as people gain mastery of their own financial histories. These testimonies, often many during the course of the assembly, also reveal to others how a problem once understood as individual is actually collective.

Within the testimony and the space of the assembly, we see the convergence of a variety of different practices and traditions. The assembly is obviously a key device in many movements, particularly during our age of austerity and outrage.[4] But we can perhaps apprehend a novel marriage of several lineages. There are traces here of Indigenous strategies that insist on sharing knowledge and resources. Traditions of the *minga,* for example, didn't impose the same boundaries between public and private: if one family was experiencing hardship, it was incumbent upon the community to assist in service to the collective. In the space of the assembly, what was once guarded as private now becomes shared, exposed, but also ordered, made legible, and thus actionable. But we also see the influence of the city's autonomous and feminist struggles. The site of the assembly, Centro Social Seco, was created through previous struggles for anticapitalist space in an increasingly capitalist city, as neighborhood youth activists in the Retiro area demanded sites of sociality and exchange.[5] Their generation had emerged out of the bleak struggles of the early 1980s, when the city was ravaged by heroin, to demand alternative forms of social activity and insist on the importance of the neighborhood. Within autonomous, anticapitalist struggles, the assembly has been the key site for decision-making through consensus.[6] Meanwhile, against some of the masculinist tendencies of radical urban activism, the city's potent feminist movement had fought to move beyond recognition toward an ethos of care, evident in the work of *acogida.*[7]

We can also bear witness to the influence of feminist traditions in the insistence on the testimony as a means of establishing commonalities upon which to build action and mutual support. Joséfina, for example, found listening to people's narratives a means by which she could relate to a movement she initially dismissed as immigrant: "[The next] time I went by myself. I started to listen to the stories. I start to realize that their anxieties are my anxieties. A house, a mortgage, children. In the background their problem is my problem, and it doesn't matter if they're from Senegal, Chile, Ecuador." In her retelling, these stories form the necessary crude material that allowed her to see beyond race and class. As an upper-middle-class woman who had come of age in the *Movida*—the exuberant and profane cultural movement that emerged after Franco's death—she was tolerant and progressive. Yet her politics worked in abstraction but not in substance: when confronted with a situation in which she was called upon to recognize commonality in the face of difference, she literally fled. It took listening to these voices, on surface so different from her own, for her to recognize a tolerance and mutuality that went beyond cosmopolitan ideals of hip egalitarianism.

The testimony is also an opportunity to release emotion. The airing of internal anguish is an important component in translating shame and fear into action and resistance. Fear and sadness can consume and demobilize, devouring the *afectada's* mental and emotional life, banishing her to the isolation of civil death. Thus, in the space of the assembly certain devices attempt to channel that fear and sorrow into indignation and anger. At the start of every assembly, someone galvanizes the crowd through the sermon of "This is not a crisis, this is a scam!" In reimagining the terms of this political economic reality, *afectadas* can begin to externalize their emotions, directing them not inward to their own perceived deficiencies, but outward, toward the cracks and faults in the system. Betsy described her early days in the PAH: "Suddenly I no longer felt that guilt. They had defrauded me. I had that strength. I feel good with myself. I'm gonna fight until the end." Joining the space of the assembly, she transformed her guilt and shame into anger, finding strength in the process. We see in her words, moreover, how anger and indignation can serve as impetus for action. She moves easily from discussing her internal sense of self, which she has rid of shame, into her will to fight. Heightened emotions thus become productive fuel for future action.

Emotion is a means, too, of building solidarity. Through the translation of sorrow and fear into anger and action, members of the collective find a common enemy. This identification of a commonality allows for people from wildly different backgrounds to make alliances. The sharing of emotion, the *desahogo* (literally, an un-drowning, e.g., alleviation), also allows people to become enmeshed in each other's lives in unexpected ways. I went several times to the

Empowerment and Mutual Aid Workshop, a kind of group counseling session. Over the course of two or three hours, we shared the hidden details of our lives, in part simply because we had no other outlet to release these feelings. As a young single person living far from home, I too experienced bouts of isolation and loneliness, not uncommon to the researcher during fieldwork in a foreign place. We shared strategies for combatting such feelings. Despite the distinct origins of our emotions, I could recognize some part of the experience others were going through. This exchange of emotion made us suddenly intimate co-conspirators and allies. The raw display of emotion allowed empathy to be released as we sat in a circle in the light of the early spring sunshine those Sundays. There we recognized a common vocabulary that transcended status or situation.

> He repeated the mantra of the "estafa," as if by endless repetition the shame and fear would dissipate, replaced with indignation and action. . . . Various afectados [then] presented their cases. Each one got up to tell their tales of woe to the assembly.
> —Fieldnotes. March 3, 2013

> I've found great friends there. Who I never would have spoken to in the outside world. Neither to Maria nor Iñaki. Because we are different and we are different worlds. But it turns out that there is a place of encounter where you discover other people.
> —Joséfina. *Afectada*. Activist.

Slowly these encounters and exchanges crafted new social ties and rhythms of solidarity. When I met Iñaki for the first time, we were in a large Chinese restaurant in a heavily Ecuadorian and Peruvian neighborhood down the block from the CONADEE. I had gone with three women from the PAH, two Spaniards and an Ecuadorian. There we met several other women active in the collective, Ecuadorians and Peruvians. Iñaki joined us at some point in the meal, the lone male at a table full of women gossiping easily of both activism and romance. This lunch continues to occupy a bright spot in my memories of fieldwork, as an unexpected moment of convergence. We were on Hermanos Garcia Noblejas, a street I had never been to, in a neighborhood that was foreign to me. As I sat at a table with women who ranged from dewy-eyed recently minted graduates to graying retirees, we chattered on like old friends. That afternoon was illustrative of the new friendships that have emerged within the space of the collective, in addition to the openness with which these *afectada*-activists receive newcomers.

Throughout my interviews, people described to me the ways in which participation and activity had broadened their horizons in ways they never imagined possible, mostly through the creation of new, unexpected friendships. There emerged an alternative social network based on care, mutual support, empowerment, and relationality that crossed traditional lines of race, class, and gender. During my fieldwork, it was impossible to feel alone. At the end of a morning session, for example, Margarita would turn to me and say, "If you have nothing to do, come with me." We'd take the metro to a meeting in a different part of town, stroll through the center browsing shops, or head to her house for a late lunch.

Over a year later, when I returned to Madrid for a short period of follow-up fieldwork during the summer of 2014, an *afectada*'s husband died of a heart attack in the middle of the night. That afternoon, I had been with Begoña, the *afectada,* and a host of others after a lengthy meeting. In the warm gloaming of a summer evening, we sat around plastic tables outside the local watering hole near Seco, sipping cold white wine and mini bottles of beer. Several hours later, Begoña's husband was dead. The next day, as the news spread over email and WhatsApp, people began to make their way to the crematorium in Carabanchel. Plagued by a torrential early summer rain, I made my way up the hill with Sofia and Alonso, Carlota and Margarita. Others joined as we struggled up the muddy driveway to the cool marble and glass of the crematorium, where we shivered in wet clothes. People spilled out the room designated for Begoña's family; many were familiar faces from the PAH, all offering warm embraces of condolence to the grieving widow.

Solidarity here is defined by showing up, of bearing witness to others' triumphs and misfortunes, of constantly providing support wherever it is required. This ontology is reflected in Mabel's constant activity. She said to me, "I try to help other people." She went on, "I feel compelled" because there are so many families going through horrible situations. She makes multiple trips across Madrid every day: in the northern courts, she accompanies someone at a hearing, only to dash to a suburban bank branch to help counsel an *afectada* as she attempts to negotiate the terms of her mortgage. Similarly, in defining the PAH, Joséfina illustrates this idea of solidarity as active participation, as a physical exercise of showing up. She stated: "I know that if tomorrow Iñaki needs me, I'll be there, the same as Iñaki for me." Such a description privileges

personal relationships and the needs of others above one's own wants and desires. This "showing up" can often be uncomfortable, thankless, requiring endless movement from one point of the city to the next. Yet it is the crude material that defines a radical politics of solidarity above and beyond sentiments of
empathy and care.

Years later when Aida described to me the *minga,* I could see clearly how it
translated to a particular ethos that marked the PAH, where life and its pleasures and problems are to be shared. She was describing rural life in the high
plains of the Andes, among very modest communities. That reality seemed
so far removed from urban Spain, with its insistence on endless speculation,
concrete utopias, and fantasies of modernity. The modest communities here
were members of the hollowed-out working class, the descendants of people
who also once came from rural stock. They had their own traditions of organizing, sharing, and solidarity. Austerity and crisis brought together disparate traditions, from different parts of the globe and emerging out of diverse
communities—Indigenous, anti-Francoist, labor unions, feminist struggles,
anticapitalism, and radical autonomous politics—to produce new forms of collective action.

The Plural Imagination

While the assembly became the central space to build solidarity within the
PAH, the collective engaged in a number of techniques to effect further political
change and garner outside support from the public. When the PAH first began
to attract national attention in 2011, news media and the public were entranced
by the spectacle of activities intended to stop evictions—the "*stop desahucio.*"
This action, physically stopping an eviction, would regularly draw scores of activists to defend the doorways of modest homes in mostly working-class neighborhoods across Spain. While this was the most ferocious and visible line of
action, it was accompanied by a series of other tactics of delay and blockage.

Its eclectic repertoire combines a number of different tactics that seek both
spectacular disobedience and more subtle negotiation. This exhaustive arsenal recalls other successful movements, including Indigenous organizing in
South America. In particular, its ability to marry grassroots street activism with
a focus on electoral politics and official spheres of justice recalls many of the
techniques that characterized that earlier movement. Both movements, as with
many successful popular mobilization, seek to effect change within different

fronts. As I argue later on, however, the specific legal imaginary that inflects much of the PAH's practices is a direct legacy of Indigenous organizing.

Blocking Evictions and Reclaiming Homes: The Radical Imagination

Blocking an eviction is the hallmark of the PAH. Here activists seek to create a physical barrier around the entrance of the dwelling in order to prevent the entrance of the judicial commission—deployed by the regional courts—and the police. While the commission is the official entity charged with dispossession, the police perform the physical labor of removal. In depicting these urban events, the media grew sympathy for the PAH's cause. As one activist interlocutor related to me, blocked evictions were potent as they revealed transversal themes—that of house and home—that transcend race, class, or political affiliation. Further, the action—made visible in the media, on Facebook and Twitter—reveals in stark detail the collusion between state power and the financial system. Here state entities in the form of the police and the courts are called upon to do the bidding of the banks in carrying out dispossession.[8] In doing so, moreover, blocking an eviction unveils the inherent violence of both institutions.

The act translates understandings of the public nature of private ruin into action. Broadcast on television and social media, blocking an eviction is extremely public, with consequences that extend beyond the confines of the *hogar* (hearth and home). It demands society see foreclosure and eviction as social epidemic rather than the result of personal irresponsibility and poor judgment. Here the collective works together to save one household, revealing the symbiosis between community and individual as mutually constitutive. Second, it is a visible insistence on the primacy of a home's use value. Blocking an eviction insists that the right to housing supersedes the right to property—by the time of the eviction, the bank is proprietor. In a country littered with empty housing, these acts draw attention to the contradictions of that system, arguing for the social function of housing above and beyond its use as a tool for the perpetuation of capitalist economies. Finally, this act of insurgency rejects the prevailing institutional logic of the government and the judiciary. In physically preventing egress to the police, activists confront a system they view as illegitimate.

The politics of both refusal and spectacular disobedience animates the practice of home reclamation, which also seeks to dismantle further the traditional political economy of housing. Here the PAH's *Obra Social* seizes space for families that have been evicted. This practice has been particularly potent in Catalonia and often consists of a mass occupation of an abandoned building. Many of these buildings were the physical remains of the bubble, unfinished speculative shells that might, in the eyes of activists, be made to work to serve social ends. Like a *stop desahucio,* home reclamation involves careful planning and strategizing in addition to daring acts of physical labor. Often the occupation is planned for an extended period of time. Groups are careful to identify buildings that belong either to a bank or to a major developer. Thus, occupying a building draws similar attention to the inequity of the Spanish housing system, while also insisting on the primacy of use value. Reclamation, too, is an act of refusal, as it confronts decades of housing policy that has privileged access to ownership over occupation and habitability. Occupation actions demand these structures be removed from the marketplace of opaque transactions and securitization, the "bad bank," and the bailout of industry over the suffering of everyday urban dwellers.[9]

Both blocking an eviction and reclaiming homes are acts of spectacular disavowal. For young, often male activists, stopping an eviction is an experience in which they find voice and power. While the families they defend might be of far different demographic backgrounds, their experience of loss is one to which they can relate. For the young generation that took to the streets in May 2011, a future of comfort and upward mobility had also experienced foreclosure. Institutions—the state, the university—had promised a life better than that of the previous generation. Crisis revealed such promises to be lies, and those institutions quickly lost their legitimacy. Thus both eviction and reclamation become sites in which activists can express their disgust with the extant demands of the contemporary political economy. Here there is the promise to make anew a system of cohabitation outside and against dominant models, autonomous from the predations of state and financial power, akin to David Graeber's celebrated "radical imagination."[10] These actions are done in opposition to existing frameworks and, in the case of squatting, seek to create alternatives autonomous from dominant systems of dwelling in the city. A similar imagination animates the work of the *Obra Social,* which attempts to not only rehouse families but also remove physical units from the existing logics of the market and the city.

There are, however, limitations to this form of disobedience. While spectacular in their physicality and often, too, their brutality, most *stop desahucios* actions provide only a temporary solution for the household, usually allowing for some extra time before the court issues another order of eviction. The family must then live in legal limbo. Similarly, many occupied dwellings are temporary shelters as, once detected, authorities pursue legal means to remove new inhabitants. Further, these actions do little to redress the issue of debt, engaging only with the question of one's right to shelter. Both acts create visibility for the problem of evictions and precarious housing, but don't provide a comprehensive solution. Spectacle, while shedding light on the structural and physical violence of the Spanish property system, also does little to address the larger political economic situation, as it can only deal with one case at a time. While they operate in opposition to the dominant modes of dwelling in and creating the city, calling out those modes as corrupt, they do not in themselves dismantle hegemonic systems of housing and urbanism. In addition, they are enervating experiences that take a toll on the bodies and psyches of activists and *afectadas,* even putting those bodies directly in harm's way. Police brutality and the risk of arrest are ever-present threats during these actions.

Who can participate in the spectacular politics of refusal? Indeed, it is not an option open for all. Both blocking an eviction and the occupation of a building require physical labor, flexible schedules, and individual daring. Questions of age, gender and domestic responsibilities, employment circumstances, and personal preference can prevent participation. As someone who suffers from a lifetime of sleep issues, I was hesitant to stay overnight with a household to await the judicial commission's early morning arrival, a common practice in stopping evictions. If I had children or aging parents at home, my participation would also be precluded. Sometimes there is also fear of entanglements with the law. For immigrants worried about their legal status in Spain, there was always the question of any penalties that might befall them for participating in such acts. In one case, a Congolese family resisted advice of some activists to wait until the date of the eviction to stage a *stop desahucio.* As undocumented immigrants, they were afraid that route would only lead to internment and potentially deportation. Finally, while both blocking an eviction and occupying homes insist in their bravado on an elusive right to housing, neither dismantles the financial architecture that undergirded this landscape of crisis.

"This Bank Defrauds People": The Economic Imagination
While activists engage in blocking evictions and occupying homes to demand the right to housing, the PAH also confronts the financial system. Central to its arsenal of resistance has been the constant, direct engagement with banks, either through civil negotiations or spectacular disruption. Confronting the

financial system is a particular tactic that combines both an aggressive politics of resistance and a more accommodating strategy of bureaucratic fatigue.

In that latter paradigm, *afectadas* doggedly pursue their goals through bureaucratic means. The path toward saving a home from eviction is paved in paperwork. Here individuals make regular trips to the bank and the courts to file pieces of paper, small petitions to suspend the foreclosure or date of eviction. These documents might contain myriad information, from one's health status to current economic woes to impact statements from social workers and counselors. Often the public testimony is transcribed and included as further evidence of harm. The logic behind this strategy is twofold. While some of it is born out of the *afectada's* own desperation to save her home, it is also motivated by a desire to inundate the banks with paperwork as a kind of just desserts. During the process of foreclosure, those same banks dump information upon their clients, in addition to overwhelming them with various forms of contact: late-night phone calls and personal visits complement unending streams of paper, culminating in the thick stack of the *tocho*. This deluge is but an extension of the initial experience of taking out a loan, during which the banks would oversaturate their clients with reams of paperwork, each documenting a different requirement, such as life insurance, death insurance, repatriation insurance, and mandatory credit and debit cards. Interlocutors describe the minor thrill of subjecting their banks to a similar kind of deluge, which they are required by law to address. Thus this tactic seeks not only to allow for someone to avoid eviction, but also for her to exact a kind of bureaucratic revenge.

There is also a process of learning that takes place in these financial itineraries. In endless trips between one's home, the bank, and the courts, *afectadas* encounter the everyday aspects of large multinational financial institutions. Navigating financial mazes can be highly chaotic and confusing, as Spanish banks, often in partner with the state, have undergone constant restructuring. With restructuring after public bailouts, some banks have ceased to exist, others have been absorbed or collapsed into larger entities, some have merged, and some have been parceled off to other parties. With the creation of the "bad bank" for toxic assets, moreover, some people have found their foreclosed home has been passed on to this other institution. Finally, as banks securitized mortgages and sold off debt, many people now have to fight debts that have been passed on to international third parties, including Blackstone. Thus people encounter a tangled, increasingly intricate web of transactions, securitizations, and contemporary global financial practices. These multiple trips, demands, clarifications, and activist narratives seek to untangle this web to make legible a complex financial landscape, revealing the constitutive pieces to this intricate puzzle.

While these small acts of negotiation attempt to force the bank to agree to activist demands through micro-interventions, other more spectacular actions seek disruption. A creative array of activity falls under this latter rubric, with the explicit goal of inconveniencing financial institutions. For example, various groups of *afectadas* have occupied a bank office for the morning, demanding to speak to the director and holding an impromptu assembly. Other actions might include "blocking" a bank. In June 2014 I went with a group in Barcelona to a local branch of Catalunya Caixa. Each of us entered individually with some absurd request: one woman wanted change for 100 euros entirely in one- and two-cent coins, while I asked inane questions about opening a bank account for foreigners. At a certain point, exasperated with our questions, the bank realized they were subject to a targeted action, and shut the gate dividing the front door from the street. We remained outside until the bank closed at 2, having effectively prevented them from working for the morning. As we prepared to abandon the office for the afternoon, the security guard—thus far steadfastly opposed to our entrance—quietly whispered to one of the more vocal activists. He had been struggling to pay his mortgage and wanted to know his options. These more spectacular acts attempt to alter, albeit briefly, the standard operating procedures of the Spanish capitalist system. But they also, once again, publicize the cause, drawing others to the collective.

This tactic confronts what the anthropologist Hannah Appel has termed, in relation to Occupy Wall Street, the "economic imagination."[11] Examining the various economic practices of groups associated with OWS, Appel reveals how activists articulated new positions vis-à-vis finance and its institutions. Rather than feel helpless and hapless in the face of debt and the machinations of financial institutions, people found ways to act upon and penetrate systems usually rendered opaque and cloistered to everyday citizens. Similarly, in engaging with financial institutions, the PAH reimagines the terrain of possibility, crafting new tools to advance their claims. It rejects the notion of the bank as an impenetrable monolith, beholden only to the whims and expertise of bankers. Instead it is something to be acted upon, disrupted, and made to stand accountable for its actions. In doing so, the collective reveals such entities to be not behemoths of faceless authority, but rather porous with the potential to be confronted and subverted. This tactic renders the bank into an opponent, but one that is beholden to the demands of the client. It also sees in constant, minute, and unglamorous struggles the potential for political openings to advance a particular claim. It does so with the implicit threat that should the bank breach certain terms, spectacular disobedience—mass protest, occupation, blocking—is all but guaranteed.

Legislative Changes and the Institutional Imagination

Stopping evictions is a tactic that is concerned with the intimate confines of the domestic sphere, the city block, and the neighborhood. Meanwhile, agitation in the banks confronts the ways in which housing has been subjected to financialization and attempts disruption while also drawing attention to this cause. Such spectacular actions not only defend the privacy of the home, but also incite neighbors to participate in the struggle. By making a household's anguish visible, such actions implicate the surrounding area in these contestations. But the PAH also attempts to change policy through more technical means and institutional pressure/lobbying at the national scale.

Central to its broad support was the elaboration of a popular legislative initiative. By Spanish law, any group can force an initiative to go before the Spanish Congress, which then votes on whether it will be heard or not, prior to an approval vote. An *iniciativa legislativa popular* (ILP—popular legislative initiative) requires 500,000 signatures to be presented to Congress, which then decides whether it will invite speakers to defend positions, or veto the proposal altogether. Utilizing its national network of platforms, the PAH decided in 2012 to collect signatures for such a vote to go before the legislature. The proposal called for a moratorium on evictions, the introduction of *dación en pago*—debt forgiveness in exchange for surrender of the housing unit—and the creation of public housing stock.

While the goal was to substantively alter existing policy, the deployment of this practice of collecting signatures achieved several other ends that were critical in shifting public consensus. First of all, everyday encounters between activists and the broader nonactivist public served effectively to educate people on the evictions issue. The collective, working with other activist groups and leftist organizations, set up stands throughout public spaces in major Spanish cities. Activists also canvassed neighborhoods and attended events in the interest of informing the public and building support. Face-to-face discussions here allowed for a process of teaching and learning. Those members of PAH and 15M, some of them inexperienced in activism, developed sophisticated vocabularies for transmitting personal experiences of financial ruin, enunciating political messages that spread outward. Here individual stories of the devastation of foreclosure—economic loss compounded by familial discord, divorce, battles with depression, gendered violence, and terror at unknown futures—became powerful means to reveal the human cost of the crisis. These moments of encounter fostered empathy: passersby got a small but personal glimpse into the lived reality of foreclosure and eviction. The stories resonated in part because of the long shadow cast by the crisis. Even individuals who did not confront mortgage or housing problems had been touched by economic decline in some way, big or small, such as shrunk bank accounts, cut pensions, slashed wages, reduced hours, or forced early retirements. Crisis in its myriad forms has spread throughout society, provoking both vulnerability and greater sympathy for the struggle.

In Madrid this strategy was key in bringing together a diversity of activists. After over a month of occupation, the 15M movement decided to devolve efforts to the neighborhoods as a means of continuing its momentum. As a result, neighborhood assemblies formed to address the needs and conditions of their local communities. Assemblies met in squatted social centers, deepening and in some cases establishing links between anarchist squatters and their newly activated neighbors.[12] The tactic of devolving to the neighborhood speaks to Madrid's activist histories, as it seeks to emulate the struggles of the 1960s and '70s in which the neighborhood, and then the neighborhood association, became key loci to advance demands. The emergence of neighborhood assemblies reflects a reality in which the neighborhood is the de facto scale of political action and grassroots organizing. Local 15M assemblies addressed housing as one of the many issues facing their neighborhoods, and they worked symbiotically with the PAH Madrid to prevent evictions. When the campaign for the ILP began, the PAH Madrid and neighborhood assemblies collaborated on signature efforts. With intense links to their communities, these assemblies could reach additional publics. These efforts allowed for 15M groups and the PAH Madrid to mutually support one another, building bridges between the issue-based platform and the neighborhoods.

I would regularly attend assemblies in Tetuán, where I saw this dynamic firsthand. If a case of eviction came to the assembly, activists would send them to the PAH for legal aid and specific mortgage-related education and empowerment. Within the neighborhood, however, the 15M assembly would begin to gather support from the immediate community to leverage at the bank branch and ensure the family under threat of eviction had their immediate needs met.

Similarly, if a case of eviction in the Tetuán neighborhood passed through the PAH Madrid, activists would direct the *afectada* to also pursue aid within her local assembly. Through WhatsApp channels and Twitter, moreover, activists could easily connect new cases with sites of action and modes of struggle.

Meanwhile, at the national scale, the ILP effort allowed the PAH to build its network. The national PAH was forced to foster its channels of communication and organizational framework. Through online activity and periodic statewide meetings, the various local initiatives that made up the broader collective shared ideas, built trust, and developed further lines of action. Utilizing this arena, which connected local issues with national policy discussions, local PAH chapters could coordinate simultaneous actions that would reverberate within both urban space and statewide dialogues. These various networks of solidarity—both local and national, through online spaces and urban place—drew more activists into the PAH's fold. In February of 2013, as the ILP was to go before Congress, the PAH announced they had collected almost 1.5 million signatures—nearly a million more than required, far exceeding any other signature collection.

During the campaign for the ILP, as Congress awaited a vote on the proposal, the PAH adopted a new tactic, the *escrache*—a particular form of calling out persons in power—which has no real translation into English. Argentine activists, after the Dirty War, elaborated this method as a means of uncovering the military officials responsible for disappearances and deaths, who nonetheless went on to live peaceful lives.[13] Groups of activists would descend outside the house of the official to denounce to the community the presence of a war criminal within their midst. The PAH elected to use the *escrache* to call out politicians on the right who intended not to vote in favor of the ILP by going to their homes. The decision produced a particular "moral framing" that set up the conflict between activists and the state as one of antagonism.[14] I went to one of the first *escraches*. Activists, *afectadas*, lawyers, and others sympathetic to the cause gathered outside the Manuel Becerra metro stop in the posh Salamanca area. From there we marched southeast into the Fuente de Berro section of the neighborhood, where chic blocks of flats give way to single-family homes. We descended on the home of the then-vice president Soraya Sáenz de Santamaría. Police soon arrived, and many scattered. The tactic, since then, has been polemical, as many members of the media and public denounced the practice as infringing on people's privacy. But it also served to bring together radical acts of disobedience with the slow work of changing policy. It was done so, too, under the pretense that politicians had not respected the sanctity of the home for the scores of *afectadas* facing eviction. As such, they should be accorded the same disregard for divisions between their public roles and private lives.

Despite such struggles, the ILP was ultimately unsuccessful. While the initiative had the support of every other political party, the conservative party ultimately rejected the ILP in early April 2013, using its absolute majority. But its provisions maintained the broad support of the public: *El País* commissioned a survey that found 90 percent of readers agreed that borrowers should be offered loan forgiveness.[15] That support did not come naturally, but rather as a result of this constant agitation, which brought activist struggles, social concerns, and everyday lives into immediate proximity. Street organizing and political pressure acted symbiotically, shifting public opinion and building a network of outrage.

Here again emerges a particular imagination around the state and its institutions. In reflecting on the possibility for radical democracy and social justice, the philosopher Chantal Mouffe advocates for a combination of parliamentary and extraparliamentary struggles.[16] She imagines change to occur through engagement with both the oppositional politics of street protest and the mechanisms of elections and institutions of liberal democracy.[17] Similarly, the PAH identifies the local, regional, and national levels of the state as important targets for intervention. Operating within a fairly young democracy, the movement argues the Spanish state must work for and on behalf of its citizens. Such a logic is in contrast to some of the ideologies that animated 15M, whereby activists decried engagement with the state as a means of validating an institution that had long lost its legitimacy. Further, it reads the various layers of the state as under constant transformation through negotiation between various actors. Rather than reject entirely the current Spanish state, the PAH instead insists on calling out its various lacunae and silences. Here again we can see connections to the Indigenous movement in Ecuador. That former struggle sought not just to make visible the conditions of a segment of the population, but also to engage with and transform the state. The state, while a problematic entity, is also an important and singular nucleus of power.

Justice and the Legal Imagination

In addition to challenging the predominant housing system within the streets, the banks, and the legislature, the PAH set about using the space of the law as a terrain of contestation. Over the course of 2009–12, Ecuadorian activists found they could extend the date of eviction by filing appeals that automatically granted extensions. From that practice, they began to delve deeper into this tactic, filing numerous lawsuits with the courts. While often these suits would end in dismissal, doggedly pursuing this strategy slowly created political openings. First of all, with the imposition of austerity measures, the courts faced staffing shortages at a time when they were experiencing an unprecedented level of lawsuits related to speculation, fraud, and unpaid bills—the legal hangover of the economic boom. Thus filing a lawsuit might postpone the inevitable eviction simply because the documents would have to wind themselves slowly through the morass of the legal system.

More important, however, have been those suits that come before sympathetic judges. In such cases, individual lawsuits that address one particular aspect of the mortgage or contest some part of the eviction proceedings have had the good fortune to be assigned to a specific court. The most emblematic case of this type involved Mohamed Aziz, a Moroccan immigrant living in a small town in Catalunya.[18] After losing his house to the bank, Aziz filed a suit against the bank Catalunya Caixa in the Commercial Court #3 in Barcelona, arguing about the abusive terms of the mortgage. In the estimation of the lawyer, the mortgage was a bad faith contract: its terms essentially set the debtor up to fall behind on the payments. It was a mortgage designed to fail in the eyes of the court. The judge for Barcelona's Commercial Court referred the case to the Court of Justice of the European Union. He believed it was possible Spanish mortgage law did not fully comply with EU-wide directives on consumer protection in the realm of contracts. The European court agreed in March 2013, declaring the abusive clauses in most mortgages a violation of multinational policy edicts . The ruling in Aziz's case immediately affected the legal arena, as PAH lawyers worked to elaborate different kinds of statements to present to the courts that would document abusive clauses. Through such targeted, individual interventions, the collective has pushed back forcefully against the banks. With each new court judgment against the banks, the PAH has one more tool to advance their claims.

Similar to its economic imagination, the PAH here utilizes a specific legal imagination to advance its agenda in deliberate ways. In both cases, the law and the economy are realms that can be acted upon, contested, infiltrated, and made to work in activists and *afectadas'* favor. Relations between the everyday and what Calavita has termed "the legs of the law" are complicated in contemporary Spain. The law is rife with ambiguities, which proliferate in many cases as a means of obfuscation. Both ordinary people and the elite can display laissez faire attitudes toward matters of rules and regulations, and regularly exploit ambiguities with little fear of reprisal.[19] The law, in promoting gray areas and silences, thus allows for the proliferation of extralegal behavior, and "the state is a principal, conspicuous or inconspicuous, participant in the formation and functioning" of the informal.[20] At the same time, legal silences and absences have created new openings for social agitation and outside actors, which we can observe most clearly within the "historical memory" movement.[21] In that instance, Spain's transition to democracy encouraged a pact of silence and "forgetting" of the Franco era and its many crimes.[22] Yet international law insists on human rights and the investigation of such acts of historical violence. These tensions and contradictions between national and international law, cultural practice and experiences of grievous harm (in the case of both Fascist violence and contemporary housing inequities) can stymie and frustrate, but they also provide agile openings for enterprising individuals.[23] The anthropologist Lee Douglas writes: "this [legal] absence is a roadblock, but it is also quite generative."[24] Because the rules are contradictory, ambiguous, and difficult to follow, they can be challenged, called into question, or subjected to scrutiny to demand hard and fast definition. Furthermore, this rendering sees the law as scalar, operating through the national and then the international sphere to become a space of justice and the accordance of rights and recognition. Here the law might offer protection from the unduly punitive tentacles of the regional and national state, a tool made all the more powerful because it is fundamentally *of the state.* Using the state against itself could be a means of demonstrating these contradictions while demanding the law serve the interest of private individuals.

We can see the influence of early Andean activism within these tactics and their eclecticism. For that community, the struggle against eviction was not just a question of housing and shelter. Rather, it implicated that "essence of the capitalist system," in addition to the trenchant and long-standing question of human rights. Indeed, what was at stake was a struggle for justice after collusion between banks and the state had wrested many years of equity from a marginalized community. As such, this situation implicated the state, existing legal doctrine, and illegal practices targeted at a minority group. Just as Indigenous groups demanded protection under the law, so too did mortgaged Andean demand acknowledgment of grave injustice. Saving one's home was only one part of the issue; the other was legal reckoning of the wrongdoing perpetrated by the bank, which had conspired to wrest millions of euros from unsuspecting customers.

As many have noted with regard to Indigenous struggles in Ecuador, the path to rights and recognition was often forged through direct engagement with the state and its institutions.[25] In the wake of environmental destruction, for example, the courts were an important venue for restitution. Similarly, engaging directly with the mechanisms of electoral politics also afforded increased access and rights. The very terms of democratic political engagement—the courts, the legislature, and the presidency—became battlegrounds for the elaboration of strategies of resistance and change. Working outside and against this system, through a politics of withdrawal as favored by scholars such as Michael Hardt and Toni Negri, would have been counterproductive.[26] The entire basis of their struggle was legal and institutional recognition; street politics and spectacle alone could not accomplish that task.

Engaging with these state institutions can be deeply problematic. As anthropologist Audra Simpson has written about within several contexts of Indigeneity, such engagement implicitly confers legitimacy upon historical systems of oppression.[27] As she writes regarding the Australian court decision to recognize aboriginal claims to land, such instances only shore up lengthier narratives of belonging made possible through historical, biased impressions then turned into universal truths. Yet in the face of complete erasure, such tactics are singular tools for recognition.[28] Furthermore, institutions confer protection in ways that popular protest and refusal alone cannot. The deep and horizontal democracy as it is imagined within many contemporary social movements can often reproduce the very power imbalances they seek to unmake, particularly in regards to minority voices and struggles.[29] While imperfect arenas for change, institutions provide political openings unavailable elsewhere.[30]

Finally, the lessons of the Indigenous movement revealed how activism had to be promiscuous and eclectic. The stakes over environmental degradation and political erasure are incredibly high. Thus no nonviolent practice for resistance and restitution is out of bounds. Activists couldn't be ideologically wedded to one form of protest over another; in a situation that is literally life or death, such questions of ideology can become frivolous distractions from the real terms of the conversation. In the early days of the struggle over evictions, 15M activists faulted the PAH in Madrid for having collaborated with institutions such as the FRAVM, a traditional instrument of the left-wing parties in the city. The response from *afectadas* was sharp: theirs was too great a struggle to worry about party affiliations and questions of autonomy from institutions—they wanted justice however they might achieve it.

These various modes of activism, which encapsulate both anticapitalist spectacle and institutional engagement, became interdependent. Many *afectadas* recognize the important work of young activists not directly affected by housing precarity who nonetheless risk their physical safety to block an eviction. Yvette revealed how her activism works in concert with and is enabled by the radical acts of others: "Many activists give their bodies [to the struggle], there are a lot of people who have the solidarity to defend us. . . . I take to the streets because I am fed up, I am tired, and I take to the streets because I have the support of those activists." Such a statement reveals the symbiotic relationship between her activism and that of young people willing to literally use their bodies to fight this system. In interviews, lawyers for the collective uniformly argued for the mutual dependence of disruptive street politics and institutional agitation: their legal victories are made possible through the visibility that comes from protests, bank occupations, or blocking an eviction, a campaign that placed this issue into the public eye in the first place. Working through the streets, the courts, and the legislature has forced national consensus on housing to shift rapidly, in addition to fostering interdependence between those repertoires.

The PAH's diverse repertoires, moreover, remind us that homeownership is a system that relies on numerous others in order to "work." Rather than constitute an ur-model, property in land and real estate requires the law, finance, statecraft, and everyday sensibilities in order for it to function. These myriad systems are all implicated in its perpetuation, and thus must be confronted when tackling the question of homeownership's violent exclusions. Its everyday common sense, its "ruse of consent,"[31] are also necessary, as I detail in the final section below.

Against Dispossession

While Madrid's crisis begat novel forms of contestation and organizing, so too did it bring about physical changes and a new urbanism of devastation. The vast new neighborhoods at the periphery once promised domestic futures and untold wealth. Now, however, they were ghostly shells, some buildings largely empty while others went unfinished. There, wide boulevards led through a sparse forest of brick buildings toward nowhere. Occupancy rates could barely reach 50 percent. Planners' wager on 300,000 new units now appeared a cruel joke. A lacy corona of cranes marked the city's skyline, visual reminders of untold new ruins. The municipal and regional governments slashed spending in an effort to deal with their own mounting debts, which emerged in part out of their adventures in speculative housing development. Trash collected on city streets as garbage services were reduced. And everywhere one looked there was empty housing, either hollowed through foreclosure and eviction or permanently vacant, visual reminders of decadence and failed policy.

Many empty units passed into the hands of the "bad bank" SAREB, the holding cell for the Spanish financial system's toxic assets.[32] Relying on taxpayer money to prevent the massive failure of the banking industry, the *banco malo* received assets from a slew of entities, including from Bankia, a bank created out of the ruinous savings bank Caja Madrid, the single greatest purveyor of mortgages during the boom.[33] As individuals experienced foreclosure, many found that their homes had passed into the hands of an opaque institution that is also 45 percent public. Similarly, Bankia and other financial institutions received billions in public funds to keep the system afloat.[34] In this new landscape of financialization, the boundaries between domestic crisis and public ruin are increasingly blurred, and dispossession by the nexus of the state-backed real estate–financial complex is suddenly evident. The crude terms of this arrangement deem that people are allowed to fail while banks are not, and those banks relying on public funds continue to mercilessly evict ordinary citizens.[35] To exacerbate the cruel irony of this situation, moreover, the SAREB began to adjudicate pieces of its enormous pile to third parties, including the son of former president Aznar.[36] What seemed likely was a long process of accumulation by dispossession.[37]

If the explosive urbanism of the boom produced certain subjectivities, wants, and desires, so too does this urbanism of crisis. Consent for propertied systems of housing was conjured in part by the landscape of abundance. In the absence of abundance and the preponderance of indebted vulnerability, that consent has broken down. It was against this landscape of severe material lack, in addition to an emergent regime of accumulation by dispossession, that I noticed a qualitative shift. In late September 2013, I sat in a cramped office of the collective with a young woman, mother to three children aged thirteen, eleven, and seven, who had arrived with her mother in search of shelter. She was more than ready to squat in an empty unit as a solution. These two women chatted amiably with Joséfina, who had become a committed activist since her early forays into the PAH. She smoked furiously while perusing the real estate website of Banco Sabadell, a bank that now owned thousands of properties throughout Madrid, often as a result of foreclosure. Standing fallow, one such unit might serve as more than adequate for the needs of this young family. The website, moreover, placed great amounts of information at the visitor's disposal as a means of enticing clients who might help the bank offload its bloated portfolio. With very little sleuthing, one could discover which empty houses in a given neighborhood pertain to which banks, and whether they were empty because of foreclosure and eviction.

Many Spanish cities have a long, radical tradition of *okupación,* or political squatting; Madrid has its own robust tradition.[38] In contrast to *chabolismo,* which roughly refers to needs-based squatting practices mostly through land invasion, *okupación* is a political act that seeks to claim urban space for a host of ends.[39] Often *okupas* seek to create sites that are liberated from the oppressive confines of capitalism and its entanglements with state rule. In Madrid the *okupa* movement flourished throughout the 1980s and '90s; most recently its legacy has been evident in the creation of a number of autonomous social centers (CSOA), which flourished after the 15M movement.[40] These centers, during crisis, have taken on renewed importance against this backdrop of austerity.[41] Providing a host of activities in neighborhoods that have been largely abandoned by state funding, they can be lively sites for sociality and exchange during the crisis. The *okupa* movement has traditionally been composed of young, often male anticapitalists, and its aims have not always been in keeping with those of the PAH. Yet during urban crisis and convergence, there has been an intermingling of these various forms of activism. Many housing meetings take place in CSOA, and many activists involved in *okupa* practices have been at the frontline of anti-evictions activity throughout the city.

Increasingly, however, women and immigrants engage in the practice of squatting as a means of finding shelter. This confluence of urban crisis with modes of contestation render that option into something legitimate. Struggling with the prospect of eviction, *afectadas* attempt to secure social housing through either the municipal or regional housing agencies, only to be put on a waitlist or have their petition denied. Indeed, those who currently live in social housing also live under the threat of eviction: Madrid's small stock is becoming wholly privatized, as both municipal and regional governments sell off portfolios to international financial entities, including Goldman Sachs and Blackstone, often for pennies on the dollar. Inhabitants are never given the chance to purchase, let alone at the bargain basement prices offered to overseas financial firms. While the state has sometimes sold properties with existing tenants, it has also carried out evictions for even the most minor infraction. These evictions have been audacious in their violence; often dozens of vans full of riot police line the street from the earliest hour of the morning to ensure the eviction order is carried out. In a moment in which people most need the security of a public social safety net, that net has rapidly unraveled.

In early 2014, shortly following the extended winter holiday season, I walked south through the center of the city to the EMVS (Empresa Municipal de la Vivienda y Suelo—Municipal Housing and Land Office). I was meeting the director of housing management and merchandising; the pretense of the interview was the recent announcement of a sizable sale to Blackstone. The director informed me she could not speak very openly on the topic, as the agreement was still being worked out. During our discussion, she assured me repeatedly that the units were on sale because they had no longer had any use for the EMVS: they were zoned for a particular demographic with rents that were below market during the boom. But the market had fluctuated, and now those rents were above market value. Instead of reclassifying these units, she claimed the EMVS could not deviate from the parameters laid out in a law that was now obsolete—she made clear that idea was unfeasible and lay well beyond the purview of her job. Yet she assured me that her doors were always open for those who might be in search of a home. In light of this transparency, she stated, "I do not understand the demands of those collectives," such as the PAH. She went on, "We work for the people. We are here to help. We want to house people."[42] Those who faced eviction from public housing were guilty of poor neighborly relations and "bad behavior," perhaps even involved in drug dealing and crime.

Yet the experiences of everyday citizens belied these assurances of openness. On numerous instances, various *afectadas,* some of them residents of EMVS buildings, would attempt to speak with people at the agency about their situations. Often they were harassed by security guards who denied them entry. On one occasion, a motley crew of activists and *afectadas* assembled in the entrance, attempting to speak with someone about their cases. The guards turned hostile, demanding they abandon the premises. One woman began to seize, writhing on the floor in agony in the grips of an epileptic fit. Another woman attempted to control the seizure while the police began to arrive. Most of the assembled had charges pressed against them for disturbing the peace, which were dropped at a later court date.

Indeed, as the crisis has swept through these urban landscapes of decadence and ruin, political action emerges not from vague notions of justice and abstract rights, but rather from direct, often conflictive contact with the violences of homeownership, perhaps encapsulated by Borja's transition from *afectado* to activist, from *propietario* to *indignado*. Through his involvement with the PAH, he engaged in his own small acts of revolution. As an experienced handyman, he began to provide locksmithing services to families looking to squat. He described to me his leap into disobedience as a response to a particularly violent eviction. A young women and her family were ordered to abandon their home, a social housing unit in a peripheral neighborhood. They had missed a payment, and the local government, eager to divest of this housing stock, began evictions proceedings. After the eviction was postponed once, an outsized deployment of riot police crushed the attempts of activists to keep the family in their home, and they were removed with force. With nowhere to go, the family sat for several days with all their belongings in the interior courtyard of their former home. In this moment, Borja relates he decided to act, "almost without thinking." He opened up an empty house for the family several days later.

This action is predicated on a particular political claim that seeks to make legible an opaque system. I discussed how Spanish systems of housing and land had to be made legible to an outside market as a goal for Europeanization (see chap. 2). If property needs to be made legible in this way for the sake of the market, so must it be made sensible to an everyday public. Here I am inspired by the work of Jacques Rancière, who discusses a "partition" or "distribution" of the "sensible," which undergirds political communities. Reflecting on this ambiguous term, Davide Panagia writes: "In order to cut up lots and allocate goods there need to be criteria in place for the proper circulation of things, and it is this sense of the proper order of things that structures what Rancière refers to as 'the order of distribution of bodies into functions corresponding to their nature.'"[43] A system such as homeownership must be recognized by all parties that take part, and the order in which objects and affects circulate must be *sensible* to those parties. My rights as a homeowner are only really in effect if my neighbor also recognizes them, which requires an aesthetic ordering. But that ordering—which also relies on notions of propriety or what is proper—is made in collaboration with the state. In this instance, however, the state has repeatedly privileged the interests and rights of banks and corporations over those of everyday citizens. And so for those citizens, people like Mabel and Betsy, there is a reordering in which previous norms and rules cease to carry heft and legitimacy. What good is the category of homeownership and, by extension, property, if it can be sold to multinational companies for pennies while numerous families go homeless, denied that same opportunity? Who owns what if public, taxpayer money is used to bail out banks that have repossessed homes? Within the context of postcrisis Madrid, that which was previously sensible to everyday citizens has dissolved, in large part because those everyday citizens have been rendered outside this system.

The insensibility of the housing market's dispossessions—evident in brutal evictions, in a young woman's epileptic fit on the floor of a government office, in the rising numbers of childhood poverty—has made other forms of housing make sense in a way that was previously unthinkable. Throughout many years of struggle, *okupas* have become fellow travelers in a politics of outrage. Their attitudes against the property market, the dominant modes of urban development, and the capitalist system now take on new legitimacy because a much wider swath of the public can see clearly their arguments. At the same time, as *afectadas* appropriate the practices of *okupas* into their arsenal of resistance, they elaborate their own lexicon to position their acts in relation to the dominant whole. Rather than the occupation of these buildings, this act is one of recuperation. During meetings sponsored by the PAH for people facing eviction from occupied dwellings, activists and *afectadas* forcefully rejected the standard descriptor of *okupa*. These families were not engaged in *okupación*. Rather they were liberating and *recuperating* dwellings for their own use. *Recuperación* meant seizing these properties from the hands of banks and speculators for the benefit of the neighborhood, the community, the family now engaged in social reproduction under duress. This politics, however, is not only about claiming space. "Recuperating" these buildings, rather, is a means of articulating a particular transformation in the way in which urban citizens relate to regimes of housing and homeownership.

For *afectadas* and activists, the contemporary insensibility of the current regime is not only harmful to everyday citizens. Rather, it also represents the fundamental corruption of private property, the public provision of services, and even the terms of urban cohabitation. For individuals such as Betsy and Margarita, two Ecuadorian single mothers, property was a means of permanence and personal advancement that might offer a bulwark against other forms of discrimination. Yet it has only led to dispossession and greater exclusion, as they have seen years of toil obliterated by an economic crisis that has still proven incredibly lucrative for a chosen few. Furthermore, while they labored both to make a wage to pay for their homes and maintain those homes in impeccable condition, the bank has not seen fit to do the same. As property owners, banks fail to carry out their obligations to the homeowners association, and the building itself suffers, falling into disrepair.[44] Evidently the bank would prefer to allow its patrimony to become new ruins rather than allow in tenants at reasonable rates. While previously homeownership encouraged cosmopolitanism and urbanity, here it is revealed as but a tool for the accumulation of capital, regardless of any use value or the preservation of urban communities.

Thus rather than allow neighborhoods of disinvestment to become ruinous deathscapes, *afectadas* transform the inherent public quality of this situation into a claim. Throughout meetings, people regularly chant the mantra of *recuperación,* reconfiguring the analytic of expulsion through an emphasis on the public. Perhaps they have been expelled from their homes, but they demand not to be expelled from the city itself—they still pay taxes, their children still attend public schools. To squat in these homes is to recuperate them—as taxpayers and citizens, these units technically belong to them, and all of Madrid, not the overseas financial conglomerate or the wealthy scion of a political family. But it also, crucially, is a political act that reads possibility. *Recuperación* seeks to recuperate the city, the neighborhood, and the *hogar*—the hearth and home—against the punitive demands of this system. As such, it stands against previous and ongoing forms of dispossession. Yet rather than articulate their actions as a form of *repossession, afectadas* reject the singularity and individualism, bound up in notions of private property, that the term implies. Recuperation privileges the community and demands we see housing as not only shelter, but also an integral piece of a diverse urban community.

Intersectional Urban Futures

The crisis revealed the city to be a site of extraction and accumulation by dispossession through the tyranny of homeownership, which rendered certain populations as outside and against dominant systems of management and rule. The collapse of the homeownership model was central to Madrid's regime of dispossession. Thus emerged, through the painstaking work of a diversity of activists, a multipronged struggle *against* homeownership. These activists transformed homeownership within its crisis into a battleground to advance new lines of action and argumentation. In elaborating forms of resistance against homeownership's crisis, the PAH has configured homeownership and by extension the city as a particular territory in which to make claims and demand recognition. In Indigenous struggles in Ecuador, the notion of *territorio* brings together land and its stewardship with shared histories, resources management, and a situated politics of solidarity and mutual aid. Territory, similarly, is about not only physical place, but also its governance and sovereignty, its modes of inhabitation, and its relations to the world at large. Such themes animate a movement that emerged out of entangled histories of activism and that prefigure a politics of dwelling together.[45]

It would be impossible to extricate the one line of action, whether a lawsuit, the occupation of an empty building, or the blocking of any eviction, and pinpoint its specific origin, the foundational moment in which it crystallized into something legible and certain. There are of course firsts—the first demonstration, the first blocked eviction, the first assembly. Yet the origins of each are muddled, made possible by coincidences of place and time. Instead, what I have done in this chapter is draw out the ways in which various modes of action and engagement have comingled and coproduced a successful social movement. This analysis insists we see the indigenous movement as an important precursor to the PAH alongside its standard Spanish antecedents. But it also makes us confront the alternative modes of engagement, action, and habitation that emerge from housing struggles.

In uncovering and denouncing dispossession through homeownership, *afectadas* revealed the perversions of the propertied order. An array of practices, from the blocking of evictions and banks to the recuperation of buildings, forced the public to reckon with the legacy of an entire economy predicated on the expansion of the housing market. The PAH, meanwhile, has been exceptionally aware of the gendered dynamics of crisis and resulting protest, advancing feminist practices and critiques.[46] Yet the ways in which urban property markets and their dispossessions work through racial and ethnic difference have largely escaped analysis. The first to dissent, Andeans served to catalyze efforts against dispossession. Their enduring presence and ongoing protest reveal the racialized nature of urban property markets even in a place in which "race" emerges only as a recent category of analysis. Indeed, Madrid's urban economics of property and place worked through such differences, as I have revealed across this account.[47] Those differences, too, helped to foment dissent, sparking one of the world's most successful housing movements.

8 Imagining Urban Futures in the Age of Uncertainty

It has been over a decade since the Great Financial Crisis decimated the city of Madrid. With the rise of austerity politics and the reregulation of credit markets, the city can no longer turn to homeownership as a magic fix. Instead, it has pursued major commercial real estate deals to position the city as the next European financial center, while also selling off historic buildings in the old city. One postcrisis landmark has been slow transformation of seven historic buildings into a palatial Four Seasons, the first of its kind in Spain. Recovery has meant a surge in tourism and weakened labor laws. The spectacular rise of the PAH, meanwhile, launched the careers of some of the most powerful and vocal politicians on the left, starting with Ada Colau who is now in her second term as Barcelona's mayor. Meanwhile, the PAH has more or less resolved the problems of mortgages, opening numerous lines for negotiation and resolution such that mortgage-related evictions are practically nil. Despite massive gains, however, many people who lost their homes to foreclosure remain worse off. Amidst growing inequality, the far-right, anti-immigrant Vox party has surged to power.

Since the events narrated in this book, housing in Madrid has become ever more precarious, as monthly rents have increased by 200 percent in some parts of the city. The government has never redressed the fundamental imbalances shaping that segment of the housing market, instead making it easier to evict renters for nonpayment. Now the evictions that plague the city are a result of failure to pay rent or illicit occupation, which both account for numerous

evictions daily. When rental contracts expire, landlords now offer new contracts with astronomical monthly increases, sometimes in an effort to evict
tenants and transform units into vacation rentals. AirBnB, as in many cities,
has consumed the rental housing market, even drawing tourists to peripheral,
working-class neighborhoods for cheap accommodations while emptying out
the historic center. The transfer of numerous units into the hands of real estate
investment trusts—new investment vehicles that own and operate vast portfolios of urban property—has further accelerated the precarity of the rental
market. Blackstone, as in the United States, is now Spain's leading landlord.

The public sector, meanwhile, remains hobbled through many rounds of
cuts. Austerity has decimated elements of the welfare society, including housing, which was never really included in the battery of goods and services provided by the Spanish state. The small public provision of urban housing has
crumbled, as in much of the North Atlantic, just as poor city-dwellers must
brave the wilds of rapacious real estate markets and predatory landlords.

The reality of the deepening housing crisis—in Madrid but also globally—
fundamentally shapes immigrant lives and livelihoods as they make their way
in the city. Immigrants are moving to new places where it is increasingly difficult to meet the basic need for shelter—a struggle for longtime urban dwellers,
too. Finance's interest in urban real estate and the return of monied classes to
the city has forced service sector workers, many of them immigrants, to the
edges of the urban fringe. Most recently, ongoing housing precarity certainly
worsened the depth and breadth of the spread of the novel coronavirus; Madrid
has been one of the hardest-hit cities in Europe. Spatial inequities, in which the
central city is gleaming and empty, while its peripheries warehouse the urban
majority, have had desperate and tragic consequences. In neighborhoods such
as Puente de Vallecas, overcrowded, multi-ethnic communities now live with
the heightened threat of epidemiological infection, a reality echoed in many
other cities across the North Atlantic. Precarious, crowded housing means
many immigrants face increased risk of death even as their labor is deemed
essential: delivery workers and day-laborers, nannies and elder caretakers all
continue to report to duty. Not to do so would mean facing greater economic
ruin, even if it means risking one's life. The eternal fear of life under the tyranny
of debt continues to impel the calculus of daily action. The virus has revealed in
its intensity and disparate impacts the way the state maintains and actively per-
petuates "the right to *expose* people to the possibility of death,"[1] by demanding
work on the one hand, while ignoring and even refusing adequate shelter on the

other. Many of the issues of housing and cohabitation thus remain unresolved and perhaps more troubling.

What, then, might be the lessons of Madrid's immigrant activists? First of all, this book reveals the necessity of placing housing at the center of our analyses of migration and the city. For scholars who study migration, urbanism, and housing, that exhortation might seem obvious. Clearly, housing matters and is a centerpiece to the immigrant urban experience. Yet there is a marked paucity of material that looks to housing as central to urban experiences of migration. As I have illuminated in this account, housing markets, dominant systems of tenure, and habitational struggles are key sites for understanding immigrant urban futures. In the case of Madrid, homeownership became a central device that organized labor, money and finance, calculations of risk and reward, and conceptions of the self within a society under transformation. It allowed people like Betsy and Mabel to gain shelter, but also to demonstrate ability for full membership. Through homeownership, they could prove to the hostile society around them that they were good wage earners, hard workers, diligent savers, and investors in a collective urban project of imagining the future. Of course, homeownership only served to further exile them to the spatial and metaphorical periphery, both because of *where* they bought and also *how* they bought. Faced with foreclosure, they saw their hard-earned gains wrested from them. In crisis, meanwhile, homeownership became a flashpoint to organize claims and articulate new politics. Finally, the housing struggles that emerged in response have provided for what integration policy could not: an arena for cooperation and inclusion, even in a moment of rising xenophobia and nativism. They also, crucially, conjoin private suffering with public outrage to demonstrate the porous boundary between domestic economies and shared horizons of possibility.

Entwined processes of migration and urbanism demand a more robust interrogation of housing as a central variable of analysis. Housing is, of course, a basic need, a commodity to exchange, a site of wealth creation, a system producing inequalities, and an engine for exclusion and even dispossession. Social scientific inquiry has long acknowledged the role of housing in driving exclusion, particularly for the city's newest arrival. Most analyses reveal how immigrant exclusion from dominant regimes of housing produces variegated experiences of sociospatial inequality. In this analysis, however, participation in those regimes, rather than facilitating inclusion and ameliorating inequality, can instead extract equity from immigrant populations and condemn them to even more extreme forms of marginalization.

Why hasn't housing been at the center of critical inquiry into migration's urban expressions? Contemporary migration scholarship is often compelled by the public spectacle of increasing diversity and multiracial realities. It is after all in public where the questions of diversity, demographic transformation, and multi-ethnic and -racial futures are most evident and pressing. As a need that has been confined to the private sphere, housing can be overlooked when examining the experiences of urban immigrants. Migrant suffering, central both to popular understandings of mobility and to the elicitation of sympathy, is often made into public spectacle, a matter of borders and camps, not housing applications, eviction orders, and overdue mortgage payments. But even while it is rendered into a private system, housing structures multiple urban publics. From schooling to health outcomes, commute times to public health orders mandating shelter in place, housing shapes our ability to survive and/or thrive in the city. The furthering of inequality, racism, and differential exposure to risk and even death is produced not only in the camp, the sea crossing, or the detention center, but also in the bank branch, the bureaucracy of forms and testimonies, the real estate section of the newspaper, and the overcrowded, substandard living conditions of many urban areas. On the other hand, the antidotes to such suffering might lie not with policy and planning, but rather within the confines of the neighborhood assembly, the apartment block, and the migrant collective.

This book demonstrates not only the centrality of housing for migrants, but also the centrality of migrants within emergent housing struggles, spaces in which they can claim rights and recognition and demand more egalitarian urban futures. Indeed, while the housing demands and despairs of immigrants mark cities, so, too, does their activism. Madrid's mortgaged migrants provide a potent example of resistance to financial devastation that collectivized personal ruin against anomic experiences of suffering. Rather than accept the terms of the private homeownership model in Spain, people like Aida Quinatoa openly questioned and then confronted its logics, articulating alternative understandings of ruin and its production. As this case reveals, immigrants offer insights into other modes of being and dwelling in the city, made necessary in a moment of deepening ecological and pandemic crises that demand new models of praxis. Whether through indigenous traditions, past activism, or experiences of racialization and exclusion, immigrant activists formulate new political vocabularies that extend the terms of extant housing debates. Yet while immigrant influence and innovation has been made evident in struggles over labor and work, notions of citizenship, ecology and environmental justice, and race and racialization, their voices are not nearly as prevalent within research on housing movements.

It is within such movements that we can articulate our collective futures and draw upon disparate forms of knowledge and activism. In Madrid, as in much of the world, housing movements now do the traditional work of the welfare state, tending to vulnerable populations in their hour of need. The retreat of the state, hollowed through austerity measures and neoliberal antigovernment edicts, means networks of mutual aid and grassroots organizing must now take up the task of care in an age of social reproduction under duress. In Madrid, as I write, an emergent web of neighborhood care groups has sprung up to minister to disparate needs during the COVID-19 pandemic. Faced with overwhelmed social services, everyday urban dwellers instead turn to informal mechanisms for survival, made visible through WhatsApp groups and street pamphleting.

Beyond the work of charity and welfarism, however, these infrastructures from below articulate radical visions for urban life and dwelling together. Groups such as the emergent Sindicato de Inquilin@s (Renters' Union) in Madrid, or CASA (Community Action for Safe Apartments) in the Bronx focus on community capabilities and local expert knowledge against the ravages of the housing market. As immigrants face some of the steepest housing hurdles in the city, so too do they articulate new arenas for multi-ethnic, anti-supremacist collective action, and incorporate alternative knowledge and modes of doing. As we confront new threats to both daily life and the task of organizing, immigrant struggles over housing can offer alternative modes of survival and wellbeing. Histories with social justice struggles, different systems of space and shelter, and ongoing marginalization and racialization allow for distinct modes of political thinking that can articulate the hypocrisies of the urban order. In the case of the PAH, Andean migrants insisted on the collective nature of private ruin, enmeshed in a web of extraction and punishment. They articulated the violence of housing as it is subject to capitalist development, in addition to its central role in producing the city of speculative excess.

Indeed, new grassroots collectives apprehend the role of housing within a much broader landscape of capitalist expansion in opposition to the communal good. Housing of course is both a central motor of the economy and a basic necessity for urban survival. As it has become the site *par excellence* for investment and speculation, it also plays an increasingly important role in determining the look and feel of our cities. Homeownership and related systems of property and land fundamentally shape how planning and policy envisions and produces the city. Housing movements, then, force us to confront the reality of the city as a speculative project of expansion. The PAH's slogan, "From the real estate bubble to the right to housing," brings together capitalist urbanization with the needs of everyday urban dwellers. In the case of Madrid, immigrant activism revealed that the concerns of the kitchen table, far from being the province of a single family going through hard times, are instead implicated within a dense fabric of urban sociality. Resulting activism stands against individualized notions of private households and domestic ruin, configuring housing as a demand to be fought for and yanked from the hands of financial interests. Housing then becomes a collective call to action, to be constantly enacted, shared, and defended, against its use as a device to produce great wealth that accords privileges to a select few.

To draw out the ways in which urban development as usual is antithetical to just shelter is not sufficient, however, just as immigrant involvement within housing struggles is not merely a question of alternative interpretations of society and space. Rather, multiethnic and multiracial housing movements force the public to contend with the differential impacts of the propertied order. Property, they demonstrate, furthers the abjection of populations made other through race, gender, and migratory origins. One of the faults of the PAH, I would argue, has been an unwillingness to address head on the question of race and ethnicity in processes of housing dispossession and the city's propertied order. At the same time, ongoing marginalization and racialization, from Madrid to Quito, Jackson, MS, to Beirut, inspire sophisticated political imaginaries and collective action that prefigure radical urban futures. Immigrant involvement in housing struggles seeks to redress legacies of exclusion that have conspired to produce differential exposure to risk and even death. Recent debates over rent strikes, moratoria, and urban budgets reliant on property taxes force a reckoning with dependency on private ownership as a means of financing and reproducing the city. Indeed, the pandemic has made evident the violence and dispossession of propertied systems upon low-income communities of immigrants, the Indigenous, and people of color, a reality many movements have long denounced. Struggles over shelter already confront and strive to abolish dominant modes of producing and dwelling in the city. So, too, do they articulate more egalitarian forms of habitation. To reimagine the city in the age of epidemiological risk and climate catastrophe, therefore, collectives such as the PAH might provide blueprints for an alternative urbanism of cooperation against the tyranny of the market. Within their insurgencies and counter-imaginaries we might find and propagate hopeful, inclusive housing and urban futures.

Notes

Chapter 1

1. I have chosen to use the term "immigrant" instead of "migrant" in this account. Debates in Europe often deploy the term "migrant," which some argue privileges mobility and stands implicitly against settlement, rendering the migrant presence as temporary. I resist that urge, but I also use "immigrant" because it is faithful to the original Spanish, *inmigrante*. In a country that has a long history of emigration, the term provides crucial distinction.

2. All mortgages in Spain, similar to most other parts of Europe, are recourse loans. As such, the house does not act as the only collateral—lenders can pursue other assets to recoup the entire amount of the loan. Considering most housing was overvalued during the boom, many borrowers were then responsible for large amounts of money after repossession of the house.

3. Drawing on the lineage of Andean area studies, I use the term to reference mostly Ecuadorians and Peruvians. Most interlocutors and early organizers were of Ecuadorian descent. At the same time, there are many ties between the Ecuadorian and Peruvian communities in Madrid, with the latter being much smaller than the former. Because of their relatively small size, many in the Peruvian community were incorporated into the Ecuadorian community. For an overview of Andean area studies, see Drake and Hershberg, *State and Society in Conflict*.

4. Iglesias Martínez, *La población de origen ecuatoriano en España*.

5. Çaglar and Schiller, *Migrants and City-Making*; Hinze, *Turkish Berlin*; Sandoval-Strausz, *Barrio America*; Barber, *Latino City*; Vitiello and Sugrue, *Immigration and Metropolitan Revitalization in the United States*; Stein, *Capital City*.

6. Rolnik, *Urban Warfare*; Potts, *Broken Cities*.

7. Bhandar, *Colonial Lives of Property*; D'Costa and Chakraborty, *The Land Question in India*; Islamoglu, *Constituting Modernity*; Zavisca, *Housing the New Russia*, 9.

8. Dikeç, "Immigrants, Banlieues, and Dangerous Things"; Merrill, *An Alliance of Women Immigration and the Politics of Race*; Çaglar and Schiller, *Migrants and City-Making*; Nicholls and Uitermark, *Cities and Social Movements*; Holmes, "Representing the 'European Refugee Crisis' in Germany and Beyond."

9. While such a statement might seem obvious, there is a surprising lack of scholarship that centers housing in examining immigrants and the city.

10. Portes and Stepick, *City on the Edge*; Leal and Alguacil, "Vivienda e inmigración"; Martínez del Olmo and Leal Maldonado, "La segregación residencial, un indicador espacial confuso en la representación de la problemática residencial de los inmigrantes económicos"; Pareja-Eastaway, "The Effects of the Spanish Housing System on the Settlement Patterns of Immigrants"; Alba and Logan, "Assimilation and Stratification in the Homeownership Patterns of Racial and Ethnic Groups"; McConnell and Marcelli, "Buying into the American Dream?"; Kauppinen, Andersen, and Hedman, "Determinants of Immigrants' Entry to Homeownership in Three Nordic Capital City Regions"; Kurz, *Home Ownership and Social Inequality in a Comparative Perspective*; Clark, *Immigrants and the American Dream*.

11. Telles and Ortiz, *Generations of Exclusion*.

12. Rugh and Hall, "Deporting the American Dream"; Diaz-Serrano and Raya, "Mortgages, Immigrants and Discrimination."

13. Taylor, *Race for Profit*.

14. McCabe, *No Place Like Home.*; Rothstein, *The Color of Law*.

15. Soto, *The Mystery of Capital*; Kwak, *A World of Homeowners*.

16. Janoschka, Sequera, and Salinas, "Gentrification in Spain and Latin America—A Critical Dialogue"; Lees, Shin, and López Morales, *Planetary Gentrification*.

17. Aalbers, *Subprime Cities the Political Economy of Mortgage Markets*; Aalbers, "Neoliberalism Is Dead . . . Long Live Neoliberalism!"; García-Lamarca and Kaika, "Mortgaged Lives"; Coq-Huelva, "Urbanisation and Financialisation in the Context of a Rescaling State"; Newman, "Post-Industrial Widgets"; Wyly et al., "American Home."

18. Soto, *The Mystery of Capital*.

19. Bowsher, "Credit/Debt and Human Capital"; Hodkinson, "The New Urban Enclosures"; Valli, "When Cultural Workers Become an Urban Social Movement."

20. García-Lamarca and Kaika, "Mortgaged Lives."

21. Moore, *Capitalism in the Web of Life*; Martin, *Financialization of Daily Life*; Zavisca, *Housing the New Russia*, 9.

22. Bourdieu's work on the construction of the French single-family housing market is instructive in thinking about the various actors, systems, and social norms that contribute to making economic supply and demand. While his analysis is more structural, it illuminates the careful interplay between different actors and subject positions. Bourdieu, *The Social Structures of the Economy*.

23. Hall, "Geographies of Money and Finance II"; Kear, "Governing Homo Sub-primicus"; Reid, "Financialization and the Subprime Subject"; Stout, *Dispossessed*; Suarez, "Debt Revolts."

24. D'Costa and Chakraborty, *The Land Question in India*; Essen and Hodkinson, "Grounding Accumulation by Dispossession in Everyday Life"; Roberts, "Financing Social Reproduction"; Roberts, *Gendered States of Punishment and Welfare*; Salemink and Rasmussen, "After Dispossession"; White and White, "Gendered Experiences of Dispossession"; Zaloom, *Indebted*.

25. Chen and Webster, "Homeowners Associations, Collective Action and the Costs of Private Governance"; Martin, *The Permanent Tax Revolt*; Mouritzen, "The Demanding Citizen"; McCabe, *No Place Like Home*.

26. Adell Argilés, Martínez López, and Alcalde Villacampa, *Dónde están las llaves?*; Martínez López and García Bernardos, *Okupa Madrid (1985–2011)*.

27. This facet of the Madrid case is distinct from the development of the housing movement in Barcelona, where longtime activists involved in other housing struggles initiated the fight against foreclosures and evictions. I discuss some of the differences and similarities, in addition to their shared histories, in the final chapter.

28. A brief but by no means exhaustive overview of recent influential work includes Nicholls, *The DREAMers*; Koopmans, *Contested Citizenship*; Nicholls and Uitermark, *Cities and Social Movements*; Pojmann, *Migration and Activism in Europe since 1945*; Nyers and Rygiel, *Citizenship, Migrant Activism and the Politics of Movement*; Das Gupta, *Unruly Immigrants Rights, Activism, and Transnational South Asian Politics in the United States*; Millner, "From 'Refugee' to 'Migrant' in Calais Solidarity Activism"; Sziarto and Leitner, "Immigrants Riding for Justice."

29. Featherstone, "Black Internationalism, Subaltern Cosmopolitanism, and the Spatial Politics of Antifascism"; Gidwani, "Subaltern Cosmopolitanism as Politics"; Dines, Montagna, and Ruggiero, "Thinking Lampedusa"; Holmes, "Representing the 'European Refugee Crisis' in Germany and Beyond"; Casas-Cortes et al., "New Keywords"; Mudu and Chattopadhyay, *Migration, Squatting and Radical Autonomy*; Martínez López, "Squatters and Migrants in Madrid."

30. Kornetis, "'Is There a Future in This Past?'"

Chapter 2

1. King, Lazaridis, and Tsardanidis, *Eldorado or Fortness?*; King, *The Mediterranean Passage*.

2. Instituto Nacional de la Estadística.

3. Coppola et al., *The Godfather*.

4. Ahmed, "Home and Away."

5. Jokisch and Pribilsky, "The Panic to Leave"; Lucero, "High Anxiety in the Andes."

6. We need only think of the Massimo Sestini image that won a World Press Photo award (http://time.com/4063972/refugee-crisis-massimo-sestini/). That image

of overcrowding and danger at sea contributes to our understandings of the current refugee crisis and the broader process of migration to Europe more generally. Never mind that the vast majority of immigrants arrive in very different circumstances such as overstaying a tourist visa. This understanding, meanwhile, helps to shore up the idea of the immigrant as either a security threat or a victim in need of humanitarian sympathy. While these reactions appear at opposite ends of a spectrum of care, they both serve to reify the immigrant as other and apart.

7. Aparicio, *Marroquíes en España*.

8. Several amnesties under the Zapatero government allowed large numbers of immigrants to regularize their status.

9. Calavita, *Immigrants at the Margins*, 45, 68.

10. Lee, "Sociological Theories of Immigration"; Loch, "Integration as a Sociological Concept and National Model for Immigrants"; Bloemraad, Korteweg, and Yurdakul, "Citizenship and Immigration."

11. Crul and Vermeulen, "The Second Generation in Europe."

12. Bloemraad, *Becoming a Citizen*; Koopmans, *Contested Citizenship*; Calavita, *Immigrants at the Margins*; Andall, *Gender, Migration and Domestic Service*.

13. Castañeda, *A Place to Call Home*.

14. Nicholls and Uitermark, *Cities and Social Movements*, 33.

15. Escobar, *Encountering Development*.

16. Bowen, *Why the French Don't Like Headscarves*; Calavita, *Immigrants at the Margins*; Uitermark, *Dynamics of Power in Dutch Integration Politics*.

17. Brubaker, *Citizenship and Nationhood in France and Germany*, 22.

18. Bruquetas-Callejo, "Immigration and Integration Policymaking in Spain."

19. Carrera, *In Search of the Perfect Citizen?*, 235.

20. The debate over national identity has heightened with the ongoing, sometimes brutal, question of Catalan status. Within that lengthy debate, the spectral and vexing question of Spanish identity is a constant flicker in the background.

21. Carrera, *In Search of the Perfect Citizen?*, 250.

22. The Partido Popular were quick to blame the bombings on the Basque terrorist group ETA. The rapid response would prove their damnation, as millions of Spaniards condemned their rush to judgment in protests throughout the country. The PP then went on to lose national elections despite previous polls predicting their victory.

23. Diario de Sesiones de la Asamblea de Madrid, 2004, 4284.

24. Diario de Sesiones de la Asamblea de Madrid, 2005.

25. Diario de Sesiones de la Asamblea de Madrid, 8640.

26. "*Cama caliente*," or warm bed, is a colloquial term for an arrangement in which the urban poor, namely immigrants, rent space in a bed for a period of eight hours, rotating with two others. Hence the bed stays warm. Such arrangements are often made in *pisos pateras*—apartments named after the ubiquitous large rowboats in which Sub-Saharan Africans make the journey across the Strait of Gibraltar, a visual synecdoche for contemporary migration to Europe.

27. Diario de Sesiones de la Asamblea de Madrid, Pub. L., No. 161, 4300.

28. Ibid., 4303.

29. Diario de Sesiones de la Asamblea de Madrid, Pub. L., No. 402, 11669.

30. Diario de Sesiones de la Asamblea de Madrid, Pub. L., No. 44, 737.

31. Diario de Sesiones de la Asamblea de Madrid, Pub. L., No. 49, 925.

32. Ibid., 928.

33. Ibid., 932.

34. Comunidad de Madrid, "Plan de Integración 2006–2008," 152.

35. Ibid., 245. Emphasis mine.

36. The emphasis on financial services within development is part of a broader trend in international development, which has sought to push people onto the ladder of progress through the extension of credit. Here, as Ananya Roy argues in *Poverty Capital,* the goal is to integrate the poor into financial markets through indebtedness. That same logic is of course at work in millennial Madrid, whereby the acquisition of a mortgage allows the poor and working classes to access membership within a booming economy.

37. Comunidad de Madrid, "Plan de Integración 2006–2008," 177.

38. This discussion of course reveals the slippery boundaries between the economy and society as they have been conceived of by both social scientists and policymakers. Critical scholars from Polanyi to Mitchell to Krippner discuss how these concepts when mapped onto actually existing phenomenon are wholly artificial and fairly insufficient in describing the world at large. Many of these discussions produce an elision between the social and economic capabilities, responsibilities, and virtues of the city's immigrant community. Krippner, *Capitalizing on Crisis*; Mitchell, "The Work of Economics"; Polanyi, *The Great Transformation.*

39. La Caixa, "Productos y servicios para inmigrantes."

40. La Caixa, *2007 Informe anual "La Caixa."*

41. En Colectivo Ioé, Igual de seres humanos, o.c., p. 122.

42. Spain also lacks a robust investment culture. Real estate has long been a central vehicle for everyday individuals to direct their extra wealth.

Chapter 3

1. A "PAU" is an acronym for a *Plan Actual Urbanística*, a specific planning device that emerged in the Spanish democratic era in order to create integrated neighborhoods with services. This particular mechanism is a response to previous rounds of urbanization, which I discuss in this chapter, in which the state built standalone housing estates with nothing more in the way of infrastructure, transportation, and so on.

2. Vallekas is the alternative, decidedly left working-class denomination for an area that has long been a hotbed of organizing and working-class solidarity.

3. López and Rodríguez, "The Spanish Model"; García, "The Breakdown of the Spanish Urban Growth Model."

4. Francisco Franco was the dictator of Spain from his civil war victory in 1939 until his death in 1975. During the early years of his dictatorship, his regime practiced

economic isolation known as autarky, in which no economic imports were accepted into the country. Spain was mired in depression, which only increased because of these autarkic conditions.

5. Richards, *A Time of Silence*; Arco Blanco, "«Morir de hambre»"; López, *Autarquía y mercado negro*.

6. Iniesta Corredor, Gonzalo Calavia, and Bernal, *Estampas de Madrid*, 10.

7. Comisaría General para la Ordenación Urbana de Madrid y sus Alrededores, "Gran Madrid."

8. Bidagor, *Orientaciones sobre la reconstrucción de Madrid*, 16.

9. Díaz, Ringrose, and Segura, *Madrid*, 525.

10. Such comparisons between cities that then act as planning rationales are consonant with the logic of "worlding" that emerges as a concept within planning and urban studies literature only recently.

11. Muguruza Otaño, *El futuro Madrid*.

12. Consejo Superior de los Colegios de Arquitectos, "Organización teorica de un distrito de 100,000 habitantes."

13. Goode, *Impurity of Blood Defining Race in Spain, 1870–1930*.

14. Richards, *A Time of Silence*.

15. "Población de Madrid," *Gran Madrid*, No. 4 (1949): 39.

16. Madrid (Spain) and Ayuntamiento, *Memoria comprensiva de la actuación del primer Ayuntamiento después de la liberación de Madrid*, 58.

17. For example, the regime pursued the construction of a triumphal arch in the Moncloa Plaza, which would act as ceremonial entrance to the *Via Imperial*. The arch is similar to archways built under Carlos III, thus serving as visual link between the regime and its Bourbon forbearers. Similarly, it pursued the rehabilitation of the Plaza de Oriente, near the historic royal palace, again as a means of allying Franco's legacy to that of the former royal empire.

18. López Díaz, "Vivienda Social y Falange."

19. Decreto Ley de 25 de noviembre de 1944, *Boletín Oficial del Estado*, No. 332, 8959–65.

20. Zavisca, *Housing the New Russia*, 7.

21. Ghertner, *Rule by Aesthetics*; Bhan, *In the Public's Interest*.

22. Ramón López de Lucio, interview. See also Sambricio, *Madrid, vivienda y urbanismo*. June 2017, Madrid.

23. Spain, Ministerio de la Vivienda, and Secretaría General Técnica, *Architecture, Housing and Urbanisation in Spain*, 71–72.

24. "El problema primero: La vivienda."

25. Decreto Ley de 25 de noviembre de 1944, 8961.

26. Consejo Superior de los Colegios de Arquitectos, "Casa de pisos en la calle de Ayala (Madrid)."

27. Douglas, *Purity and Danger: An Analysis of Concepts of Pollution and Taboo*; McClintock, *Imperial Leather*.

28. At the same time, there emerged a huge black market for construction materials. See Muñoz García, *El poder de la banca en España*.

29. Sánchez Recio and Tascón Fernández, *Los empresarios de Franco*.

30. One of the paradoxes of the autarkic period was that while Franco pursued economic isolation, he soon also encouraged the development and consolidation of the tourist industry. Thus while the country was closed off to foreign goods and capital through official channels of trade, it was increasingly interested in foreign visitors who might then spend their money on Spanish consumer goods and experiences.

31. "Plaza de España y Avenida José Antonio," *Cortijos y Rascacielos,* Nos. 75–76 (1953): 51.

32. Soria Marco, *Madrid antiguo y moderno*.

33. Bonet Correa, Mora Carbonell, and Instituto de Estudios Madrileños, *Madrid. Tomo 5*.

34. Gonick, "From Pueblo to Capital."

35. Roy and Ong, *Worlding Cities*.

36. Ministerio de Vivienda, *Sesenta mil viviendas—Plan de urgencia social de Madrid*.

37. Cronistas Villa Verde, *Cuadernos de Investigación 4: El Poblado de Absorción de Villaverde (Colonia Del Cruce)*.

38. Berlanga et al., *Bienvenido, Mister Marshall!*

39. Burriel, "Subversion of Land-Use Plans and the Housing Bubble in Spain"; López and Rodríguez, "The Spanish Model"; Coq-Huelva, "Urbanisation and Financialisation in the Context of a Rescaling State."

40. Castells, *The City and the Grassroots*.

41. Pérez Quintana and Sánchez León, *Memoria ciudadana y movimiento vecinal*.

42. Larson, "Shifting Modern Identities in Madrid's Recent Urban Planning, Architecture and Narrative."

43. The work of a number of scholars both within and outside of Spain have demonstrated the salience of memory of the civil war, on both sides of the debate, in shaping contemporary politics and culture. This reality is particularly relevant in a society in which one of the dominant political parties emerged from the Franco regime, and many of the legal and legislative structures from that era remain in effect.

44. País, "El Plan General, un modelo de urbanismo 'de izquierdas'"; País, "Antiguos altos cargos relacionados con el urbanismo critican el Plan General."

45. Compitello, "Designing Madrid, 1985–1997," 405.

46. Ofer, *Claiming the City and Contesting the State*.

47. Neuman, *The Imaginative Institution Planning and Governance in Madrid*, 103.

48. For an excellent discussion of this dynamic see Observatorio Metropolitano, *La Apuesta Municipalista: La Democracia Empieza Por Lo Cercano*.

49. Interviews with Julio Rodríguez López. Held December 2013, Aravaca, Madrid.

50. Hebbert, "Town Planning versus Urbanismo," 242.

51. Gutiérrez, *El proyecto urbano en España*.

52. López and Rodríguez, "The Spanish Model."

53. Compitello, "From Planning to Design."

54. Herráez, Cabezas López, and Pinedo Reyes, *Urbanismo y Arquitectura En El Madrid Actual*, 52. The colloquial name for the development references other

important urban arches, *Puerta de Alcala* and *Puerta de Toledo,* which were built under Carlos III. Franco created his own triumphal arch in the same style, which still sits at the entrance to the road that leads to El Escorial and the Valley of the Fallen. Such various references, sites, and histories play off one another, and establish the *Puerta de Europa* as the newest capital splendor.

55. Interview with Férmin Álvarez, former head of the department of rehabilitation and housing at the Empresa Municipal de la Vivienda in Madrid. February 2013 and January 2014, Madrid.

56. Interview with Álvarez. See also Fernández Durán, *La explosión del desorden. Castizo,* not to be confused with the same term that refers to racial mixing in the Americas, emerges from *casticismo madrileño,* a specific term used to describe the uncosmopolitan, folkloric qualities of the capital city, particularly in its historic center. It is related to the picaresque, a word that emerges from central Spain and the figure of the *picaro. Castizo* conjures up many of the city's charming traditions, such as the San Isidro festival, but is also meant to evoke an element of antiquation against more modern urban environments.

57. Almodóvar et al., *Carne trémula.*

58. Herraez, "La rehabilitación en del centro histórico de Madrid."

59. A recent social housing struggle in Madrid has emerged out of this precise situation. An old housing block in the Lavapiés neighborhood is under threat of eviction. The families who have lived there for generations have paid very miniscule amounts of rent, a holdover from Franco's rent freezes. Their landlords are the numerous offspring of an old noble family, who have cared little about the property, but have also not bothered to raise rents. The situation, in which reliable tenants had paid small amounts of rent steadily, was stable for years, and the owners saw no need to change anything. Finding new tenants to pay more, or insisting on raising the rents for the existing tenants, would have simply been a hassle that would also have required investment in the building. Then came the real estate investment trusts, who saw in such a property an enormous rent gap, and promised the owners large sums of money. Now humble families who have lived for generations in modest but reliable circumstances are facing expulsion.

60. Fernández Durán, *La explosión del desorden;* Cladera and Burns, "The Liberalization of the Land Market in Spain."

61. Cladera and Burns, "The Liberalization of the Land Market in Spain," 551.

62. Soto, *The Mystery of Capital.*

63. País, "El interés general y los particulares."

64. Salamanca, "La nueva Ley del Suelo de 1998 en el contexto del neoliberalismo postmoderno."

65. Fernández Durán, *La explosión del desorden.*

66. Harvey, *Spaces of Capital.*

67. Ordovás, *Políticas y estrategias urbanas,* 286.

68. Aznar's lineage reveals the intimate entanglements between the contemporary *populares* and their Franco-era predecessors. During the Spanish transition to

democracy, leaders on both the left and right made a tacit pact of silence—the years of austerity, oppression, and the influence of the Catholic Church in all aspects of life were to be treated as a past life, at a remove from contemporary democracy moving forward. Rather than come to terms with and then purge the remnants of rabidly right-wing demagoguery and intolerance, lawmakers envisioned a simple leap into the future. Yet those remnants simply took on the guise of democratic modernity, readying themselves for the demands of electoral party politics. As such, the contemporary Partido Popular is the not-so-distant descendant of the Franco regime.

69. País, "El PP propone liberalizar más la Ley de Suelo."

70. Ibid.

71. Salamanca, "La nueva Ley del Suelo de 1998 ," 7.

72. Cladera and Burns, "The Liberalization of the Land Market in Spain," 551.

73. Scott, *Seeing Like a State*.

74. Soto, *The Mystery of Capital*.

75. Madrid and Ayuntamiento, *Plan General de Ordenación Urbana de Madrid, 1997*.

76. País, "Soluciones al problema de la vivienda."

77. Mitchell, "The Properties of Markets Informal Housing and Capitalism's Mystery," 19.

78. Nasarre y de Goicoechea and Rodríguez-Avial, "PAUs: Programas de Actuación Urbanística Para Afrontar El Problema de La Vivienda En El Municipio de Madrid."

79. Observatorio Metropolitano, *Madrid*, 239.

80. Acerete, Shaoul, and Stafford, "Taking Its Toll."

81. Hergé, Lonsdale-Cooper, and Turner, *Tintin in America*.

82. As Park argues in a recent piece, the US mortgage was born out of an effort to dispossess native peoples of their lands. Park, "Money, Mortgages, and the Conquest of America."

83. Elyachar, *Markets of Dispossession*, 8.

Chapter 4

1. Gonick, "Fordist Absences."

2. Boyer, *Dreaming the Rational City*; England, "Changing Suburbs, Changing Women"; Hayden, *Redesigning the American Dream*; Martin-Márquez, *Disorientations*; Stoler, *Carnal Knowledge and Imperial Power*.

3. López Díaz, "Vivienda Social y Falange."

4. Consejo Superior de los Colegios de Arquitectos, "Viviendas económicas en el barrio de Usera (Madrid)."

5. López Díaz, "Vivienda Social y Falange."

6. Goode, *Impurity of Blood Defining Race in Spain, 1870–1930*.

7. Muguruza Otaño, *El futuro Madrid*, 194.

8. "Declaraciones del ministro de la vivienda, don José Luis de Arrese."

9. "Mientras no tengamos cubiertas las necesidades minimas de tantas familias, no tenemos derecho a acudir en socorro de los demas."

10. "Declaraciones del ministro de la vivienda, don José Luis de Arrese."

11. "No queremos una España de proletarios, sino de propietarios."

12. Graham and Labanyi, *Spanish Cultural Studies*, 169, 171.

13. Martín-Santos and Rey, *Tiempo de silencio*.

14. Interview with Andres Walliser. June 2017, Madrid.

15. Many of these old housing blocks are where immigrants then bought in the early and mid-2000s.

16. Castells, *The City and the Grassroots*, 218, 219, 222.

17. Pérez Quintana and Sánchez León, *Memoria ciudadana y movimiento vecinal*.

18. Amin, *Post-Fordism*; Tickell and Peck, "Accumulation, Regulation and the Geographies of Post-Fordism."

19. Castells, *The City and the Grassroots*, 217.

20. Saura, Socuéllamos Zarco, and Querejeta, *Deprisa, deprisa*.

21. Almodóvar et al., *Que he hecho yo para merecer esto?*

22. Recently activists have speculated that politicians did little to stop the ravages of heroin usage in peripheral neighborhoods because it served to demobilize a significant portion of these areas, preventing further demands for social justice and more egalitarian forms of city-making and economic development. Similar arguments have been elaborated regarding the crack epidemic in the United States and its distinct effects on the Black community during the 1980s.

23. The belief in physical transformation—in this case the large-scale construction of housing—as a means of social and cultural transformation is of course reminiscent of the utopic visions espoused by Modernist planners and thinkers. While Oscar Neimeyer and Lucio Costa sought a spatial form that might inaugurate Brazilian democracy in Brasilia, Franco instead used space to insist on his vision of Catholic authoritarianism. Both cases reveal the limits of the spatial fix, while also reminding us of the hegemony of modernist thought.

24. Zara is in many ways emblematic of the new, cosmopolitan Spain. It is the flagship brand of the Inditex empire, which is owned by Amancio Ortega. One of the richest men in the world, Ortega emerged from humble origins to create a multinational corporation with outposts all over the world. Zara is a pioneer in "fast fashion," quickly translating runway looks from Paris and New York into accessibly priced High Street goods. Its ubiquity throughout Europe is another symbol of a kind of trendy everyday Europeanization.

25. López and Rodríguez, "The Spanish Model"; Sánchez Santos, "Household Debt and Consumption Inequality"; de Barrón Arniches, *El hundimiento de la banca*; Coq-Huelva, "Urbanisation and Financialisation in the Context of a Rescaling State"; Carbo-Valverde, Marques-Ibanez, and Rodríguez-Fernández, "Securitization, Bank Lending and Credit Quality"; Observatorio Metropolitano, *Madrid*.

26. Isin, *Being Political*; Isin and Turner, *Handbook of Citizenship Studies*; Bosniak, "Citizenship Denationalized"; Balibar, *We, the People of Europe?*.

27. Holston, *Insurgent Citizenship*; Holston, *Cities and Citizenship*; Isin, *Democracy, Citizenship and the Global City*.

28. Ong, *Flexible Citizenship*, 19.

29. Leyshon and Thrift, "Geographies of Financial Exclusion"; Roberts, "Financing Social Reproduction"; Kear, "Governing Homo Subprimicus."

30. Roberts, "Financing Social Reproduction," 24.

31. Aldridge, "Habitus and Cultural Capital in the Field of Personal Finance," 7.

32. País, "Agilidad y seguridad para el mercado hipotecario."

33. Fernández Durán, *La explosión del desorden*; Sánchez Santos, "Household Debt and Consumption Inequality"; Carbo-Valverde, Marques-Ibanez, and Rodríguez-Fernández, "Securitization, Bank Lending and Credit Quality."

34. Carbo-Valverde, Marques-Ibanez, and Rodríguez-Fernández, "Securitization, Bank Lending and Credit Quality," 14.

35. The gothic tale of Caja Madrid serves to underscore this shift from public welfare provider to outsized speculators. During this moment of ostensible prosperity, Aznar chose as its head Miguel Blesa, someone with lengthy ties to the party but no experience whatsoever in the banking industry. Under Blesa's rule, the bank continuously grew their mortgage portfolio by 30% per year, even when the national average was 20%. Changes to mortgage financing, which allowed for securitization, bundling, and other technologies of debt and credit, permitted a regional savings bank charged with a social mission to emit covered bonds and lend to whomever asked for a credit. Such a climate, meanwhile, promoted an endogamous environment in which bankers, public servants, politicians, and captains of industry were all complicit in changing regulation related to banking, land use, urban development, and housing. Little separated these various siloes of power as they promoted the economy's increasing reliance on residential construction and consumption through novel credit products. De Barrón Arniches, *El hundimiento de la banca*.

36. Banks and financial entities, including UCI, also conspired with appraisers and notaries public to drive up the price of housing and occlude the kinds of punitive clauses that were included in contracts and deeds of sale. More info: https://tribunalciudadanodejusticia.wordpress.com/2017/05/13/sobretasaciones-el-sucio-origen-de-la-estafa/https://elpais.com/economia/2019/02/12/actualidad/1549968872_804078.html.

37. Clarke and Zavisca, "Housing/Housing Markets."

38. Graham and Labanyi, *Spanish Cultural Studies*.

39. The Zapatero Government famously named Carme Chacón as the first female defense minister.

40. Holmes, *Integral Europe*.

41. López and Rodríguez, "The Spanish Model."

42. Bentolila, Dolado, and Jimeno, "Reforming an Insider-Outsider Labor Market."

43. Sánchez Santos, "Household Debt and Consumption Inequality."

44. Aldridge, "Habitus and Cultural Capital in the Field of Personal Finance."

45. Clarke and Zavisca, "Housing/Housing Markets," 3.

46. Sánchez Santos, "Household Debt and Consumption Inequality."

47. Bourdieu, *The Social Structures of the Economy.*

48. Ravelli, "Financial Backlash When Local Bankers Face Social Protest."

49. Banco de España, "Survey of Household Finances (EFF): Descriptions, Methods, and Preliminary Results"; Banco de España, "Survey of Household Finances (EFF) 2005: Methods, Results and Changes Between 2002 and 2005"; Banco de España, "Survey of Household Finances (EFF) 2008: Methods, Results and Changes Since 2005."

50. Holston, *Insurgent Citizenship.*

Chapter 5

1. I will continue to use the female pronoun; PAH Madrid is explicitly feminist, and the majority of people who seek out mortgage-related aid is women.

2. The language of delinquency also of course allies an economic situation with personal failings and deviant behavior.

3. Elyachar, *Markets of Dispossession*, 30.

4. Roberts, "Financing Social Reproduction."

5. Bourdieu, *Distinction*, 387.

6. Bourdieu, *The Social Structures of the Economy*, 189.

7. Ibid.

8. Aldridge, "Habitus and Cultural Capital in the Field of Personal Finance," 8.

9. Durkheim, *Suicide*, 253.

10. Izquierdo and del Riego, "Cospedal: 'Los votantes del PP son los que pagan la hipoteca.'"

11. Zaloom, *Indebted*; Gregory, "On Money Debt and Morality."

12. An understanding of financial ruin as criminal, singular, and individual reflects broader currents that render the poor into subjects undeserving, and thus in need of punishment, the oft-repeated refrain of blaming the poor for their poverty. Katz, *The Undeserving Poor*; Slater T, "The Myth of 'Broken Britain'"; Wacquant, *Punishing the Poor.*

13. I use distortion here deliberately following arguments that insist ideology works initially through distortion or deformation. For a good discussion of distortion and ideology, see Dikeç, "Immigrants, Banlieues, and Dangerous Things."

14. Lisa Marie Cacho points to the ways in which acts of survival during crisis—in the case she uses, taking food from an empty store—are illegalized through processes of racialization. The Black man is seen as a looter, while his white counterpart is simply struggling to avoid hunger in post-Katrina New Orleans. The question of property is at the heart of the interpretations of both acts: in one, property is seen to be violated, while in the other such violation is absolved in the name of survival. Cacho, *Social Death.*

15. Gilmore, *Golden Gulag*; Roy, "Paradigms of Propertied Citizenship Transnational Techniques of Analysis"; Wacquant, *Punishing the Poor.*

16. Roy, "Dis/Possessive Collectivism."

17. LeBaron and Roberts, "Confining Social Insecurity."

18. García-Lamarca and Kaika, "Mortgaged Lives."

19. Durkheim, *Suicide*.

20. In Spanish as in other romance languages, the same word, *vergüenza,* signifies both shame and embarrassment. Bourdieu, *Distinction*, 204.

21. Gilligan, "Shame, Guilt, and Violence."

22. Biddle, "Shame," 229.

23. Heller, "The Power of Shame," 215.

24. Patterson, *Slavery and Social Death*, 38.

25. Agamben and Heller-Roazen, *Homo Sacer*.

26. Observatorio DESC and Plataforma de Afectados por la Hipoteca, "Emergencia habitacional en el estado español."

27. At times, however, the *aval* might be someone the buyer barely knew, a situation I will revisit later on.

28. I would argue that mortgage debt, because of the ways in which it seemed to ensure entry into the middle class and labor market participation, functioned in similar ways in Madrid to student debt in the United States. The unique qualities of both forms of debt—difficult to discharge, inheritable, taken out in vast quantities for goods and services of questionable quality—also make them ripe for comparison.

29. Bourdieu, *The Bachelors' Ball*.

30. In this section, I draw on an archive of PAH *fichas,* intake forms used by the collective to record information for people with fixed date of eviction. The forms, filled out in dialogue with a PAH member, recorded both mortgage and banking information, and personal circumstances, which might then be utilized to mount a defense in the bank or the courts.

31. Ismail, *Political Life in Cairo's New Quarters Encountering the Everyday State*.

32. Roy, *City Requiem, Calcutta Gender and the Politics of Poverty*.

33. Wyly and Ponder, "Gender, Age, and Race in Subprime America"; Roberts, "Financing Social Reproduction"; Roberts, *Gendered States of Punishment and Welfare*; Dymski, Hernandez, and Mohanty, "Race, Gender, Power, and the US Subprime Mortgage and Foreclosure Crisis"; Bakker, "Social Reproduction and the Constitution of a Gendered Political Economy"; Bezanson, *Gender, the State, and Social Reproduction*.

34. Observatorio DESC and Plataforma de Afectados por la Hipoteca, "Emergencia habitacional en el estado español."

35. Critical urban studies have deployed the notion of the periphery as spaces not necessarily at the physical edge, but rather metaphorical sites that are liminal to the dominant project of building the city. These sites might contain abjection and dispossession, but also their own logics and insurgencies that challenge and destabilize the "core." See, for example, Simone, *City Life from Jakarta to Dakar*.

36. Arbaci and Malheiros, "De-Segregation, Peripheralisation and the Social Exclusion of Immigrants"; Martínez del Olmo and Leal Maldonado, "La segregación residencial, un indicador espacial confuso en la representación de la problemática residencial de los inmigrantes económicos."

37. Wacquant, *Urban Outcasts*.

38. Martínez del Olmo and Leal Maldonado, "La segregación residencial, un indicador espacial confuso en la representación de la problemática residencial de los inmigrantes económicos," 59.

39. Activists created a website that mapped all the evictions that had passed through the PAH Madrid: https://viveroiniciativasciudadanas.net/2015/03/10/madrid-desahuciado/

40. The following discussions of municipal data on building conditions, etc., are based on data found here: http://www.madrid.es/portales/munimadrid/es/Inicio/Ayuntamiento/Estadistica/Areas-de-informacion-estadistica/Edificacion-y-vivienda/Censo-de-edificios-y-viviendas/Censo-de-Edificios-y-Viviendas-2001?vgnextfmt=detNavegacion&vgnextoid=d8cddc5bed1b8410VgnVCM1000000b205a0aRCRD&vgnextchannel=f93124e8951ef310VgnVCM1000000b205a0aRCRD.

41. While the question of disability and accessibility is beyond the scope of this book, the urban environments I'm describing clearly prevent all urban residents from benefiting from access and enjoyment.

42. Martín, "Imágenes Mentales Del Centro de Madrid, El Barrio de Lavapiés."

43. García García, "Inseguridad, poder y biografía en un contexto barrial. El caso de Carabanchel."

44. French, *Broken Harbor*, 97.

45. Butler and Athanasiou, *Dispossession*.

Chapter 6

1. Balibar and Wallerstein, *Race, Nation, Class.*

2. Caldwell, *Reflections on the Revolution in Europe*; Huntington, "The Clash of Civilizations?"

3. A few pieces examine Ecuadorian experiences with mortgage debt and activism. See Palomera, "How Did Finance Capital Infiltrate the World of the Urban Poor?"; Suarez, "Debt Revolts."

4. Colau and Alemany, *Vidas hipotecadas*; Haro Barba, Barba, and Blanco, "Activismo político en red"; Aguilar Fernández and Fernández Gibaja, "El movimiento por la vivienda digna en España o el porqué del fracaso de una protesta con amplia base social."

5. Fominaya, "Redefining the Crisis/Redefining Democracy."

6. Colau and Alemany, *Vidas hipotecadas*.

7. Gratton, "Ecuadorians in the United States and Spain"; Jokisch and Pribilsky, "The Panic to Leave"; Lucero, "High Anxiety in the Andes."

8. Calero, Bedi, and Sparrow, "Remittances, Liquidity Constraints and Human Capital Investments in Ecuador"; Ponce et al., "Remittances for Development?"

9. Many advertised the possibility to purchase two homes at once, one in Madrid and the other in the country of origin

10. Marina D'Or holiday village: https://www.marinador.com/en.

11. The Alcazares are fortresses dating from the medieval era in the historic towns of Toledo and Segovia, both near Madrid.

12. Such developments are part of the global spread of gated communities, which have proven particularly popular in Latin American cities, where, as Teresa Caldeira's research on Sao Paolo has revealed, for example, fears of security and crime have created new aesthetic regimes of fencing, gating, and so on. Caldeira, *City of Walls*. See also Borsdorf, Hidalgo, and Sánchez, "A New Model of Urban Development in Latin America"; Webster, Glasze, and Frantz, "The Global Spread of Gated Communities."

13. Lopez, *The Remittance Landscape*.

14. Escobar, *Encountering Development*.

15. That notion resonates with hegemonic understandings of indigenous Ecuador, for example, as Sawyer makes clear in her work. The racialization of *indios* has largely depicted them as docile and passive.

16. In her recent book, Hiba Bou Akar argues we are witnessing a turn toward "planning without development," in which the notion of development is falling away. Exurban gated communities perhaps also make us confront that logic. In an age of coming climate catastrophe, they follow older notions of progress that now spell ever greater carbon consumption. Bou Akar, *For the War Yet to Come*; see also Goldman, *Imperial Nature*.

17. Masterson-Algar, *Ecuadorians in Madrid*.

18. Sawyer, *Crude Chronicles*, 188.

19. Becker, "Indigenous Struggles for Land Rights in Twentieth-Century Ecuador"; Goodwin, "The Quest to Bring Land under Social and Political Control"; Martí i Puig, ed., *Pueblos indígenas y política en América Latina*.

20. Erazo, *Construyendo la autonomía organizaciones indígenas, gobierno y uso de la tierra en la región amazónica del Ecuador, 1964–2001*; Faas, "Reciprocity and Development in Disaster-Induced Resettlement in Andean Ecuador"; Pribilsky, "'Aprendemos a Convivir.'"

21. Aguilar Sánchez, Zeas S, and Pedro, *Territorialidad y gobernabilidad indígenas*; Becker, "Indigenous Struggles for Land Rights in Twentieth-Century Ecuador"; Radcliffe, "Gendered Frontiers of Land Control."

22. Andolina, Laurie, and Radcliffe, *Indigenous Development in the Andes*, 67.

23. Sawyer, *Crude Chronicles*, 84.

24. Ibid., 48. There has also been a robust conversation over the concept of territory within the spatial social sciences. See Blomley, "The Territory of Property"; Elden, *The Birth of Territory*; Sassen, *Territory, Authority, Rights*.

25. Centro de Educación Popular (Quito and CONFENIAE (Organization), *Defendamos nuestra tierra! Defendamos nuestra vida!*; Comision por la Defensa de los Derechos Humanos (Quito) et al., *El levantamiento indigena y la cuestion nacional*; "Levantamiento indigena"; Vallejo, *Crónica mestiza del nuevo Pachakutik*.

26. Andolina, Laurie, and Radcliffe, *Indigenous Development in the Andes*, 30. The Catholic Church has played an interesting role in the Indigenous movement. While it is a symbol of colonial histories of oppression, the Church has more recently become an advocate for struggles for emancipation, often through those parishes that embrace liberation theology. Thus it is both historical enemy and contemporary advocate, a paradoxical institution.

27. Sawyer, *Crude Chronicles*, 15.

28. Ferguson, *Give a Man a Fish*; Hardt and Negri, *Multitude*.

29. Of course these kinds of cultural ties and modes of collective life are leveraged in processes of accumulation by dispossession, as Julia Elyachar makes evident in her work. What is then dispossessed is not only actual capital, but also the kinds of sociality that previously characterized the interactions of everyday. Elyachar, *Markets of Dispossession NGOs, Economic Development, and the State in Cairo.*

30. Notaries were deeply implicated in mortgage fraud. Becoming a notary in Spain is very difficult, and they are accorded much prestige. During the boom they were also integral to the fraudulent practices of many financial entities.

31 Scott, *Seeing Like a State.*

32. García-Lamarca and Kaika, "'Mortgaged Lives.'"

33. Most lawyers have only a passing knowledge of mortgage and eviction law. The lawyers who assist the PAH also went through a process of learning, becoming masters of what was once a pretty arcane area of the law.

Chapter 7

1. There is an extensive and rich literature on the 15M movement. Work has looked at its use of urban and/or cyber space, links to the housing movement, democratization, spontaneity and autonomous movements, and connections to other movements, among other topics. See Martínez López and Bernardos, "Movimiento 15M, espacio público y luchas pro- vivienda"; Hughes, "'Young People Took to the Streets and All of a Sudden All of the Political Parties Got Old'"; Castañeda, "The Indignados of Spain"; Micó and Casero-Ripollés, "Political Activism Online"; Morell, "The Free Culture and 15M Movements in Spain"; Perugorría and Tejerina, "Politics of the Encounter"; Gonick, "Indignation and Inclusion"; Fominaya, "Debunking Spontaneity"; Fominaya, *Democracy Reloaded.*

2. Featherstone, *Solidarity*; Featherstone, "Towards the Relational Construction of Militant Particularisms."

3. Feliciantonio, "Social Movements and Alternative Housing Models."

4. Hardt and Negri, *Assembly.*

5. Pérez and Casadevante, "Superhéroes de barrio."

6. Fominaya, "Autonomous Movements and the Institutional Left."

7. Indeed, several native Spanish interlocutors came out of the feminist movement. Palomo, "Austerity Policies and the Feminist Movement in Spain."

8. Notably, the fire department has refused to participate in evictions.

9. The Bad Bank, the SAREB, was created as a holding company for the toxic assets of many of Spain's largest banks. Thousands of housing units have passed into its portfolio. Additionally, while refusing to use the terminology of "bailout," the state negotiated financial restructuring and the use of public funds to keep the national financial system afloat. This was recently once again in the news because the Banco Popular, which had received 60 million euros in public funds, was recently sold to Banco Santander for one euro after revealing extensive losses.

10. Graeber, "Occupy Wall Street Rediscovers the Radical Imagination"; Hardt and Negri, "Adventures of the Multitude"; Hardt and Negri, *Multitude*.

11. Appel, "Occupy Wall Street and the Economic Imagination."

12. Martínez and Bernardos, "Movimiento 15M, espacio público y luchas pro-vivienda."

13. Fominaya and Montañes Jiménez, "Transnational Diffusion Across Time: The Adoption of the Argentinian Dirty War 'Escrache' in the Context of Spain's Housing Crisis"; Romanos, "Evictions, Petitions and Escraches."

14. Fominaya and Montañes Jiménez, "Transnational Diffusion Across Time: The Adoption of the Argentinian Dirty War 'Escrache' in the Context of Spain's Housing Crisis," 21.

15. País, "Los desahucios unen a los votantes."

16. Mouffe, *Agonistics*.

17. The idea of radical struggle through both institutions and the streets would go on to influence the emergence of Spain's municipalist movements, which I argue came out of a marriage between various forms of activism. For more information: Gonick, "Indignation and Inclusion"; Calle Collado and Vilaregut, eds., *Territorios en democracia*; Díaz-Parra, Roca, and Martín-Díaz, "Indignados, Municipalism and Podemos."

18. País, "Hemos ganado los débiles, hemos ganado todos."

19. Calavita, *Immigrants at the Margins*.

20. Eder and Kousis, *Environmental Politics in Southern Europe*, 73.

21. The historical memory movement seeks to recuperate and name the Republican experiences of oppression and violence during the civil war and Franco era in part as a means of restorative justice.

22. Labanyi, "The Politics of Memory in Contemporary Spain."

23. For example, much of the contemporary debate around historical memory in Spain was catalyzed by the journalist Emilio Silva, who took it upon himself to carry out an exhumation of his grandfather's grave in the absence of any kind of framework for transitional justice and the remains of Franco era crimes.

24. Personal correspondence.

25. Jameson, "The Indigenous Movement in Ecuador"; Kimberling, "Indigenous Peoples and the Oil Frontier in Amazonia"; Lyons, "Case Study in Multinational Corporate Accountability"; Selverston-Scher, *Ethnopolitics in Ecuador*.

26. Hardt and Negri, *Empire*.

27. Simpson, *Mohawk Interruptus*; Simpson, "The Ruse of Consent and the Anatomy of 'Refusal.'"

28. Notably, however, Simpson writes of "refusal" as a powerful tactic for Indigenous communities in settler colonial societies that rejects the standard demand for recognition and the "ruse of consent." At the same time, the settler colonial frame, which Simpson and others use deliberately, is problematic when applied to certain Latin American contexts such as Ecuador, where the mixing or *mestizaje* was an active part of the colonial project.

29. Gonick, "Indignation and Inclusion."

30. Bakker, "Social Reproduction and the Constitution of a Gendered Political Economy"; Dale and Foster, *Feminists and State Welfare (RLE Feminist Theory)*; Fraser, "After the Family Wage."

31. Simpson, "The Ruse of Consent and the Anatomy of 'Refusal.'"

32. García-Lamarca, "Real Estate Crisis Resolution Regimes and Residential REITs."

33. De Barrón Arniches, *El hundimiento de la banca*.

34. Veloso, "Bankia, el rescate más caro en la historia de España."

35. Alejandro López, "Bankia, motor de los desahucios en Madrid."

36. Información Sensible, "La Sareb 'pasa' de Aznar Junior y Del Fondo Cerberus y Entrega La Gestión de Los Activos Inmobiliarios al Sabadell."

37. Essen and Hodkinson, "Grounding Accumulation by Dispossession in Everyday Life"; Harvey, "The Geography of Capitalist Accumulation"; Glassman, "Primitive Accumulation, Accumulation by Dispossession, Accumulation by 'Extra-Economic' Means."

38. Martínez López and García Bernardos, *Okupa Madrid (1985–2011)*; Adell Argilés, Martínez López, and Alcalde Villacampa, *Dónde están las llaves?*

39. Gonick, "Interrogating Madrid's 'Slum of Shame.'"

40. Martínez López, "The Squatters' Movement in Europe."

41. Martínez López and García Bernardos, "Ocupar las plazas, liberar edificios."

42. Interview with anonymous bureaucrat, January 2014, Madrid, Spain.

43. Panagia, "'Partage du sensible.'"

44. S. L., "El 'banco malo' pagó 30 millones a las comunidades de vecinos en 2013, un 25% más de lo previsto."

45. Boggs, "Revolutionary Process, Political Strategy, and the Dilemma of Power."

46. Gonick, "Indignation and Inclusion."

47. Gonick, "Interrogating Madrid's 'Slum of Shame.'"

Chapter 8

1. Davies, "Toxic Space and Time."

Bibliography

Aalbers, Manuel B. "Neoliberalism Is Dead . . . Long Live Neoliberalism!" *International Journal of Urban and Regional Research* 37, no. 3 (2013): 1083–90.

———. *Subprime Cities: The Political Economy of Mortgage Markets*. Malden, MA: Wiley-Blackwell, 2012.

Acerete, Basilio, Jean Shaoul, and Anne Stafford. "Taking Its Toll: The Private Financing of Roads in Spain." *Public Money and Management* 29, no. 1 (2009): 19–26.

Adell Argilés, Ramón, Miguel Martínez López, and Javier Alcalde Villacampa. *Dónde están las llaves?: el movimiento okupa : prácticas y contextos sociales*. Madrid: Los Libros de la Catarata, 2004.

Agamben, Giorgio, and Daniel Heller-Roazen. *Homo Sacer*. Stanford, CA: Stanford University Press, 1998.

Aguilar Fernández, Susana, and Alberto Fernández Gibaja. "El movimiento por la vivienda digna en España o el porqué del fracaso de una protesta con amplia base social." *Revista Internacional de Sociología* 68, no. 3 (2010): 679–704.

Aguilar Sánchez, Oswaldo, and Pedro Zeas S. *Territorialidad y gobernabilidad indígenas: capitalización de la filosofía y práctica de la planificación, gestión y gobernabilidad de las nacionalidades y pueblos del Ecuador : la unidad indígena-territorio es indivisible, sagrada e innegociable*. Quito: CODENPE, 2006.

Ahmed, Sara. "Home and Away: Narratives of Migration and Estrangement." *International Journal of Cultural Studies* 2, no. 3 (1999): 329–47.

Akar, Hiba Bou. *For the War Yet to Come: Planning Beirut's Frontiers*. Stanford, CA: Stanford University Press, 2018.

Alba, Richard D., and John R. Logan. "Assimilation and Stratification in the Homeownership Patterns of Racial and Ethnic Groups." *International Migration Review* 26, no. 4 (1992): 1314–41.

Aldridge, Alan. "Habitus and Cultural Capital in the Field of Personal Finance." *Sociological Review* 46, no. 1 (1998): 1–23.

Almodóvar, Pedro, dir. *Carne trémula*. Starring Javier Bardem, Francesca Neri, Liberto Rabal, Alberto Iglesias, and Ruth Rendell, Madrid: El Deseo S.A., 1997.

———. *Que he hecho yo para merecer esto?* Starring Carmen Maura, Verónica Forqué, Chus Lampreave, and Gonzalo Suárez. Madrid: Kaktus Producciones Cinematográficas, and Tesauro S.A., 1984.

Amin, Ash. *Post-Fordism: A Reader*. Somerset: Wiley, 2011.

Andall, Jacqueline. *Gender, Migration and Domestic Service: The Politics of Black Women in Italy*. Farnham: Ashgate, 2000.

Andolina, Robert, Nina Laurie, and Sarah A. Radcliffe. *Indigenous Development in the Andes: Culture, Power, and Transnationalism*. Durham, NC: Duke University Press, 2009.

Aparicio, Rosa. *Marroquíes en España*. Madrid: Universidad Pontificia Comillas, 2005.

Appel, Hannah. "Occupy Wall Street and the Economic Imagination." *Cultural Anthropology* 29, no. 4 (2014): 602–25.

Arbaci, Sonia, and Jorge Malheiros. "De-Segregation, Peripheralisation and the Social Exclusion of Immigrants: Southern European Cities in the 1990s." *Journal of Ethnic and Migration Studies* 36, no. 2 (2010): 227–55.

Arco Blanco, Miguel Ángel del. "«Morir de hambre»: autarquía, escasez y enfermedad en la España del primer franquismo." *Pasado y memoria*, no. 5 (2006): 241–58.

Bakker, Isabella. "Social Reproduction and the Constitution of a Gendered Political Economy." *New Political Economy* 12, no. 4 (2007): 541–56.

Balibar, Étienne. *We, the People of Europe?: Reflections on Transnational Citizenship*. Princeton, NJ: Princeton University Press, 2009.

Balibar, Etienne, and Immanuel Maurice Wallerstein. *Race, Nation, Class: Ambiguous Identities*. New York: Verso, 1991.

Banco de España. "Survey of Household Finances (EFF) 2005: Methods, Results and Changes Between 2002 and 2005." *Economic Bulletin* (January 2008): 2–34.

———. "Survey of Household Finances (EFF) 2008: Methods, Results and Changes Since 2005." *Economic Bulletin* (January 2011): 90–123.

———. "Survey of Household Finances (EFF); Descriptions, Methods, and Preliminary Results." *Economic Bulletin* (January 2005): 2–21.

Barber, Llana. *Latino City: Immigration and Urban Crisis in Lawrence, Massachusetts, 1945–2000*. Chapel Hill: University of North Carolina Press, 2017.

Becker, Marc. "Indigenous Struggles for Land Rights in Twentieth-Century Ecuador." *Agricultural History* 81, no. 2 (2007): 159–81.

Bentolila, Samuel, Juan J. Dolado, and Juan F. Jimeno. "Reforming an Insider-Outsider Labor Market: The Spanish Experience." *IZA Journal of European Labor Studies* 1, no. 1 (2012): 4.

Bezanson, Kate. *Gender, the State, and Social Reproduction: Household Insecurity in Neo-Liberal Times*. Toronto: University of Toronto Press, 2006.

Bhan, Gautam. *In the Public's Interest: Evictions, Citizenship, and Inequality in Contemporary Delhi*. Athens: University of Georgia Press, 2016.

Bhandar, Brenna. *Colonial Lives of Property: Law, Land, and Racial Regimes of Ownership*. Durham, NC: Duke University Press, 2018.

Biddle, Jennifer. "Shame." *Australian Feminist Studies* 12, no. 26 (1997): 227–39.

Bidagor, P. *Orientaciones sobre la reconstrucción de Madrid*. Madrid: I.T.C.E., 1941.

Bloemraad, Irene. *Becoming a Citizen: Incorporating Immigrants and Refugees in the United States and Canada*. Berkeley: University of California Press, 2006.

Bloemraad, Irene, Anna Korteweg, and Gökçe Yurdakul. "Citizenship and Immigration: Multiculturalism, Assimilation, and Challenges to the Nation-State." *Annual Review of Sociology* 34, no. 1 (2008): 153–79.

Blomley, Nicholas. "The Territory of Property." *Progress in Human Geography* 40, no. 5 (2016): 593–609.

Boggs, Carl. "Revolutionary Process, Political Strategy, and the Dilemma of Power." *Theory and Society* 4, no. 3 (1977): 359–93.

Bonet Correa, Antonio, Vicente Mora Carbonell, and Instituto de Estudios Madrileños. *Madrid. Tomo 5*. Madrid: Espasa-Calpe, 1980.

Borsdorf, Axel, Rodrigo Hidalgo, and Rafael Sánchez. "A New Model of Urban Development in Latin America: The Gated Communities and Fenced Cities in the Metropolitan Areas of Santiago de Chile and Valparaíso." *Cities* 24, no. 5 (2007): 365–78.

Bosniak, Linda. "Citizenship Denationalized." *Indiana Journal of Global Legal Studies* 7, no. 2 (2000): 447–509.

Bourdieu, Pierre. *Distinction: A Social Critique of the Judgement of Taste*. Abingdon: Routledge, 2013.

———. *The Bachelors' Ball: The Crisis of Peasant Society in Béarn*. Chicago: University of Chicago Press, 2008.

———. *The Social Structures of the Economy*. New York: John Wiley and Sons, 2014.

Bowen, John R. *Why the French Don't Like Headscarves: Islam, the State, and Public Space*. Princeton, NJ: Princeton University Press, 2010.

Bowsher, Josh. "Credit/Debt and Human Capital: Financialized Neoliberalism and the Production of Subjectivity." *European Journal of Social Theory* 22, no. 4 (2018): 513–32.

Boyer, M. Christine. *Dreaming the Rational City: The Myth of American City Planning*. Cambridge, MA: MIT Press, 1986.

Brubaker, Rogers. *Citizenship and Nationhood in France and Germany*. Cambridge, MA: Harvard University Press, 1992.

Bruquetas-Callejo, M. "Immigration and Integration Policymaking in Spain." *IMISCOE Working Paper*, no. 21 (2008).

Burriel, Eugenio L. "Subversion of Land-Use Plans and the Housing Bubble in Spain." *Urban Research and Practice* 4, no. 3 (2011): 232–49.

Butler, Judith, and Athena Athanasiou. *Dispossession: The Performative in the Political*. New York: John Wiley and Sons, 2013.

Cacho, Lisa Marie. *Social Death: Racialized Rightlessness and the Criminalization of the Unprotected*. New York: NYU Press, 2012.

Çaglar, Ayse, and Nina Glick Schiller. *Migrants and City-Making: Dispossession, Displacement, and Urban Regeneration*. Durham, NC: Duke University Press, 2018.

Calavita, Kitty. *Immigrants at the Margins: Law, Race, and Exclusion in Southern Europe*. Cambridge: Cambridge University Press, 2005.

Caldeira, Teresa P. R. *City of Walls: Crime, Segregation, and Citizenship in São Paulo*. Berkeley: University of California Press, 2000.

Caldwell, Christopher. *Reflections on the Revolution in Europe: Immigration, Islam, and the West*. New York: Knopf Doubleday Publishing Group, 2009.

Calero, Carla, Arjun S. Bedi, and Robert Sparrow. "Remittances, Liquidity Constraints and Human Capital Investments in Ecuador." *World Development* 37, no. 6 (2009): 1143–54.

Calle Collado, Ángel, and Ricard Vilaregut, eds. *Territorios en democracia: el municipalismo a debate*. Barcelona: Icaria editorial, 2015.

Carbo-Valverde, Santiago, David Marques-Ibanez, and Francisco Rodriguez-Fernandez. "Securitization, Bank Lending and Credit Quality: The Case of Spain." ECB Working Paper n. 1329. Rochester, NY: Social Science Research Network, April 4, 2011.

Carrera, Sergio. *In Search of the Perfect Citizen?: The Intersection Between Integration, Immigration, and Nationality in the EU*. Leiden: BRILL, 2009.

Casas-Cortes, Maribel, Sebastian Cobarrubias, Nicholas De Genova, Glenda Garelli, Giorgio Grappi, Charles Heller, Sabine Hess, et al. "New Keywords: Migration and Borders." *Cultural Studies* 29, no. 1 (2015): 55–87.

Castañeda, Ernesto. *A Place to Call Home: Immigrant Exclusion and Urban Belonging in New York, Paris, and Barcelona*. Stanford, CA: Stanford University Press, 2018.

———. "The Indignados of Spain: A Precedent to Occupy Wall Street." *Social Movement Studies* 11, no. 3–4 (2012): 309–19.

Castells, Manuel. *The City and the Grassroots: A Cross-Cultural Theory of Urban Social Movements*. Berkeley: University of California Press, 1983.

Centro de Educación Popular (Quito, Ecuador), and CONFENIAE (Organization). *Defendamos nuestra tierra! Defendamos nuestra vida!* Quito, Ecuador: CEDEP: CONFENIAE, 1985.

Chen, Simon C. Y., and Chris J. Webster. "Homeowners Associations, Collective Action and the Costs of Private Governance." *Housing Studies* 20, no. 2 (2005): 205–20.

Cladera, Josép Roca, and Malcolm C. Burns. "The Liberalization of the Land Market in Spain: The 1998 Reform of Urban Planning Legislation." *European Planning Studies* 8, no. 5 (October 1, 2000): 547–64.

Clark, William A. V. *Immigrants and the American Dream: Remaking the Middle Class*. New York: Guilford Press, 2003.

Clarke, Hannah, and Jane Zavisca. "Housing/Housing Markets." In *Wiley Blackwell Encyclopedia of Consumption and Consumer Studies*, ed. Daniel Thomas Cook and J. Michael Ryan, 1–3. New York: Wiley-Blackwell, 2015.

Colau, Ada, and Adrià Alemany. *Vidas hipotecadas: de la burbuja immobiliaria al derecho a la Vivienda*. Madrid: Cuadrilátero de Libros, 2013.

Colectivo Ioé, Carlos Pereda, Miguel Ángel de Prada, and Walter Actis. 2007. *"Igual de seres humanos" : historias de inserción de migrantes con problemas en la Comunidad Valenciana*. Valencia: CeiMigra, 2007.

Comisaría General para la Ordenación Urbana de Madrid y sus Alrededores. "Gran Madrid: boletín informativo de la Comisaría General para la Ordenación Urbana de Madrid y sus alrededores." *Gran Madrid : boletín informativo de la Comisaría General para la Ordenación Urbana de Madrid y sus alrededores*. 1, no. 1 (1948).

Comisión por la Defensa de los Derechos Humanos (Ecuador). *El levantamiento indígena y la cuestión nacional*. Quito: Editorial Abya Yala, 1996.

Compitello, Malcolm Alan. "Designing Madrid, 1985–1997." *JCIT Cities* 20, no. 6 (2003): 403–11.

———. "From Planning to Design: The Culture of Flexible Accumulation in Post-Cambio Madrid." *Arizona Journal of Hispanic Cultural Studies* 3, no. 1 (1999): 199–219.

Comunidad de Madrid. "Plan de Integración 2006–2008." Consejería de Inmigración y Cooperación de la Comunidad de Madrid, 2006.

Consejo Superior de los Colegios de Arquitectos. "Casa de pisos en la calle de Ayala (Madrid)." *Revista nacional de arquitectura*. 5, nos. 58–59 (1946): 204–6.

———. "Organización teorica de un distrito de 100,000 habitantes." *Revista nacional de arquitectura* 5, nos. 49–50 (1946): 6.

———. "Viviendas económicas en el barrio de Usera (Madrid)." *Revista nacional de arquitectura* 3.2, no. 35 (1944): 392–94.

Coppola, Francis Ford, dir. *The Godfather: II*. Starring Al Pacino, Robert Duvall, Diane Keaton, Robert De Niro, Talia Shire, et al. Los Angeles: Paramount Pictures, 1974.

Coq-Huelva, Daniel. "Urbanisation and Financialisation in the Context of a Rescaling State: The Case of Spain." *Antipode* 45, no. 5 (2013): 1213–31.

Cronistas Villa Verde. *Cuadernos de Investigación 4: El Poblado de Absorción de Villaverde (Colonia Del Cruce)*. Cuadernos de Investigación 4. Madrid, 2011. mcmoriademadrid.es/buscador php?accion=VerFicha&id=265324&num_id=3&num_total=9

Crul, Maurice, and Hans Vermeulen. "The Second Generation in Europe." *International Migration Review* 37, no. 4 (2003): 965–86.

Dale, Jennifer, and Peggy Foster, eds. *Feminists and State Welfare. RLE Feminist Theory*. New York: Routledge, 2012.

Das Gupta, Monisha. *Unruly Immigrants: Rights, Activism, and Transnational South Asian Politics in the United States*. Durham, NC: Duke University Press, 2008.

Davies, Thom. "Toxic Space and Time: Slow Violence, Necropolitics, and Petrochemical Pollution." *Annals of the American Association of Geographers* 108, no. 6 (2018): 1537–53.

D'Costa, Anthony P., and Achin Chakraborty. *The Land Question in India: State, Dispossession, and Capitalist Transition*. Oxford: Oxford University Press, 2017.

de Barrón Arniches, Iñigo. *El hundimiento de la banca: crónica de cómo gestores, supervisores y políticos provocaron la mayor crisis en la historia del sistema financiero español*. Madrid: Los Libros de la Catarata, 2012.

"Declaraciones del ministro de la vivienda, don José Luis de Arrese." *ABC*. September 16, 1958, Madrid edition.

Di Feliciantonio, Cesare. "Social Movements and Alternative Housing Models: Practicing the 'Politics of Possibilities' in Spain." *Housing, Theory and Society* 34, no. 1 (2017): 38–56.

Diario de Sesiones de la Asamblea de Madrid, Pub. L. No. 44, § Comisión de Integración y Cooperación (2007).

———. No. 49, § Comisión de Integración y Cooperación (2007).

———. No. 161, § Comisión de Estudio sobre la Inmigración en la Comunidad de Madrid (2004).

———. No. 402, § Comisión de Estudio sobre la Inmigración en la Comunidad de Madrid (2005).

Díaz, Santos Juliá, David R. Ringrose, and Cristina Segura. *Madrid: Historia de una capital*. Madrid: Alianza Editorial, 2000.

Díaz-Parra, Ibán, Beltrán Roca, and Emma Martín-Díaz. "Indignados, Municipalism and Podemos: Mobilisation and Political Cycle in Spain after the Great Recession." In *Challenging Austerity: Radical Left and Social Movements in the South of Europe*, ed. Beltrán Roca, Emma Martín-Díaz, and Ibán Díaz-Parra, 70–89. New York: Routledge, 2017.

Diaz-Serrano, Luis, and Josép M. Raya. "Mortgages, Immigrants and Discrimination: An Analysis of the Interest Rates in Spain." *Regional Science and Urban Economics* 45 (2014): 22–32.

Dikeç, Mustafa. "Immigrants, Banlieues, and Dangerous Things: Ideology as an Aesthetic Affair." *Antipode* 45, no. 1 (2013): 23–42.

Dines, Nick, Nicola Montagna, and Vincenzo Ruggiero. "Thinking Lampedusa: Border Construction, the Spectacle of Bare Life and the Productivity of Migrants." *Ethnic and Racial Studies* 38, no. 3 (2015): 430–45.

Douglas, Mary. *Purity and Danger: An Analysis of Concepts of Pollution and Taboo*. New York: Praeger, 1966.

Drake, Paul W., and Eric Hershberg. *State and Society in Conflict: Comparative Perspectives on Andean Crises*. Pittsburgh: University of Pittsburgh Press, 2006.

Durkheim, Émile. *Suicide*. New York: Free Press, 1966.

Dymski, Gary, Jesus Hernandez, and Lisa Mohanty. "Race, Gender, Power, and the US Subprime Mortgage and Foreclosure Crisis: A Meso Analysis." *Feminist Economics* 19, no. 3 (2013): 124–51.

Eder, Klaus, and M. Kousis. *Environmental Politics in Southern Europe: Actors, Institutions and Discourses in a Europeanizing Society*. Berlin: Springer Science and Business Media, 2001.

"El problema primero: La vivienda." *Informaciones*. December 15, 1944.

Elden, Stuart. *The Birth of Territory*. Chicago: University of Chicago Press, 2013.

Elyachar, Julia. *Markets of Dispossession: NGOs, Economic Development, and the State in Cairo.* Durham, NC: Duke University Press, 2005.

England, Kim V. L. "Changing Suburbs, Changing Women: Geographic Perspectives on Suburban Women and Suburbanization." *Frontiers: A Journal of Women Studies* 14, no. 1 (1993): 24–43.

Erazo, Juliet S. *Construyendo la autonomía organizaciones indígenas, gobierno y uso de la tierra en la región amazónica del Ecuador, 1964–2001.* Quito, Ecuador: Ediciones Abya-Yala , 2008.

Escobar, Arturo. *Encountering Development: The Making and Unmaking of the Third World.* Princeton, NJ: Princeton University Press, 2012.

Essen, Chris, and Stuart Hodkinson. "Grounding Accumulation by Dispossession in Everyday Life: The Unjust Geographies of Urban Regeneration under the Private Finance Initiative." *International Journal of Law in the Built Environment* 7, no. 1 (2015): 72–91.

Faas, Albert. "Reciprocity and Development in Disaster-Induced Resettlement in Andean Ecuador." Graduate Theses and Dissertations, January 1, 2012. https://scholarcommons.usf.edu/etd/4317.

Featherstone, David. "Black Internationalism, Subaltern Cosmopolitanism, and the Spatial Politics of Antifascism *Annals of the Association of American Geographers* 103, no. 6 (2013): 1406–20.

———. *Solidarity: Hidden Histories and Geographies of Internationalism.* London: Zed Books, 2012.

———. "Towards the Relational Construction of Militant Particularisms: Or Why the Geographies of Past Struggles Matter for Resistance to Neoliberal Globalisation." *Antipode* 37, no. 2 (2005): 250–71.

Ferguson, James. *Give a Man a Fish: Reflections on the New Politics of Distribution.* Durham, NC: Duke University Press, 2015.

Fernández Durán, Ramón. *La explosión del desorden: La metrópoli como espacio de la crisis global.* Madrid: Editorial Fundamentos, 1996.

Fominaya, Cristina Flesher. "Autonomous Movements and the Institutional Left: Two Approaches in Tension in Madrid's Anti-Globalization Network." *South European Society and Politics* 12, no. 3 (2007): 335–58.

———. "Debunking Spontaneity: Spain's 15-M/Indignados as Autonomous Movement." *Social Movement Studies* 14, no. 2 (2015): 142–63.

———. *Democracy Reloaded: Inside Spain's Political Laboratory from 15-M to Podemos.* New York: Oxford University Press, 2020.

———. "Redefining the Crisis/Redefining Democracy: Mobilising for the Right to Housing in Spain's PAH Movement." *South European Society and Politics* 20, no. 4 (2015): 465–85.

Fominaya, Cristina Flesher, and Antonio Montañés Jimenéz. "Transnational Diffusion Across Time: The Adoption of the Argentinian Dirty War 'Escrache' in the Context of Spain's Housing Crisis." *Spreading Protest: Social Movements in Times of Crisis* (2014): 19–41.

Fraser, Nancy. "After the Family Wage: Gender Equity and the Welfare State." *Political Theory* 22, no. 4 (1994): 591–618.

French, Tana. *Broken Harbor: A Novel.* New York: Penguin, 2012.

García, Marisol. "The Breakdown of the Spanish Urban Growth Model: Social and Territorial Effects of the Global Crisis." *International Journal of Urban and Regional Research* 34, no. 4 (2010): 967–80.

García Berlanga, Luis, dir. *Bienvenido, Mister Marshall!* Starring Luis Emilio Calvo-Sotelo, Lolita Sevilla, Manolo Morán, and José Isbert. Unión Industrial Cinematográfica, 1953.

García García, Sergio. "Inseguridad, poder y biografía en un contexto barrial. El caso de Carabanchel." Digibug, Universidad de Granada, May 2008. http://digibug.ugr .es/handle/10481/7062.

García-Lamarca, Melissa. "Real Estate Crisis Resolution Regimes and Residential REITs: Emerging Socio-Spatial Impacts in Barcelona." *Housing Studies* (May 26, 2020): 1–20. DOI: 10.1080/02673037.2020.1769034.

García-Lamarca, Melissa, and Maria Kaika. "'Mortgaged Lives': The Biopolitics of Debt and Housing Financialisation." *Transactions of the Institute of British Geographers* 41, no. 3 (2016): 313–27.

Ghertner, D. Asher. *Rule by Aesthetics: World-Class City Making in Delhi.* New York: Oxford University Press, 2015.

Gidwani, Vinay K. "Subaltern Cosmopolitanism as Politics." *Antipode* 38, no. 1 (2006): 7–21.

Gilligan, James. "Shame, Guilt, and Violence." *Social Research: An International Quarterly* 70, no. 4 (2003): 1149–80.

Gilmore, Ruth Wilson. *Golden Gulag: Prisons, Surplus, Crisis, and Opposition in Globalizing California.* Berkeley: University of California Press, 2007.

Glassman, Jim. "Primitive Accumulation, Accumulation by Dispossession, Accumulation by 'Extra-Economic' Means." *Progress in Human Geography* 30, no. 5 (2006): 608–25.

Goldman, Michael. *Imperial Nature: The World Bank and Struggles for Social Justice in the Age of Globalization.* New Have, CT: Yale University Press, 2008.

Gonick, Sophie. "From Pueblo to Capital: Francisco Franco, the Autarchy, and the 'Gran Madrid.'" Undergraduate thesis, A.B., Harvard College, 2005.

———. "Fordist Absences: Madrid's Right to Housing Movement as Labor Struggle." *International Labor and Working-Class History* 93 (2018): 91–100.

———. "Indignation and Inclusion: Activism, Difference, and Emergent Urban Politics in Postcrash Madrid." *Environment and Planning D: Society and Space* 34, no. 2 (2016): 209–26. https://doi.org/10.1177/0263775815608852.

———. "Interrogating Madrid's 'Slum of Shame': Urban Expansion, Race, and Place-Based Activisms in the Cañada Real Galiana." *Antipode* 47, no. 5 (2015): 1224–42.

Goode, Joshua. *Impurity of Blood Defining Race in Spain, 1870–1930.* Baton Rouge: Louisiana State University Press, 2009.

Goodwin, Geoff. "The Quest to Bring Land under Social and Political Control: Land Reform Struggles of the Past and Present in Ecuador." *Journal of Agrarian Change* 17, no. 3 (2017): 571–93.

Graeber, David. "Occupy Wall Street Rediscovers the Radical Imagination." *The Guardian*, September 25, 2011.

Graham, Helen, and Jo Labanyi. *Spanish Cultural Studies: An Introduction: The Struggle for Modernity.* New York: Oxford University Press, 1995.

Gratton, Brian. "Ecuadorians in the United States and Spain: History, Gender and Niche Formation." *Journal of Ethnic and Migration Studies* 33, no. 4 (2007): 581–99.

Gregory, Chris A. "On Money Debt and Morality: Some Reflections on the Contribution of Economic Anthropology." *Social Anthropology* 20, no. 4 (2012): 380–96.

Gutiérrez, Victoriano Sainz. *El proyecto urbano en España: Génesis y desarrollo de un urbanismo de los arquitectos.* Seville: Universidad de Sevilla, 2006.

Hall, Sarah. "Geographies of Money and Finance II: Financialization and Financial Subjects." *Progress in Human Geography* 36, no. 3 (2012): 403–11.

Hardt, Michael, and Antonio Negri. "Adventures of the Multitude: Response of the Authors." *Rethinking Marxism* 13, nos. 3–4 (2001): 236–43.

———. *Assembly.* Oxford: Oxford University Press, 2017.

———. *Empire.* Cambridge, MA: Harvard University Press, 2000.

———. *Multitude: War and Democracy in the Age of Empire.* New York: Penguin Press, 2004.

Haro Barba, Carmen, and Víctor Sampedro Blanco. "Activismo político en Red: Del movimiento por la Vivienda Digna al 15M." *Teknokultura. Revista de Cultura Digital y Movimientos Sociales* 8, no. 2 (2011): 157–75.

Harvey, David. "The Geography of Capitalist Accumulation: A Reconstruction of the Marxian Theory*." *Antipode* 7, no. 2 (1975): 9–21.

———. *Spaces of Capital: Towards a Critical Geography.* Hoboken, NJ: Taylor and Francis, 2012.

Hayden, Dolores. *Redesigning the American Dream: The Future of Housing, Work, and Family Life.* New York: W. W. Norton, 1984.

Hebbert, Michael. "Town Planning versus Urbanismo." *Planning Perspectives* 21, no. 3 (2006): 233–51.

Heller, Agnes. "The Power of Shame." *Dialectical Anthropology* 6, no. 3 (1982): 215–28.

Hergé, Leslie Lonsdale-Cooper, and Michael R Turner. *Tintin in America.* London: Mammoth, 2013.

Herráez, Carmen Fernández, Araceli Cabezas López, and Pablo Pinedo Reyes. *Urbanismo y Arquitectura En El Madrid Actual.* Madrid, Spain: Comunidad de Madrid, Consejería de Educación y Cultura, Dirección General de Centros Docentes, 1998.

Herraez, Sigfrido. "La rehabilitación en del centro histórico de Madrid." *Informes de la Construcción* 51, no. 465 (2000): 41–46.

Hinze, Annika Marlen. *Turkish Berlin: Integration Policy and Urban Space.* Minneapolis: University of Minnesota Press, 2013.

Hodkinson, Stuart. "The New Urban Enclosures." *City* 16, no. 5 (2012): 500–518.

Holmes, Douglas R. *Integral Europe: Fast-Capitalism, Multiculturalism, Neofascism.* Princeton, NJ: Princeton University Press, 2010.

Holmes, Seth M. "Representing the 'European Refugee Crisis' in Germany and Beyond: Deservingness and Difference, Life and Death." *American Ethnologist* (2016): 12–24.

Holston, James. *Cities and Citizenship.* Durham, NC: Duke University Press, 1999.

———. *Insurgent Citizenship: Disjunctions of Democracy and Modernity in Brazil.* Princeton, NJ: Princeton University Press, 2008.

Hughes, Neil. "'Young People Took to the Streets and All of a Sudden All of the Political Parties Got Old': The 15M Movement in Spain." *Social Movement Studies* 10, no. 4 (2011): 407–13.

Huntington, Samuel P. "The Clash of Civilizations?" *Foreign Affairs* 72, no. 3 (1993): 22–49.

Iglesias Martínez, Juan. *La población de origen ecuatoriano en España: Características, necesidades y expectativas en tiempos de crisis.* Madrid: Embajada del Ecuador en España, 2015.

Iniesta Corredor, Alfonso, Leónides Gonzalo Calavia, and Jesús Bernal. *Estampas de Madrid: Historia, arte, leyendas.* Sevilla: Publicaciones Digitales, 2002.

Isin, Engin F. *Being Political: Genealogies of Citizenship.* Minneapolis: University of Minnesota Press, 2002.

———. *Democracy, Citizenship and the Global City.* New York: Routledge, 2013.

Isin, Engin F., and Bryan S. Turner. *Handbook of Citizenship Studies.* Thousand Oaks, CA: SAGE, 2002.

Islamoglu, Huri. *Constituting Modernity: Private Property in the East and West.* London: I. B. Tauris, 2004.

Ismail, Salwa. *Political Life in Cairo's New Quarters: Encountering the Everyday State.* Minneapolis: University of Minnesota Press, 2006.

Izquierdo, Luis, and Carmen del Riego. "Cospedal: 'Los votantes del PP son los que pagan la hipoteca.'" *La Vanguardia*, April 16, 2013. https://www.lavanguardia.com/politica/20130417/54372496568/cospedal-votantes-dejan-comer-antes-hipoteca.html.

Jameson, Kenneth. "The Indigenous Movement in Ecuador." *Latin American Perspectives* 38, no. 1 (2011): 63–73.

Janoschka, Michael, Jorge Sequera, and Luis Salinas. "Gentrification in Spain and Latin America—a Critical Dialogue." *International Journal of Urban and Regional Research* 38, no. 4 (2014): 1234–65.

Jokisch, Brad, and Jason Pribilsky. "The Panic to Leave: Economic Crisis and the 'New Emigration' from Ecuador." *International Migration* 40, no. 4 (2002): 75–102.

Katz, Michael B. *The Undeserving Poor: America's Enduring Confrontation with Poverty. Fully updated and revised.* New York: Oxford University Press, 2013.

Kauppinen, Timo M., Hans Skifter Andersen, and Lina Hedman. "Determinants of Immigrants' Entry to Homeownership in Three Nordic Capital City Regions." *Geografiska Annaler: Series B, Human Geography* 97, no. 4 (2015): 343–62.

Kear, Mark. "Governing Homo Subprimicus: Beyond Financial Citizenship, Exclusion, and Rights." *Antipode* 45, no. 4 (2013): 926–46

Kimberling, Judith. "Indigenous Peoples and the Oil Frontier in Amazonia: The Case of Ecuador, Chevrontexaco, and Aguinda v. Texaco." *New York University Journal of International Law and Politics* 38 (2005): 413.

King, Russell. *The Mediterranean Passage: Migration and New Cultural Encounters in Southern Europe*. Liverpool: Liverpool University Press, 2001.

King, Russell, Gabriella Lazaridis, and Charalambos Tsardanidis, eds. *Eldorado or Fortness?: Migration of Southern Europe*. Houndmills: Palgrave Macmillan, 2002.

Koopmans, Ruud. *Contested Citizenship: Immigration and Cultural Diversity in Europe*. Minneapolis: University of Minnesota Press, 2005.

Kornetis, Kostis. "'Is There a Future in This Past?' Analyzing 15M's Intricate Relation to the Transición." *Journal of Spanish Cultural Studies* 15, nos. 1–2 (2014): 1–16.

Krippner, Greta R. *Capitalizing on Crisis: The Political Origins of the Rise of Finance*. Cambridge, MA: Harvard University Press, 2011.

Kurz, Karin. *Home Ownership and Social Inequality in a Comparative Perspective*. Stanford, CA: Stanford University Press, 2004.

Kwak, Nancy H. *A World of Homeowners: American Power and the Politics of Housing Aid*. Chicago: University of Chicago Press, 2015.

La Caixa. "Productos y servicios para inmigrantes." Comunicación Externa. La Caixa, Barcelona, Spain, July 2007. https://docplayer.es/17414803-Productos-y-servicios-para-inmigrantes.html.

———. *2007 Informe annual "La Caixa."* Barcelona, Spain, 2008. https://juanst.com/wp-content/uploads/2008/05/la-caixa-2007.pdf.

Mier, Carlos. "La Sareb 'pasa' de Aznar Junior y Del Fondo Cerberus y Entrega La Gestión de Los Activos Inmobiliarios al Sabadell." *Periodista Digital,* November 14, 2014. https://www.periodistadigital.com/periodismo/internet/20141105/sareb-pasa-hijo-aznar-fondo-cerberus-entrega-gestion-activos-inmobiliarios-sabadell-noticia-689401879890/ (accessed May 11, 2015).

Labanyi, Jo. "The Politics of Memory in Contemporary Spain." *Journal of Spanish Cultural Studies* 9, no. 2 (2008): 119–25.

Larson, Susan. "Shifting Modern Identities in Madrid's Recent Urban Planning, Architecture and Narrative." *Cities* 20, no. 6 (2003): 395–402.

Leal, Jesús, and Aitana Alguacil. "Vivienda e inmigración: Las condiciones y el comportamiento residencial de los inmigrantes en España." *Anuario CIDOB de la Inmigración* (2012): 126–56.

LeBaron, Genevieve, and Adrienne Roberts. "Confining Social Insecurity: Neoliberalism and the Rise of the 21st Century Debtors' Prison." *Politics and Gender* 8, no. 1 (2012): 25–49.

Lee, Chris. "Sociological Theories of Immigration: Pathways to Integration for U.S. Immigrants." *Journal of Human Behavior in the Social Environment* 19, no. 6 (2009): 730–44.

Lees, Loretta, Hyun Bang Shin, and Ernesto José López Morales. *Planetary Gentrification. Hoboken, NJ: John Wiley and Sons,* 2017.

"Levantamiento indigena." *Utopías,* no. 71 (January 2000): 50–52.

Leyshon, Andrew, and Nigel Thrift. "Geographies of Financial Exclusion: Financial Abandonment in Britain and the United States." *Transactions of the Institute of British Geographers* 20, no. 3 (1995): 312–41.

Loch, Dietmar. "Integration as a Sociological Concept and National Model for Immigrants: Scope and Limits." *Identities* 21, no. 6 (2014): 623–32.

López, Alejandro. "Bankia, motor de los desahucios en Madrid." *eldiario.es.* Accessed January 31, 2015. http://www.eldiario.es/zonacritica/Bankia-motor-desahucios-Madrid_6_11608843.html (accessed January 31, 2015).

López, Carlos Barciela. *Autarquía y mercado negro: El fracaso económico del primer franquismo, 1939–1959.* Madrid: Crítica, 2003.

López Díaz, Jesús. "Vivienda social y Falange: Ideario y construcción en la década de los 40." *Scripta Nova. Revista Electrónica de Geografía y Ciencias Sociales* 7, no. 146 (May 27, 2007).

López, Isidro, and Emmanuel Rodríguez. "The Spanish Model." *New Left Review* 2, no. 69 (2011): 5–29.

Lopez, Sarah Lynn. *The Remittance Landscape: Spaces of Migration in Rural Mexico and Urban USA.* Chicago: University of Chicago Press, 2015.

Lucero, José Antonio. "High Anxiety in the Andes: Crisis and Contention in Ecuador." *Journal of Democracy* 12, no. 2 (2001): 59–73.

Lyons, Maxi. "Case Study in Multinational Corporate Accountability: Ecuador's Indigenous Peoples Struggle for Redress, A." *Denver Journal of International Law and Policy* 32 (2004 2003): 701.

Madrid, and Ayuntamiento. *Plan General de Ordenación Urbana de Madrid, 1997.* Madrid: Ayuntamiento, 1997.

Madrid (Spain), and Ayuntamiento. *Memoria comprensiva de la actuación del primer Ayuntamiento después de la liberación de Madrid.* Madrid: Sección de Cultura e Información, Artes Gráf. Municipales, 1945.

Martí i Puig, Salvador, ed. *Pueblos indígenas y política en América Latina: El reconocimiento de sus derechos y el impacto de sus demandas a inicios del siglo XXI. Interrogar la actualidad.* Barcelona: Fundació CIDOB, 2007.

Martin, Isaac William. *The Permanent Tax Revolt: How the Property Tax Transformed American Politics.* Stanford, CA: Stanford University Press, 2008.

Martin, Randy. *Financialization of Daily Life.* Philadelphia: Temple University Press, 2002.

Martínez del Olmo, Almudena, and Jesús Leal Maldonado. "La segregación residencial, un indicador espacial confuso en la representación de la problemática residencial de los inmigrantes económicos: El caso de la Comunidad de Madrid." *ACE: Arquitectura, Ciudad y Entorno,* 3, no. 8, (2008): 53–64.

Martínez López, Miguel Angel. "Squatters and Migrants in Madrid: Interactions, Contexts and Cycles." *Urban Studies* 54, no. 11 (2017): 2472–89.

———. "The Squatters' Movement in Europe: A Durable Struggle for Social Autonomy in Urban Politics." *Antipode* 45, no. 4 (2013): 866–87.

Martínez López, Miguel Angel, and Angela García Bernardos. "Ocupar las plazas, liberar edificios [The occupation of squares and the squatting of buildings]." *ACME: An International Journal for Critical Geographies* 14, no. 1 (2015): 157–84.

———. *Okupa Madrid (1985–2011): Memoria, reflexión, debate y autogestión colectiva del conocimiento*, Madrid: Seminario de Historia política y social de las Okupaciones en Madrid-Metrópolis, 2014.

———. "Movimiento 15M, espacio público y luchas pro-vivienda." *Zainak: Cuadernos de Antropología-Etnografía*, no. 36 (2013): 87–105.

Martin-Márquez, Susan. *Disorientations: Spanish Colonialism in Africa and the Performance of Identity*. New Haven, CT: Yale University Press, 2008.

Martín-Santos, Luis, and Alfonso Rey. *Tiempo de silencio*. Madrid: Grupo Planeta (GBS), 2005.

Masterson-Algar, Araceli. *Ecuadorians in Madrid: Migrants' Place in Urban History*. New York: Springer, 2016.

McCabe, Brian J. *No Place Like Home*. Oxford: Oxford University Press, 2016.

McClintock, Anne. *Imperial Leather: Race, Gender, and Sexuality in the Colonial Contest*. New York: Routledge, 1995.

McConnell, Eileen Diaz, and Enrico A. Marcelli. "Buying Into the American Dream? Mexican Immigrants, Legal Status, and Homeownership in Los Angeles County*." *Social Science Quarterly* 88, no. 1 (2007): 199–221.

Merrill, Heather. *An Alliance of Women: Immigration and the Politics of Race*. Minneapolis: University of Minnesota Press, 2006.

Micó, Josép-Lluís, and Andreu Casero-Ripollés. "Political Activism Online: Organization and Media Relations in the Case of 15M in Spain." *Information, Communication and Society* 7, no. 7 (2014): 1–14.

"Mientras no tengamos cubiertas las necesidades minimas de tantas familias, no tenemos derecho a acudir en socorro de los demas." *ABC*. December 3, 1958, Madrid edition.

Millner, Naomi. "From 'Refugee' to 'Migrant' in Calais Solidarity Activism: Re-Staging Undocumented Migration for a Future Politics of Asylum." *JPGQ Political Geography* 30, no. 6 (2011): 320–28.

Ministerio de Vivienda. *Sesenta mil viviendas—Plan de urgencia social de Madrid*. Documentary film, 17:08, black and white. Madrid: Ministerio de Vivienda, 1959. https://www.rtve.es/alacarta/videos/documentales-b-n/sesenta-mil-viviendas -plan-urgencia-social-madrid/2847741/.

Mitchell, Timothy. "The Properties of Markets Informal Housing and Capitalism's Mystery." Cultural Political Economy Working Paper no. 2. Institute for Advanced Studies in Social and Management Sciences, University of Lancaster, 2003.

———. "The Work of Economics: How a Discipline Makes Its World." *European Journal of Sociology / Archives Européennes de Sociologie* 46, no. 2 (2005): 297–320.

Moore, Jason W. *Capitalism in the Web of Life: Ecology and the Accumulation of Capital.* New York: Verso Books, 2015.

Morell, Mayo Fuster. "The Free Culture and 15M Movements in Spain: Composition, Social Networks and Synergies." *Social Movement Studies* 11, nos. 3–4 (2012): 386–92.

Mouffe, Chantal. *Agonistics: Thinking the World Politically.* New York: Verso Books, 2013.

Mouritzen, Poul E. "The Demanding Citizen: Driven by Policy, Self-Interest or Ideology?" *European Journal of Political Research* 15, no. 4 (1987): 417–35.

Mudu, Pierpaolo, and Sutapa Chattopadhyay. *Migration, Squatting and Radical Autonomy: Resistance and Destabilization of Racist Regulatory Policies and B/Ordering Mechanisms.* New York: Routledge, 2016.

Muguruza Otaño, Pedro. *El futuro Madrid: (conferencias pronunciadas en el Aula Magna): febrero–mayo de 1944.* Madrid: Instituto de Estudios de Administración Local, 1945.

Muñoz García, Juan. *El poder de la banca en España.* Madrid: Zero, 1970.

Nasarre y de Goicoechea, Fernando, and Luis Rodríguez-Avial. "PAUs: Programas de Actuación Urbanística para afrontar el problema de la vivienda en el municipio de Madrid." *Urbanismo,* no. 24, February (1995): 6–25.

Neuman, Michael. *The Imaginative Institution Planning and Governance in Madrid.* Farnham, Surrey: Ashgate, 2010.

Newman, Kathe. "Post-Industrial Widgets: Capital Flows and the Production of the Urban." *International Journal of Urban and Regional Research* 33, no. 2 (2009): 314–31.

Nicholls, Walter J. *The DREAMers: How the Undocumented Youth Movement Transformed the Immigrant Rights Debate.* Stanford, CA: Stanford University Press, 2013.

Nicholls, Walter J., and Justus Uitermark. *Cities and Social Movements: Immigrant Rights Activism in the US, France, and the Netherlands, 1970–2015.* New York: John Wiley and Sons, 2016.

"No queremos una España de proletarios, sino de propietarios." *ABC.* May 2, 1959.

Nyers, Peter, and Kim Rygiel. *Citizenship, Migrant Activism and the Politics of Movement.* New York: Routledge, 2012.

Observatorio DESC, and Plataforma de Afectados por la Hipoteca. "Emergencia habitacional en el estado español." Barcelona, Spain: Observatorio DESC, 2013. http://afectadosporlahipoteca.com/2013/12/17/informe-emergencia-habitacional/.

Observatorio Metropolitano. *La apuesta municipalista: La democracia empieza por lo cercano.* Madrid: Traficantes de Sueños, 2014.

———. *Madrid: ¿la suma de todos?: globalización, territorio, desigualdad.* Madrid: Traficantes de Sueños, 2007.

Ofer, Inbal. *Claiming the City and Contesting the State: Squatting, Community Formation and Democratization in Spain (1955–1986).* Milton Park, UK: Taylor and Francis, 2017.

Ong, Aihwa. *Flexible Citizenship: The Cultural Logics of Transnationality.* Durham, NC: Duke University Press, 1999.

Ordovás, María José González. *Políticas y estrategias urbanas: la distribución del espacio privado y público en la ciudad.* Madrid: Editorial Fundamentos, 2000.

País, Ediciones El. "Agilidad y seguridad para el mercado hipotecario." *EL PAÍS*, March 21, 1982.

———. "Antiguos altos cargos relacionados con el urbanismo critican el Plan General." *EL PAÍS*, July 17, 1983.

———. "El interés general y los particulares." *EL PAÍS*, October 21, 1993.

———. "El Plan General, un modelo de urbanismo 'de izquierdas.'" *EL PAÍS*, March 9, 1985.

———. "El PP propone liberalizar más la Ley de Suelo." *EL PAÍS*, October 4, 1995.

———. "'Hemos ganado los débiles, hemos ganado todos.'" *EL PAÍS,* March 14, 2013.

———. "Los desahucios unen a los votantes." *EL PAÍS*, February 17, 2013.

———. "Soluciones al problema de la vivienda." *EL PAÍS*, February 10, 1997.

Palomera, Jaime. "How Did Finance Capital Infiltrate the World of the Urban Poor? Homeownership and Social Fragmentation in a Spanish Neighborhood." *International Journal of Urban and Regional Research* 38, no. 1 (2014): 218–35.

Palomo, Eva. "Austerity Policies and the Feminist Movement in Spain." *Globalizations* 13, no. 6 (2016): 925–27.

Panagia, Davide. "'Partage du sensible': The Distribution of the Sensible." In *Jacques Rancière: Key Concepts*, ed. Jean-Philippe Deranty, 107–15. New York: Routledge, 2014.

Pareja-Eastaway, Montserrat. "The Effects of the Spanish Housing System on the Settlement Patterns of Immigrants." *Tijdschrift Voor Economische En Sociale Geografie* 100, no. 4 (2009): 519–34.

Park, K.-Sue. "Money, Mortgages, and the Conquest of America." *Law and Social Inquiry* 41, no. 4 (2016): 1006–35.

Patterson, Orlando. *Slavery and Social Death: A Comparative Study.* Cambridge, MA: Harvard University Press, 1982.

Pérez, Alfredo Ramos, and José Luis Fernández de Casadevante. "Superhéroes de barrio: La juventud y el derecho a la ciudad desde una Iniciativa Barrial." *Revista de Estudios de Juventud*, no. 95 (2011): 93–107.

Pérez Quintana, Vicente, and Pablo Sánchez León. *Memoria ciudadana y movimiento vecinal: Madrid 1968–2008.* Madrid: Catarata, 2008.

Perugorría, Ignacia, and Benjamín Tejerina. "Politics of the Encounter: Cognition, Emotions, and Networks in the Spanish 15M." *Current Sociology* 61, no. 4 (2013): 424–42.

"Plaza de España y Avenida José Antonio," *Cortijos y Rascacielos*, nos. 75–76 (1953): 51.

"Población de Madrid," *Gran Madrid,* no. 4 (1949): 38–42.

Pojmann, W. *Migration and Activism in Europe since 1945.* New York: Springer, 2008.

Polanyi, Karl. *The Great Transformation: The Political and Economic Origins of Our Time.* Boston: Beacon Press, 2001.

Ponce, Juan, Lliana Olivié Aldasoro, and Mercedes Onofa. "Remittances for Development?: A Case Study of the Impact of Remittances on Human Development in Ecuador." *Elcano Newsletter*, September 17, 2008.

Portes, Alejandro, and Alex Stepick. *City on the Edge: The Transformation of Miami.* Berkeley: University of California Press, 1993.

Potts, Deborah. *Broken Cities: Inside the Global Housing Crisis.* London: Zed Books, 2020.

Pribilsky, Jason. "'Aprendemos a Convivir': Conjugal Relations, Co-Parenting, and Family Life among Ecuadorian Transnational Migrants in New York and the Ecuadorian Andes." *GLOB Global Networks* 4, no. 3 (2004): 313–34.

Radcliffe, Sarah A. "Gendered Frontiers of Land Control: Indigenous Territory, Women and Contests over Land in Ecuador." *Gender, Place and Culture* 21, no. 7 (2014): 854–71.

Ravelli, Quentin. "Financial Backlash When Local Bankers Face Social Protest." In *Finance at Work*, ed. Valérie Boussard, 108–22. London: Routledge, 2017.

Reid, Carolina K. "Financialization and the Subprime Subject: The Experiences of Homeowners during California's Housing Boom." *Housing Studies* 32, no. 6 (2017): 793–815.

Richards, Michael. *A Time of Silence: Civil War and the Culture of Repression in Franco's Spain, 1936–1945.* Cambridge: Cambridge University Press, 1998.

Roberts, Adrienne. "Financing Social Reproduction: The Gendered Relations of Debt and Mortgage Finance in Twenty-First-Century America." *New Political Economy* 18, no. 1 (2013): 21–42.

———. *Gendered States of Punishment and Welfare: Feminist Political Economy, Primitive Accumulation and the Law.* New York: Routledge, 2016.

Rolnik, Raquel. *Urban Warfare.* New York: Verso Books, 2019.

Romanos, Eduardo. "Evictions, Petitions and Escraches: Contentious Housing in Austerity Spain." *Social Movement Studies* 13, no. 2 (2014): 296–302.

Rothstein, Richard. *The Color of Law: A Forgotten History of How Our Government Segregated America.* New York: Liveright Publishing, 2017.

Roy, Ananya. *City Requiem, Calcutta Gender and the Politics of Poverty.* Minneapolis: University of Minnesota Press, 2003.

———. "Dis/possessive Collectivism: Property and Personhood at City's End." *Geoforum* 80 (2017): A1–A11.

———. "Paradigms of Propertied Citizenship Transnational Techniques of Analysis." *Urban Affairs Review* 38, no. 4 (2003): 463–91.

———. *Poverty Capital: Microfinance and the Making of Development.* New York: Routledge, 2010.

Roy, Ananya, and Aihwa Ong. *Worlding Cities: Asian Experiments and the Art of Being Global.* Malden, MA: Wiley-Blackwell, 2011.

Rugh, Jacob S., and Matthew Hall. "Deporting the American Dream: Immigration Enforcement and Latino Foreclosures." *Sociological Science* 3 (2016): 1053–76.

Salamanca, Onofre Rullán. "La nueva Ley del Suelo de 1998 en el contexto del neoliberalismo postmoderno." *Investigaciones Geográficas*, no. 22 (1999): 5–22.

Salemink, Oscar, and Mattias Borg Rasmussen. "After Dispossession: Ethnographic Approaches to Neoliberalization." *Focaal*, no. 74 (2016): 3–12.

Sambricio, Carlos. *Madrid, vivienda y urbanismo: 1900–1960*. Madrid: Ediciones AKAL, 2004.

Sánchez Recio, Glicerio, and Luis Julio Tascón Fernández. *Los empresarios de Franco: Política y economía en España, 1936–1957*. Alicante: Publicaciones Universidad de Alicante, 2003.

Sánchez Santos, José Manuel. "Household Debt and Consumption Inequality: The Spanish Case." *Economies* 2, no. 3 (2014): 147–70.

Sandoval-Strausz, A. K. *Barrio America: How Latino Immigrants Saved the American City*. New York: Basic Books, 2019.

Sassen, Saskia. *Territory, Authority, Rights: From Medieval to Global Assemblages*. Princeton, NJ: Princeton University Press, 2008.

Saura, Carlos, dir. *Deprisa, deprisa*. Starring Berta Socuéllamos Zarco and Elías Querejeta. Barcelona: Manga Films, 2002.

Sawyer, Suzana. *Crude Chronicles: Indigenous Politics, Multinational Oil, and Neoliberalism in Ecuador*. Durham, NC: Duke University Press, 2004.

Scott, James C. *Seeing Like a State: How Certain Schemes to Improve the Human Condition Have Failed*. New Haven: Yale University Press, 1998.

Selverston-Scher, Melina. *Ethnopolitics in Ecuador: Indigenous Rights and the Strengthening of Democracy*. Coral Gables, FL: North-South Center Press at the University of Miami, 2001.

Simone, A. M. *City Life from Jakarta to Dakar: Movements at the Crossroads*. New York: Routledge, 2010.

Simpson, Audra. *Mohawk Interruptus: Political Life Across the Borders of Settler States*. Durham, NC: Duke University Press, 2014.

———. "The Ruse of Consent and the Anatomy of 'Refusal': Cases from Indigenous North America and Australia." *Postcolonial Studies* 20, no. 1 (2017): 18–33.

"El 'banco malo' pagó 30 millones a las comunidades de vecinos en 2013, un 25% más de lo previsto." *El Boletín*, February 27, 2014. http://www.elboletin.com/economia/93879/banco-malo-pago-millones-comunidades-vecinos.html (accessed May 11, 2015).

Slater, Tom. "The Myth of 'Broken Britain': Welfare Reform and the Production of Ignorance." *Antipode* 46, no. 4 (2014): 948–69.

Soria Marco, Bonifacio. *Madrid antiguo y moderno*. Madrid: Editorial García Enciso, 1959.

Soto, Hernando de. *The Mystery of Capital: Why Capitalism Triumphs in the West and Fails Everywhere Else*. New York: Basic Books, 2000.

Spain, Ministerio de la Vivienda, and Secretaría General Técnica. *Architecture, Housing and Urbanisation in Spain*. Madrid: Ministerio de la Vivienda, Secretaría General Técnica, 1963.

Stein, Samuel. *Capital City: Gentrification and the Real Estate State*. New York: Verso, 2019.

Stoler, Ann Laura. *Carnal Knowledge and Imperial Power: Race and the Intimate in Colonial Rule*. Berkeley: University of California Press, 2002.

Stout, Noelle M. *Dispossessed: How Predatory Bureaucracy Foreclosed on the American Middle Class*. Berkeley: University of California Press, 2019.

Suarez, Maka. "Debt Revolts: Ecuadorian Foreclosed Families at the PAH in Barcelona." *Dialectical Anthropology* 41, no. 3 (2017): 263–77.

Sziarto, Kristin M., and Helga Leitner. "Immigrants Riding for Justice: Space-Time and Emotions in the Construction of a Counterpublic." *Political Geography* 29, no. 7 (2010): 381–91.

Taylor, Keeanga-Yamahtta. *Race for Profit: How Banks and the Real Estate Industry Undermined Black Homeownership*. Chapel Hill: UNC Press Books, 2019.

Telles, Edward M., and Vilma Ortiz. *Generations of Exclusion: Mexican-Americans, Assimilation, and Race*. New York: Russell Sage Foundation, 2008.

Tickell, Adam, and Jamie A. Peck. "Accumulation, Regulation and the Geographies of Post-Fordism: Missing Links in Regulationist Research." *Progress in Human Geography* 16, no. 2 (1992): 190–218.

Uitermark, Justus. *Dynamics of Power in Dutch Integration Politics: From Accommodation to Confrontation*. Amsterdam: Amsterdam University Press, 2012.

Vallejo, Raúl. *Crónica mestiza del nuevo Pachakutik: (Ecuador del levantamiento indígena de 1990 al Ministerio Etnico de 1996)*. College Park: Latin American Studies Center, University of Maryland, 1996.

Valli, C. "When Cultural Workers Become an Urban Social Movement: Political Subjectification and Alternative Cultural Production in the Macao Movement, Milan." *Environment and Planning A* 47, no. 3 (2015): 643–59.

Velosos, Moncho, "Bankia, el rescate más caro en la historia de España: 23.465 millones de euros." *ABC, May 26, 2012*. http://www.abc.es/20120526/economia/abci-bankia-nacionalizacion-ayudas-publicas-201205252315.html (accessed May 12, 2015).

Vitiello, Domenic, and Thomas J. Sugrue. *Immigration and Metropolitan Revitalization in the United States*. Philadelphia: University of Pennsylvania Press, 2017.

Wacquant, Loïc. *Punishing the Poor: The Neoliberal Government of Social Insecurity*. Durham, NC: Duke University Press, 2009.

———. *Urban Outcasts: A Comparative Sociology of Advanced Marginality*. Malden, MA: Polity, 2008.

Webster, Chris, Georg Glasze, and Klaus Frantz. "The Global Spread of Gated Communities." *Environment and Planning B: Planning and Design* 29, no. 3 (2002): 315–20.

White, Julia, and Benjamin White. "Gendered Experiences of Dispossession: Oil Palm Expansion in a Dayak Hibun Community in West Kalimantan." *Journal of Peasant Studies*. 39, nos. 3–4 (2012): 995–1016.

Wyly, Elvin K., Mona Atia, Holly Foxcroft, Daniel J. Hamme, and Kelly Phillips-Watts. "American Home: Predatory Mortgage Capital and Neighbourhood Spaces of Race and Class Exploitation in the United States." *Geografiska Annaler: Series B, Human Geography* 88, no. 1 (2006): 105–32.

Wyly, Elvin, and C. S. Ponder. "Gender, Age, and Race in Subprime America." *Housing Policy Debate* 21, no. 4 (2011): 529–64.

Zaloom, Caitlin. *Indebted: How Families Make College Work at Any Cost.* Princeton, NJ: Princeton University Press, 2019.

Zárate Martín, Antonio M. "Imágenes mentales del centro de Madrid, el barrio de Lavapiés." *Boletín de La Real Sociedad Geográfica*, no. 137 (2001): 403–22.

Zavisca, Jane R. *Housing the New Russia.* Ithaca, NY: Cornell University Press, 2012.

Index